IMAGES
of America

DEERPARK

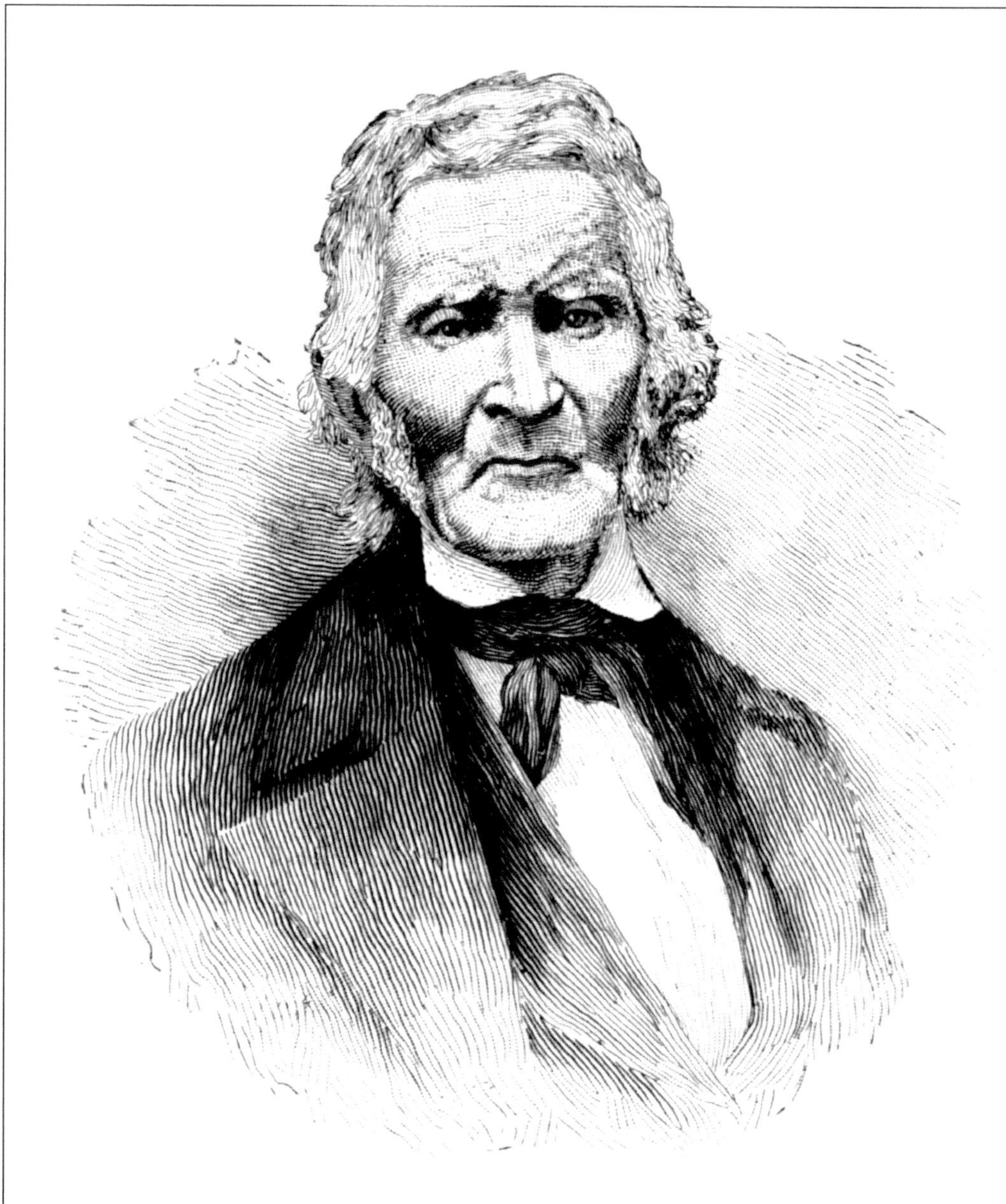

Peter Ezekiel Gumaer (1771–1869), surveyor, farmer, Delaware and Hudson Canal lock tender, sometime banker, and author of *The History of Deerpark* (an account of the area's first settlers), was probably Deerpark's first historian. At the age of 16, he studied surveying under Moses DeWitt. For many years, he mapped, surveyed, and authored legal documents in the Deerpark area. To date, not one of his surveys has been overturned. (Author's collection.)

IMAGES
of America

DEERPARK

Brian J. Lewis

ARCADIA
PUBLISHING

ISBN 978-0-7385-1107-8

Published by Arcadia Publishing
Charleston, South Carolina

Printed in the United States of America

Library of Congress Catalog Card Number: 2002109042

For all general information contact Arcadia Publishing at:
Telephone 843-853-2070
Fax 843-853-0044
E-mail sales@arcadiapublishing.com
For customer service and orders:
Toll-Free 1-888-313-2665

Visit us on the Internet at www.arcadiapublishing.com

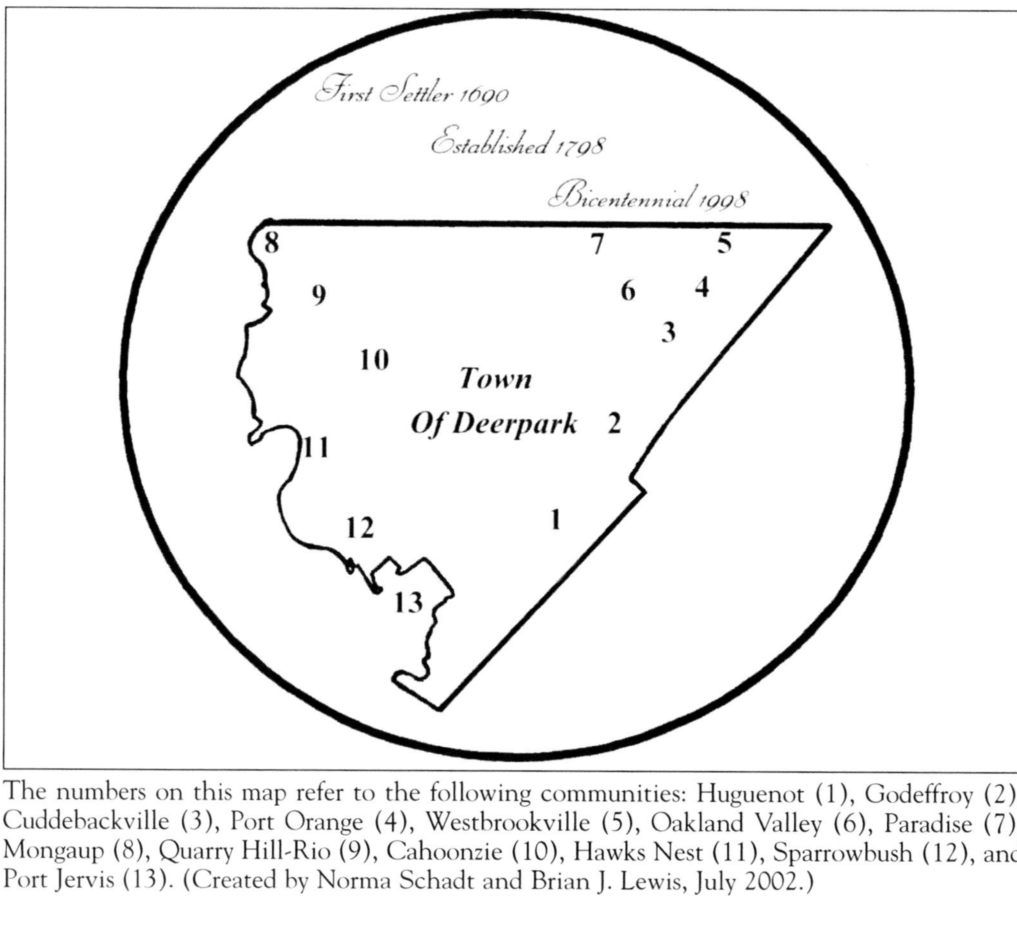

The numbers on this map refer to the following communities: Huguenot (1), Godeffroy (2), Cuddebackville (3), Port Orange (4), Westbrookville (5), Oakland Valley (6), Paradise (7), Mongaup (8), Quarry Hill-Rio (9), Cahoonzie (10), Hawks Nest (11), Sparrowbush (12), and Port Jervis (13). (Created by Norma Schadt and Brian J. Lewis, July 2002.)

CONTENTS

ACKNOWLEDGMENTS

I would like to thank and express my gratitude to many people. First, a special thank-you to my grandparents John K. and Mary E. Lewis, who are responsible for passing on to me the legacy of my family's 150- to 200-year history in this town and surrounding areas. They taught me to appreciate the history of the town of Deerpark. Second, thanks go to Matt and Carol Osterberg for their friendship, support, and encouragement to take on this project. The success of Matt Osterberg's *Images of America: Port Jervis*, which included several photographs from my collection, inspired me to write *Deerpark*. Third, this book would never have come together without the help and guidance of Peter Osborne and Norma Schadt. I thank them both for all the time they spent guiding me through the process of locating photographs, identifying subjects, and gathering information. A special thank-you goes to Norma Schadt for writing the introduction.

As with any major undertaking, many people are essential for the completion and success of the project. Many thanks go to Demetre Bové, Jean Amatucci Fox, Peter Osborne, and Norma Schadt for caption review. I am very grateful to the individuals and organizations that made their photograph collections available to me for inclusion in this work, for sharing their memories, and for helping out in many ways: Bob Aber, Diane Archer, Nancy Coleman-Bello, Glenn R. Conklin, Nancy Conod, Nancy Dunn, Judy Lewis, Bill Flieger, Rosalind Hesleitner, Ruth Hurr, Harold Moore, Krauss Photo, Matt and Carol Osterberg, Tom Patterson, Jerry and Margaret Peill, Norma and Willard Schadt, Margie Sierski, Robbie Smith, Doris Swinton, Nancy Vocci, Robert and Janice Zeller, the Minisink Valley Historical Society, the Town of Deerpark historian's office, and the Neversink Valley Area Museum.

The following works played a very important part in writing the captions: *The Pioneers of Quarry Hill*, by Maurice L. Patterson; *History of Sparrowbush and Vicinity*, by the Reverend Reece Robinson Hill; *The Minisink Valley Express*, by Gerald M. Best; *Coalboats to Tidewater: The Story of the D & H Canal*, by Manville B. Wakefield; "Roebling's Sixth Bridge Neversink," by Malcolm A. Booth; *Minqua Park*, a real estate booklet; "Hydraulic-Electric Development of the Neversink Light & Power Company," reprinted from the *Electrical World and Engineer*, August 8, 1903; *Summer Days on the Port Jervis, Monticello & NY Railroad*, 1901; "An Essay of the History of Sparrowbush," by Timothy Husson; "Description of Sparrowbush," Port Jervis *Evening Gazette*, May 29, 1869; *Old Orange Houses*, by Mildred Parker Seese; "Reflections on the Hawk's Nest," by Harry Van Inwegen, newspaper and date unknown; "History of the Cuddebackville Reformed Church," *Union Gazette*, November 17, 1937; "Rio Methodist Church History," *Union Gazette*, September 29, 1948; "School Days of Another Era," by Ina Case, Port Jervis *Union Gazette*, December 24, 1969; scenes of the first major auto accident in the Port Jervis area, newspaper and date unknown; and *Huguenot Springs House*, hotel booklet, 1863.

INTRODUCTION

Time present and time past
Are both perhaps present in time future,
And time future contained in time past.
—Thomas Stearns Eliot (1888–1963)

Deerpark, a rural town in the southwestern corner of Orange County, is nestled among lakes, streams, rivers, and mountains, bounded by the Delaware, Neversink, and Mongaup Rivers, the Shawangunk Mountains, and the wetlands of the Basha Kill. Geography has been a major factor in the town's growth and development. In early America, covered wagons carrying pioneer stock trundled westward from the Hudson River to settle in this frontier land. Deerpark's name comes from a settler named McDaniel, who enclosed his land with a brush fence. His neighbors called it McDaniel's Deerpark. Soon, the entire area was known as Deerpark.

Seven hamlets—Cahoonzie, Cuddebackville, Godeffroy, Huguenot, Rio, Sparrowbush, and Westbrookville—make up the Town of Deerpark. The origins of these names reflect the history of the town. Cahoonzie is located on land where Chief Cahoonzie of the Cahoonshee Indians is buried. Cuddebackville is named for William Cuddeback, who was related to the first descendants and a colonel in the War of 1812. Godeffroy is named for Adolphus E. Godeffroy, who built an extensive estate in the area that now bears his name. Huguenot originally was called Sindeaquan by the Lenni Lenape Indians and Peenpack by the earliest settlers. Later, the hamlet was named in honor of the Huguenot refugees who came here seeking religious freedom. Rio was known as Quarry Hill. Bluestone was mined and shipped via the Delaware and Hudson Canal to New York City for its sidewalks. When the town requested a post office, it was notified that there was another town named Quarry Hill in New York. Because a post office cannot bear a person's name, the name Rio was used to honor Ben Ryal, the postmaster who was instrumental in organizing the post office. Sparrowbush originated from Henry L. Sparrow, a large land owner, whose land was called Sparrow's Bosh, meaning Sparrow's slope or Sparrow's Bosk, meaning Sparrow's thicket. In time, it was changed to Sparrowbush. Westbrookville was named for Dirck Van Keuren Westbrook, an early settler. Fort Westbrook, dating back to the American Revolution, still stands.

The peaceful Lenni Lenape Indians were the area's first inhabitants. Chief Penhorn's tribe inhabited fine meadowland on the east side of the Neversink River. In 1690, William Tietsoort, the first European inhabitant in the valley, was asked to move here by the Lenni Lenape to build a blacksmith shop. In 1697, a 1200-acre patent of land was granted to Jacob Codebeck, Thomas Swartwout, Anthony Swartwout, Bernardus Swartwout, Jan Tyse, Peter Germar (Gumaer), and David Jamison. The men were of sturdy Dutch farming families that lived peacefully with the Lenni Lenape. With the early rumblings of the French and Indian War, the local residents were asked to form a militia in preparation for the possibility of war. This broke the trust of the Lenni Lenape, who subsequently moved west. Many families traveled along the Old Mine Road, America's oldest 100-mile road, to settle in this fertile valley watered by pristine rivers. They were not, however, to live in peace. A disputed boundary line between New York and New Jersey cut across the entire town. Both states wanted the best farmlands. Fighting, kidnaping, killing, and property destruction on both sides took place during the New Jersey and New York border war. Finally, on September 1, 1773, the king of England established the present boundary line.

In 1798, the state legislature created Sullivan and Rockland Counties from land in Orange and Ulster Counties. In order to maintain the size of Orange County, five towns from Ulster County were incorporated into Orange. The southern part of Deerpark was already part of Orange County. The northern part was added to create Deerpark as we know it today.

Fighting for the British during the War of Independence, Col. Joseph Brant, a Mohawk chief, and his raiders attacked the residents of the valley on October 13, 1778. Their order of attack went from Huguenot to Fort DeWitt in Cuddebackville. Brant, 27 Tories, and 60 Indians returned again on July 20, 1779. It was this raid that led to the major battle at Minisink Ford, where many local militiamen lost their lives. The "Painted Apron Story" at the Black Rock School, a local folk tale about Joseph Brant, has become a part of our history. When the War of Independence ended, some residents left this valley to follow the westward pioneer's dream. The abandoned land enabled those who remained to enlarge their holdings.

The construction of the Delaware and Hudson Canal (1828–1898) changed the Town of Deerpark. Primarily, it was constructed to provide much-needed Pennsylvania anthracite coal to New York City. Bluestone, cement, and lumber were shipped as well. The route of the canal through Deerpark was determined by the relative ease of construction through this valley. New and old industries expanded. Quarries, tanneries, lumbermills, boatyards, supply stores, blacksmith shops, and carpenter shops were busy places along the canal. Homes, schools, churches, and public buildings were built. Many of these buildings remain throughout the town. The town's make-up changed once again with the advent of the railroad. In 1868, the Monticello & Port Jervis Railroad Company brought many people here to enjoy our natural beauty, creating a thriving resort industry. Commercial dairying in the Neversink Valley became a viable occupation because farms within a convenient distance of a railroad had a milk stop, where trains stopped to pick up milk cans to be shipped to New York City.

The automobile brought even more people to the town. Among them was D.W. Griffith. Between 1909 and 1915, he made many films using the majestic mountains and flowing rivers as natural backdrops. The Neversink Valley Area Museum in Cuddebackville regularly shows classic silent movies. The recognition of our history is an ongoing part of our community. The Neversink Valley Area Museum has exhibits about life on the Delaware and Hudson Canal, including canal boat rides. School children visit the museum to learn about the Lenni Lenape. The town has restored an 1863 brick schoolhouse for community use. Other one- room schools have been converted into private homes.

This book shows many of the ancestors of present-day residents and how the local environs have shaped their lives. Geography is important to the town's identity. Camps teach about the environment. The nature conservancy's extensive holdings protect environmentally fragile sections of the Neversink River. The Orange County Land Trust cares for the Basha Kill wetlands. The Orange County Parks Department has established a park to preserve a section of the Delaware and Hudson Canal that still holds water. New York State has designated Route 97 and the Hawk's Nest along the Delaware River as a scenic by-way. The New York State Department of Environmental Conservation has set aside land for an eagle preserve. Visitors and residents have the opportunity to enjoy fishing, hunting, canoeing, rafting, camping, hiking, and bird-watching. Reflecting on our past gives us pause to think about our future. Changes are already in progress. An interpretive center near the Mongaup River and a walking and biking trail along the abandoned Delaware and Hudson Canal are in planning stages.

Our past influences our present and future. Brian's deep roots in the community and his love of its history have been a driving force in producing this book. May you all enjoy this picturesque travel to times past.

—Norma Schadt, Deerpark Town Historian, June 2002

One

Homesteads, Hotels, and Town Views

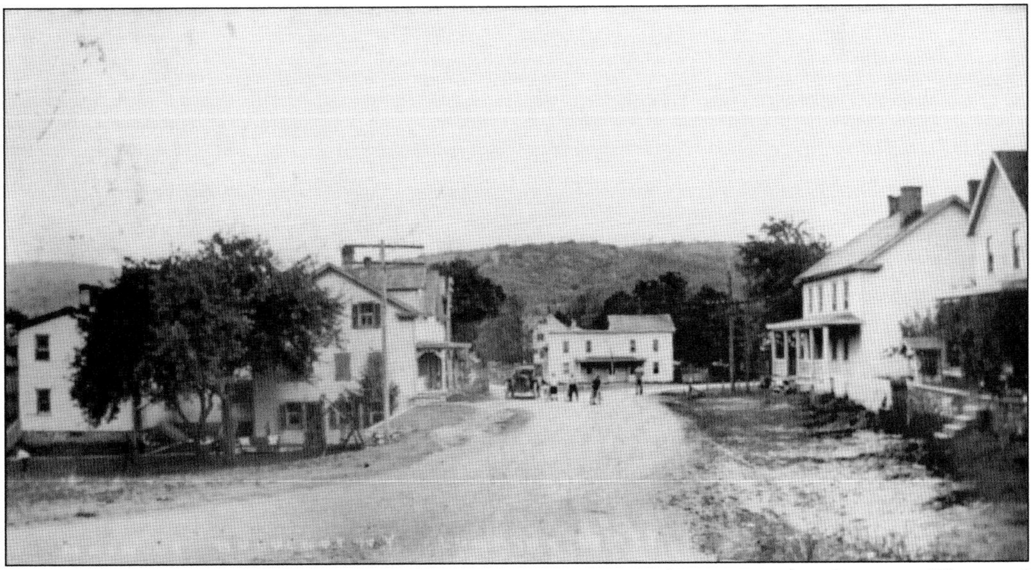

In 1910, this intersection of the hamlet of Huguenot was known as the Corners. The road coming from the left was old Route 209 (believed to be the Old Mine Road). The building on the left was, and is still, the Trading Post. (Author's collection.)

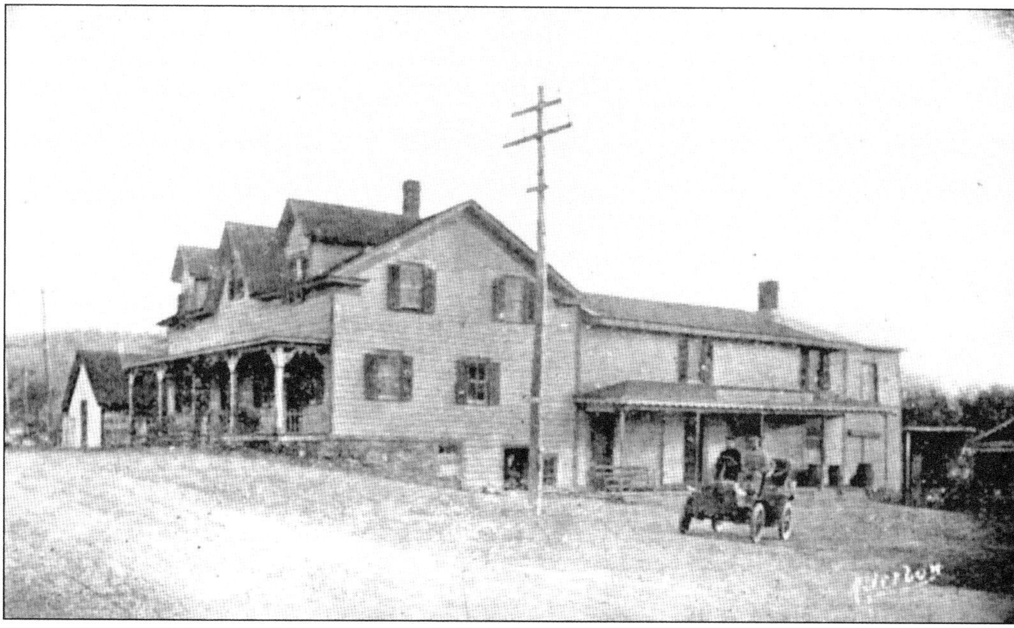

This c. 1905 postcard shows the Trading Post once located on the Delaware and Hudson Canal. Canawlers (the traditional name of canal workers) and townspeople purchased their goods here. In 1900, the canal was filled in, the bridge was removed, and the road was built. The store also housed the post office until 1936. (Author's collection.)

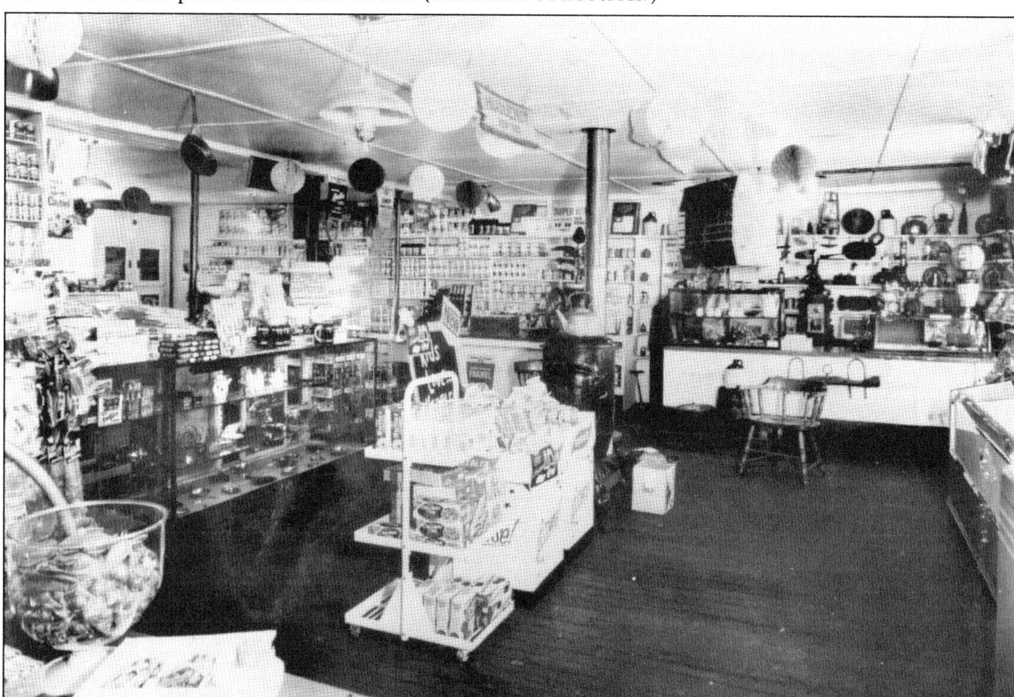

This interior view of the store in the 1940s shows an old-time potbellied stove, other old items, and modern merchandise. The store was a central part of the community, where people met and exchanged gossip. (Deerpark Historian's Office, Reiser Collection.)

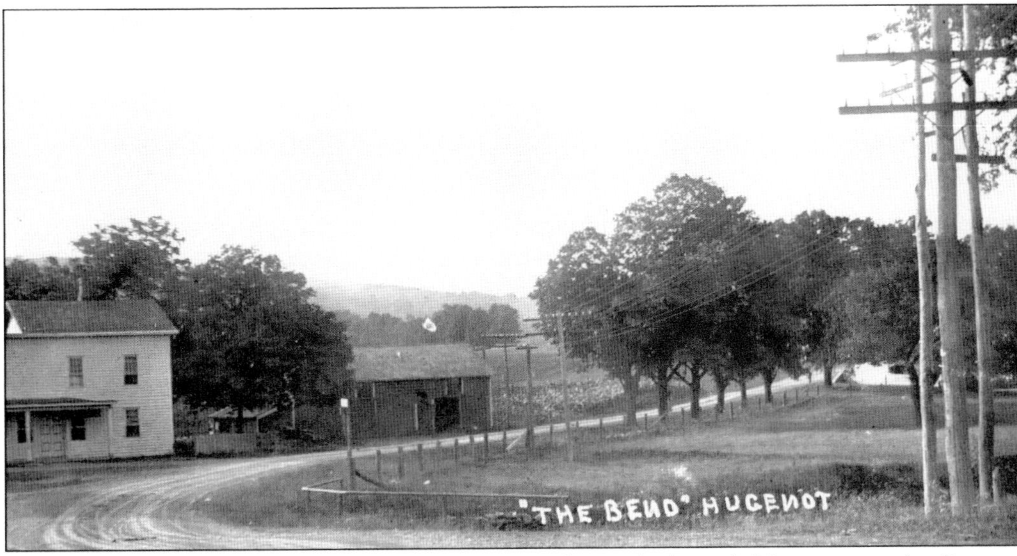

The Bend, old Route 209 (now called Grange Road), winds through Huguenot at the Corners. The house on the left was razed sometime in the 1950s. One might find it amusing that the photographer titles this old postcard "'The Bend' Hugenot," misspelled and with a backward *n*. (Minisink Valley Historical Society.)

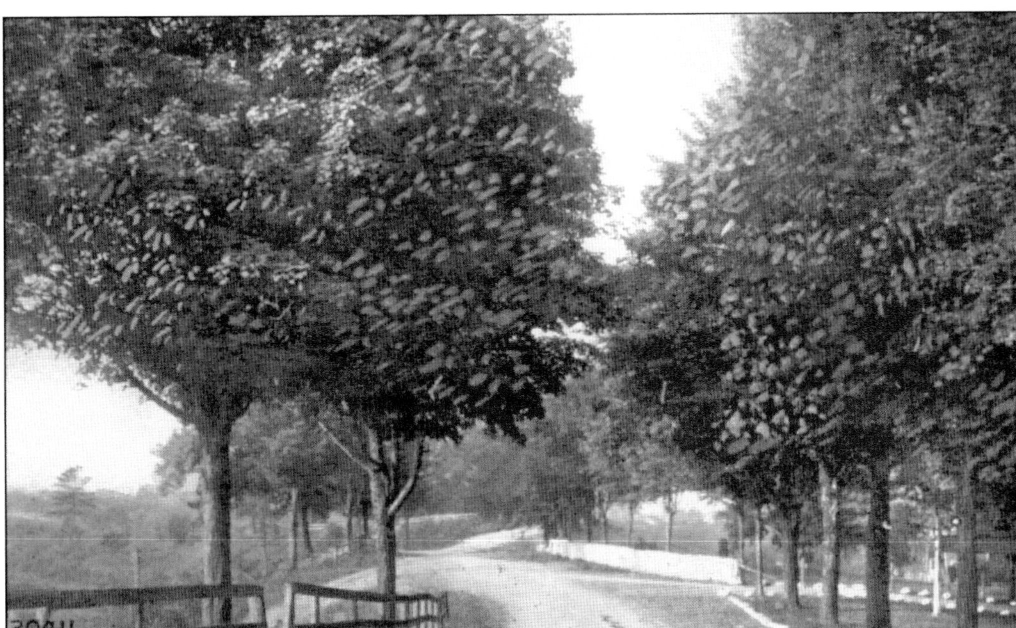

Until the 1960s, Route 209 was lined with trees creating a tunnel-like effect. This view is in front of the Hotel Huguenot, looking toward Port Jervis, in 1910. (Author's collection.)

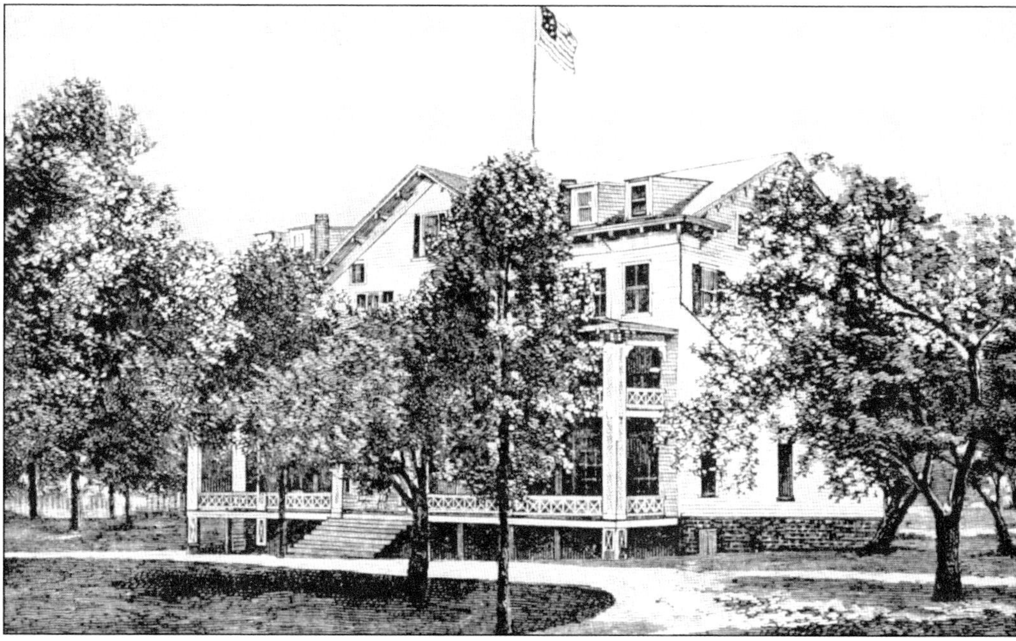

The Mineral Spring House at Huguenot had several names: the Huguenot Springs House (1863), the Spring House (1880s), the Huguenot, and the Hotel Huguenot. This Victorian trade card describes the hotel as "A pleasantly located summer resort. The water of the celebrated Chalybeate Mineral Springs, possessing valuable healthful qualities, can be had free of charge." The hotel burned on November 18, 1979. (Author's collection.)

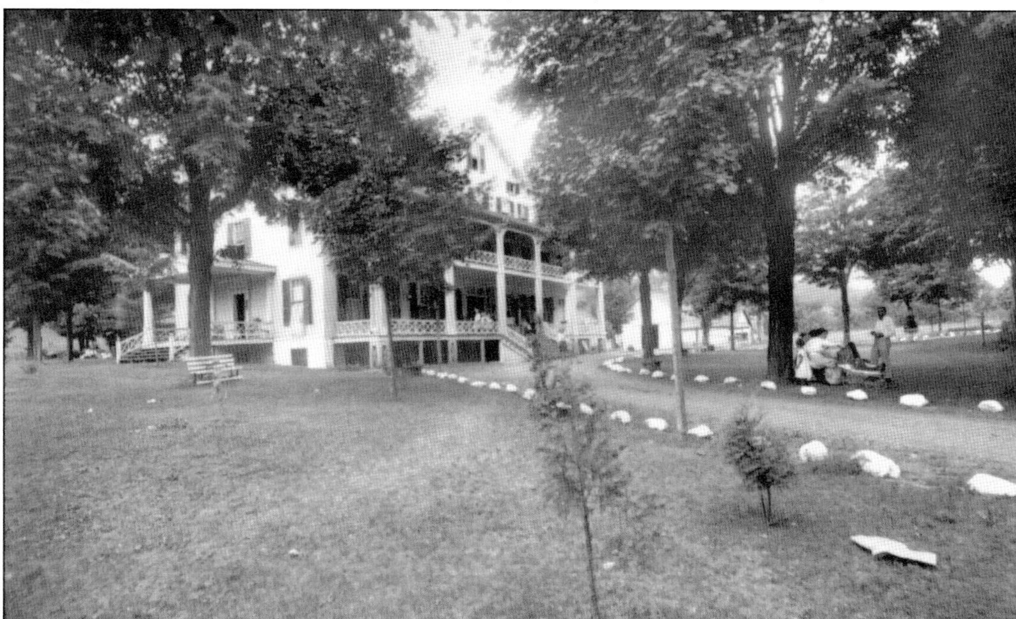

This photograph, taken in the 1890s or early 1900s, shows the Hotel Huguenot and families relaxing under shade trees on the front lawn, perhaps having arrived by a surrey seen parked next to the carriage house. The hotel was a favorite place for banquets and often featured local musicians. (Minisink Valley Historical Society.)

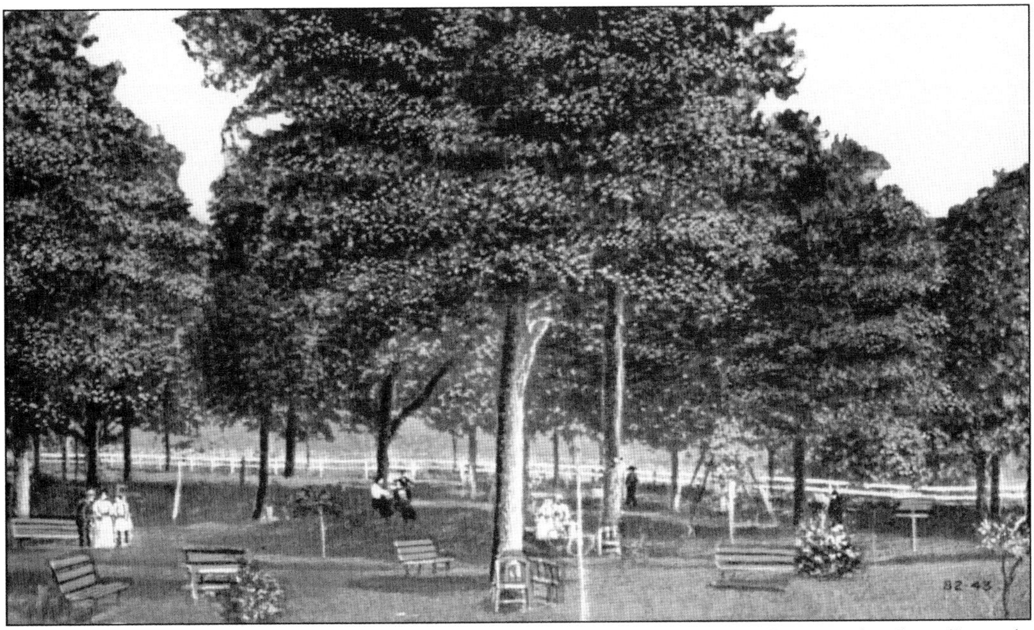

Guests relax on the front lawn of the Hotel Huguenot in 1916. During the hotel's early years, people came to take the waters. According to a flyer, "The waters of the Huguenot Chalybeate Springs are being extensively introduced and used as a remedy for those afflicted with Rheumatism, Dyspepsia, Scrofula, Liver and Kidney complaints, want of action in the Digestive and Urinary Organs, Diseases peculiar to Females, and as a general Purifier of the Blood." (Author's collection.)

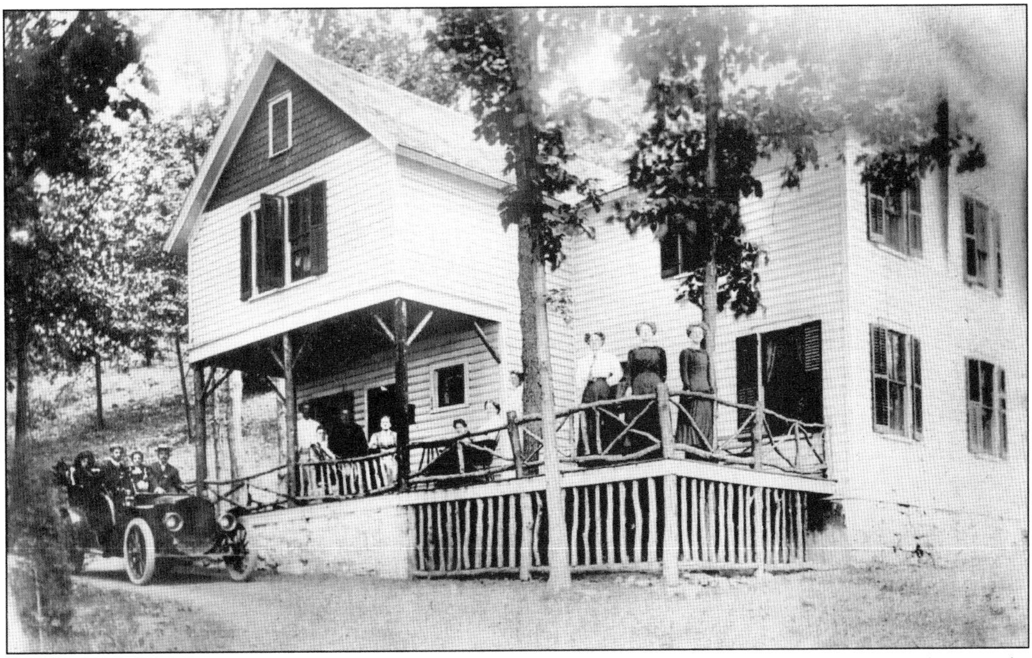

Mrs. Anderson (owner), Hedda Hanson, Mrs. Presbrey, and others are pictured on the porch, according to this 1910 postcard. A 1903 map shows the Pine Grove Inn and Cottages located between the Hotel Huguenot and Ruth's Place on Route 209. (Author's collection.)

PINE GROVE INN and (4) COTTAGES

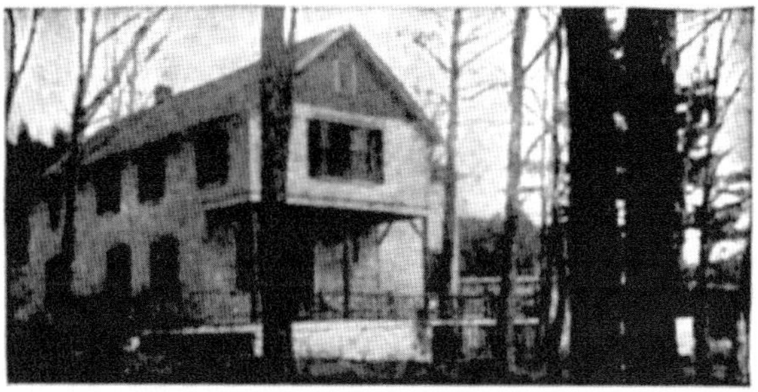

The Pine Grove furnished cottages (5) up in the mountains of Orange Co. at Huguenot, N. Y., are for rent singly to private families or together to a club or Summer Colony.

The main cottage or Inn (see picture of exterior and end of living room) consists of a large living room with rough stone fire-place, dining room with seating capacity for 24 people, a commodious pantry stocked with decorated table service, glass and silverware, for 35 people; store room with large refrigerator; Winter and Summer kitchens with range, sink, tables and utensils complete; on the second floor are eight sleeping rooms. Cottages No. 2, No. 3, No. 4 and No. 5, each contain a large living room with open fire-place, first floor bed-room; on the second floor three bed-rooms; floors of hardwood; ample piazzas.

Rents, fully furnished, from $200 to $500 for the season.

Huguenot is situated on the east spur of the Schwangunk Mountains, 1,000 feet above sea level, four miles over a fine macadam road from Port Jervis on the main line of the Erie Railroad, 2½ hours from New York City.

After a personal inspection of these cottages and the section generally I am able to recommend the place as being very near to ideal for one who is trying to decide where to locate this Summer. Besides the unsurpassed views, pure mountain air and spring water you have for enjoyment canoeing on the famous Neversink River; trouting in several streams within a few minutes' walk; a mountain lake with its shores of white sand where bass and pickerel fishing is at its best and where bathing is superb; drives and walks most picturesque; abundant partridge and deer shooting in the adjacent woods if you can stay late enough for it.

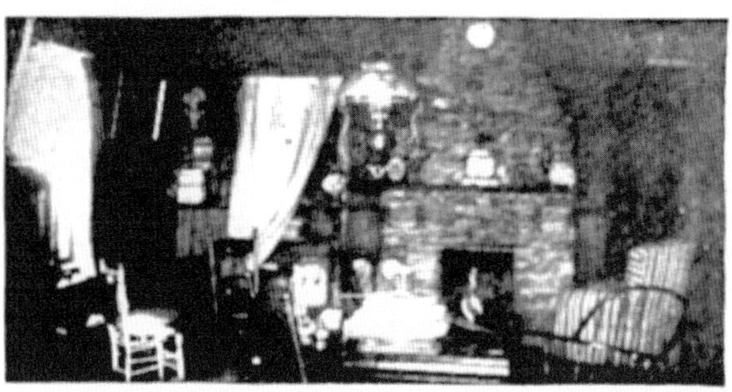

E. E. SLOCUM, Country Property Specialist
141 Broadway, N. Y. City

This advertisement for the Pine Grove Inn and Cottages appeared in June 1907. (Author's collection.)

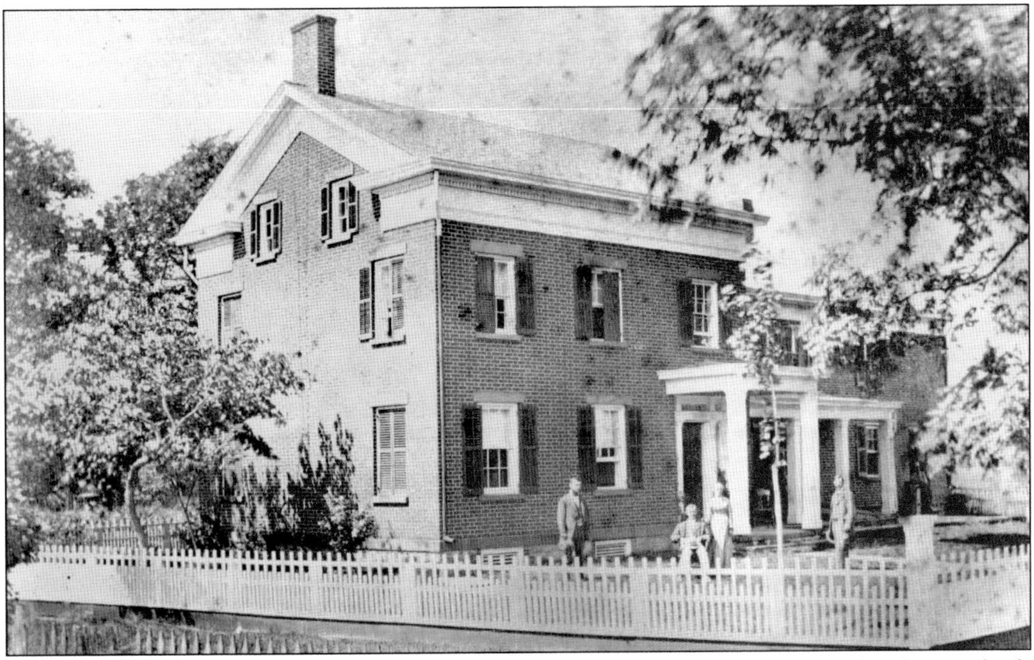

The Seneyaughquan Farm, property owned by generations of the Swartwout family, was built by Peter P. Swartwout in 1845. The house was built of bricks made from clay found on the farm. Seen here are, from left to right, Peter P. Swartwout, builder; Dr. Henry B. Swartwout (seated), son of Peter and the first mayor of Port Jervis; Hannah Cuddeback, wife of Peter; and Benjamin Cuddeback Swartwout, grandfather of Charles H. Swartwout, the last owner. This photograph was taken *c.* 1880. The farm is now owned by the Orange County Department of Parks and Recreation. (Deerpark Historian's Office, Swartwout Collection.)

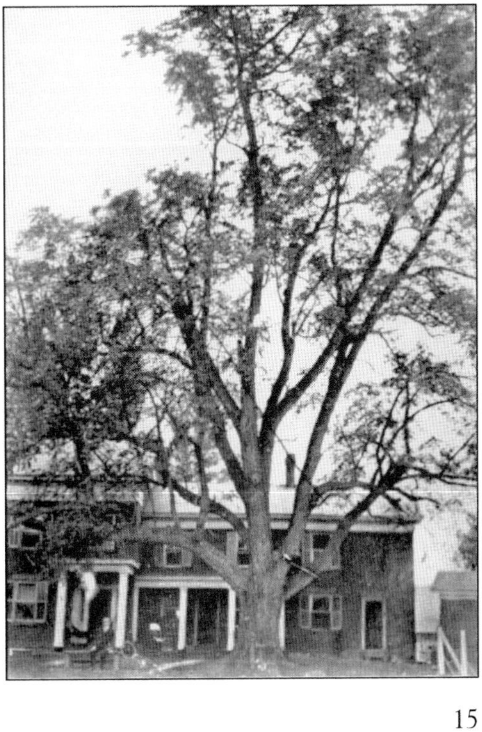

This 200-year-old walnut tree stood at the Seneyaughquan Farm. Although this tree, pictured in the 1920s, is no longer standing, it is said that trees descended from it can still be found on the property. (Author's collection.)

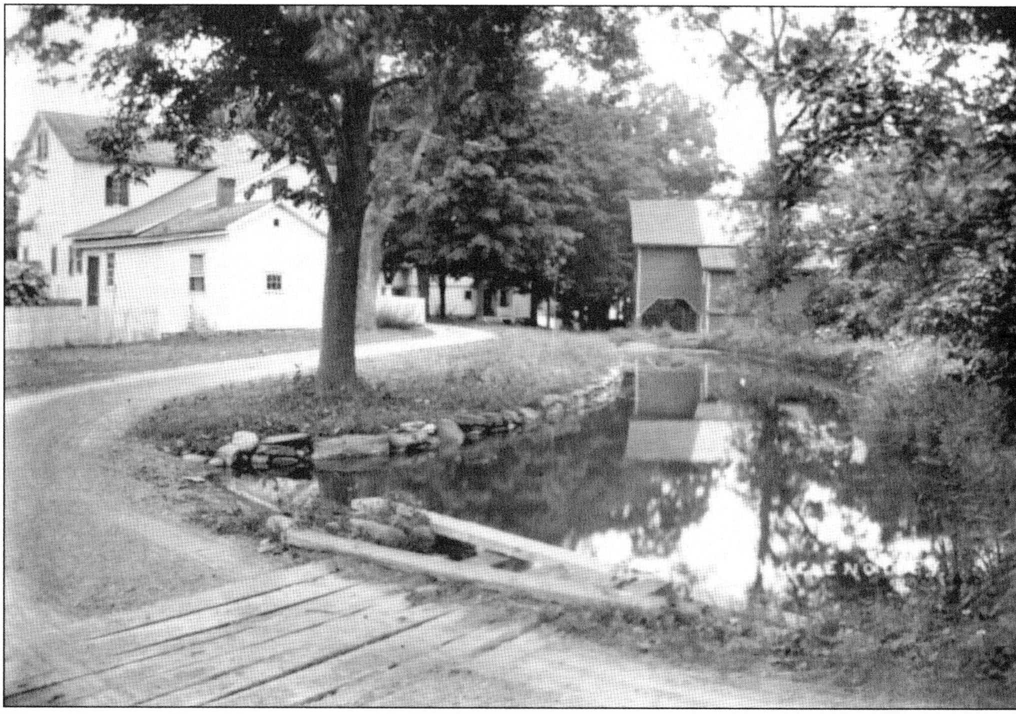

The old gristmill in Huguenot was located on Big Pond Road. This early-1900s view from the small plank bridge shows the original path that Big Pond Road followed. The old farmhouse, built in the late 1700s, is still standing. The road has been redirected toward the mill. Some parts of the mill foundation and the original bridge remain. (Minisink Valley Historical Society.)

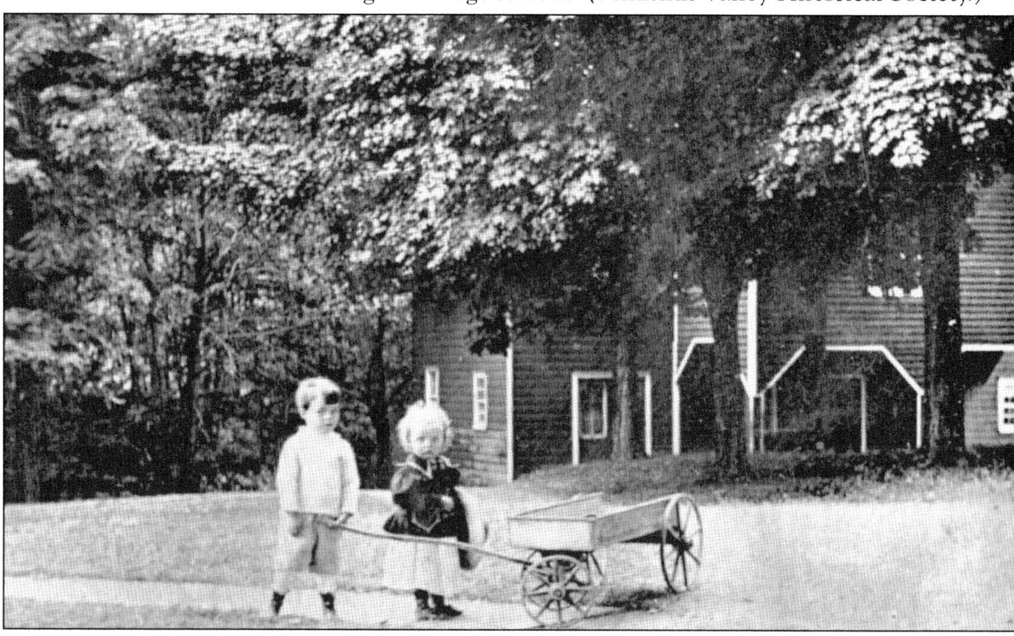

This postcard, dated 1922, shows two children "Going to Mill." It is also a closeup of the old Huguenot gristmill. Wagons would drive under the loading bay. The old mill was burned down by an arsonist in the late 1950s to early 1960s. (Author's collection.)

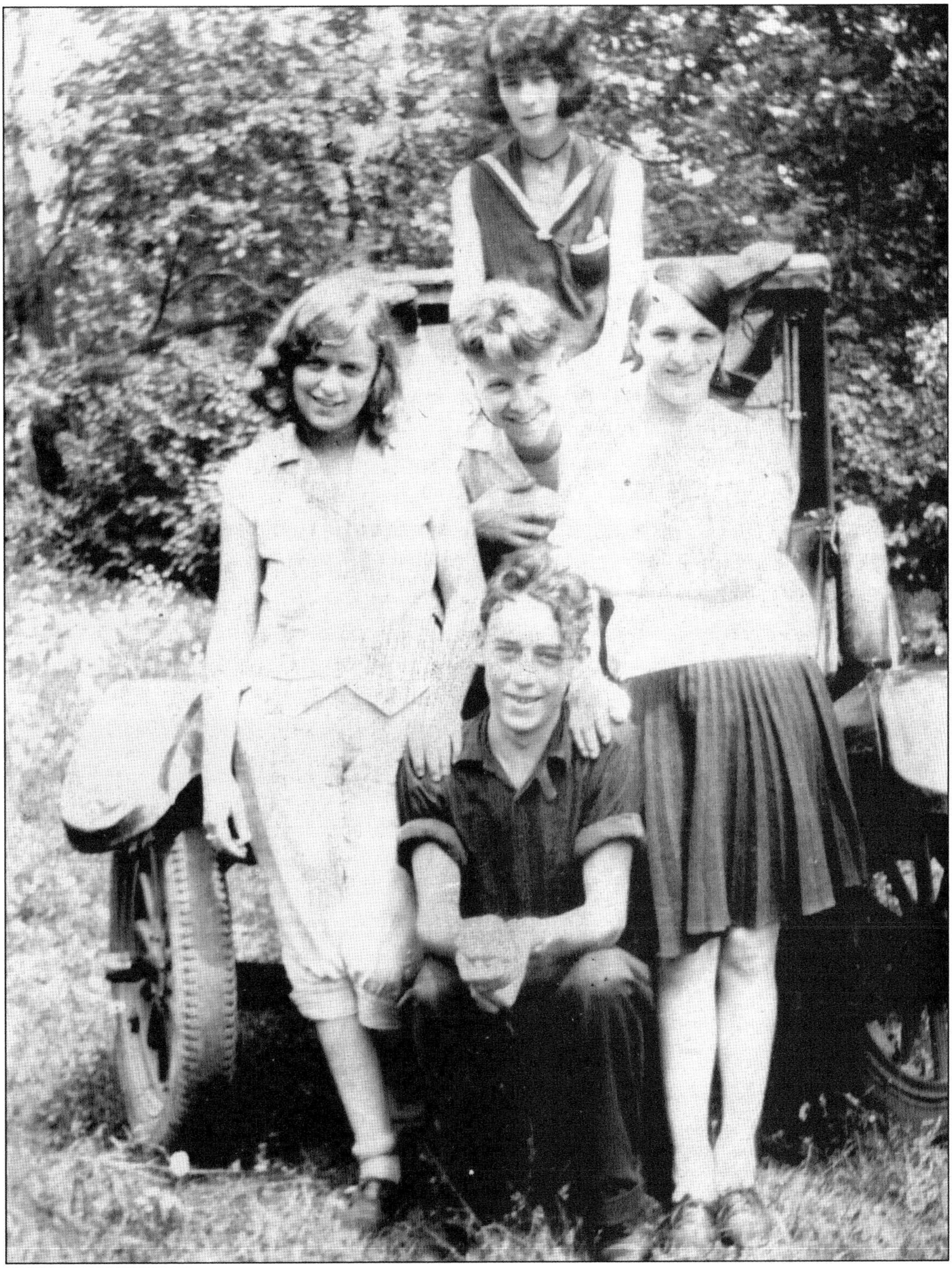

These young people were having "a grand ol' time," according to Margaret E. Aughton Cherry. One day in 1927, they decided to go camping, and they drove up Big Pond Road, pulled over, and camped near the side of the road. Seen here are, from left to right, the following: (front row) David Edwards; (middle row) Margaret Cherry, Charlie Burrows, and unidentified (David's girlfriend); (back row) Alice Edwards Burrows. Franklin Cherry, Margaret's husband, took this photograph. (Author's collection.)

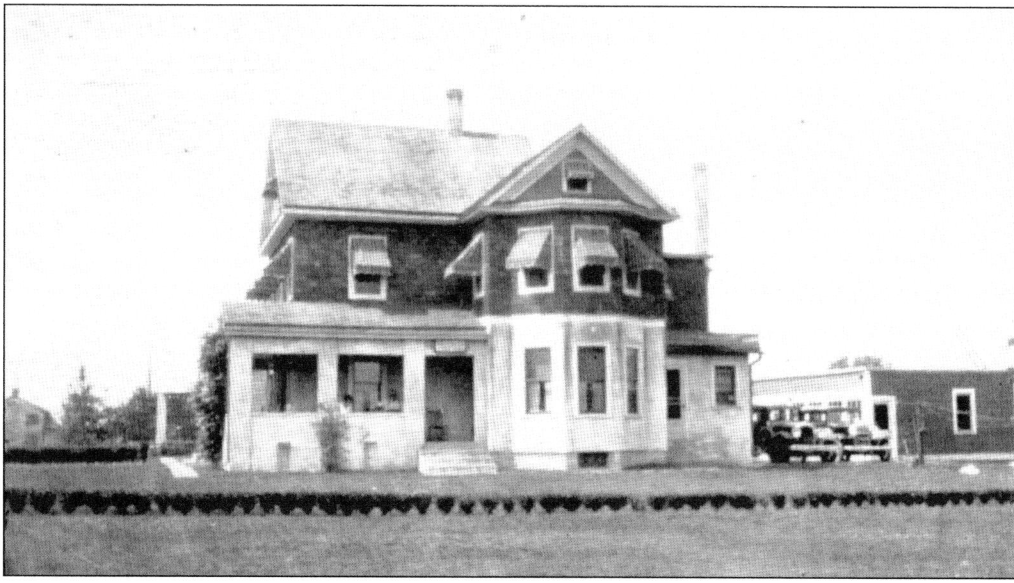

Many generations of the Space family have lived along this stretch of Route 209. This house, near the corner of Route 209 (6N) and Peenpack Trail, is just one example of the homes and farmhouses that took in boarders. It was called End-O-Day and was run at the time by Mrs. C.W. Space. The Huguenot Post Office was located in the front room of Harriet Space's residence, just behind the End-O-Day. Harriet Space retired as postmaster in 1969, and Betty Rolff took over. The post office moved to the present site in 1971. (Author's collection.)

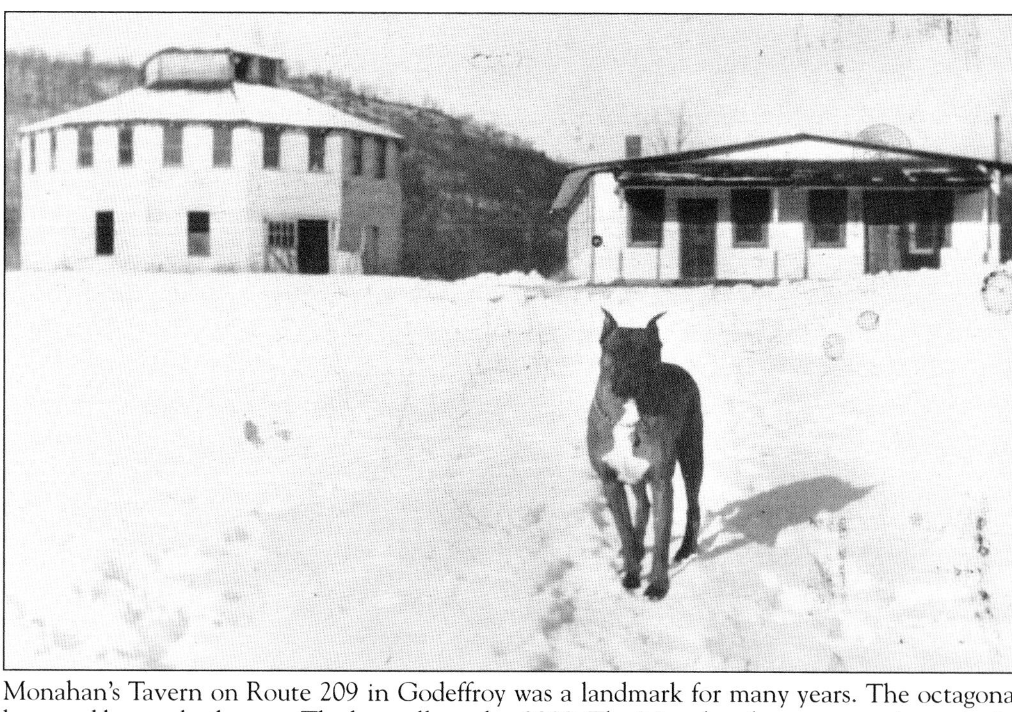

Monahan's Tavern on Route 209 in Godeffroy was a landmark for many years. The octagonal barn and bar are both gone. The bar collapsed *c.* 2000. The Monahan boxers were always in the bar and were well known throughout the community. (Deerpark Historian's Office.)

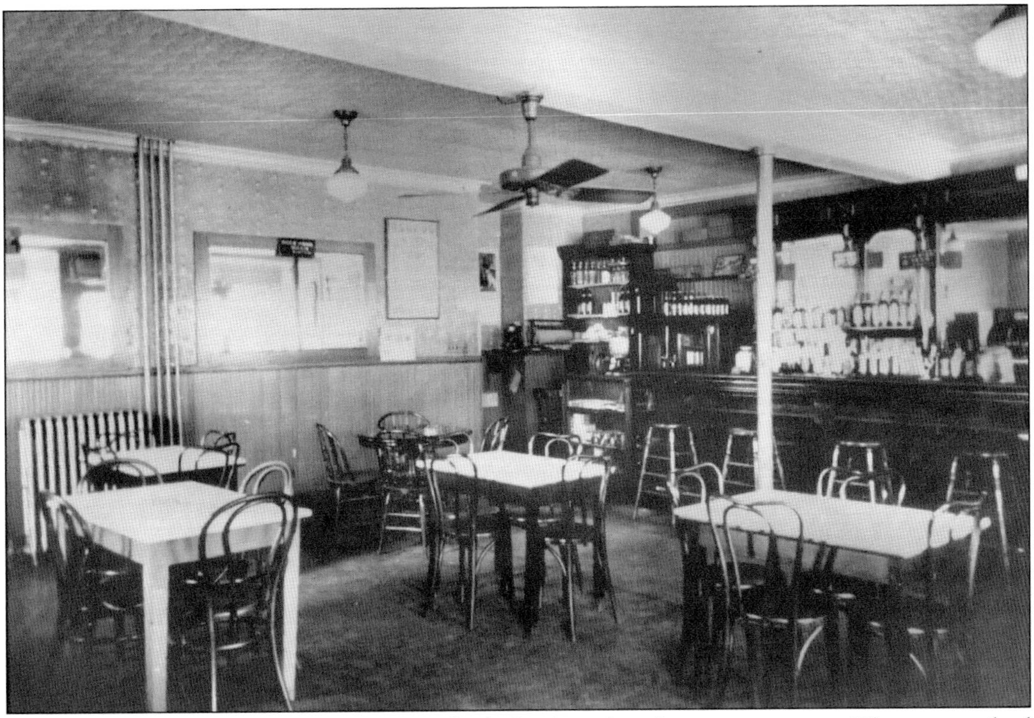

Everyone said that Monahan's Tavern had the best hamburgers in town. The tavern had beautiful tin ceilings and a classic hardwood bar with mirrors. (Deerpark Historian's Office.)

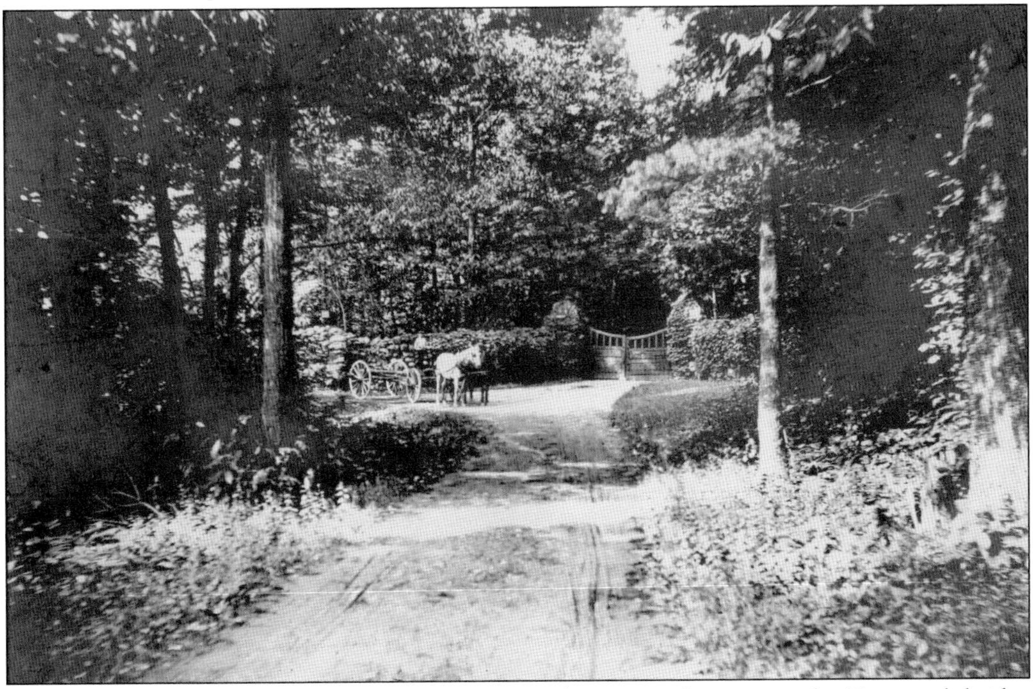

The common saying is a grand estate needs a grand entrance. Just across the Neversink bridge on Guymard Turnpike in Godeffroy stand two stone walls and pillars. Beyond the gates stood a mansion owned by the Otis Plock family. (Deerpark Historian's Office, Myers Collection.)

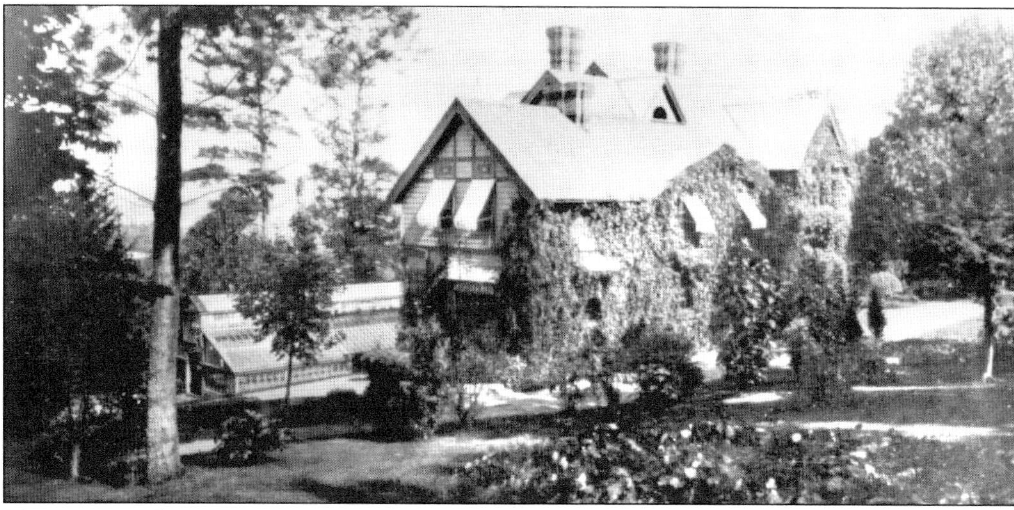

The mansion, known as Minqua Park, consisted of more than 800 acres between the Neversink River and the Erie Railroad. The buildings were designed by Henry J. Hardenberg, Esq., a well-known New York architect. According to an old real estate flyer, "No expense was spared, all and everything was of the best. It was completely finished in hardwood throughout—has all modern improvements as hot and cold water, gas, bath rooms, and water closets." This photograph from 1877 shows the vine-covered mansion and its large glass greenhouse. (Deerpark Historian's Office, Myers Collection.)

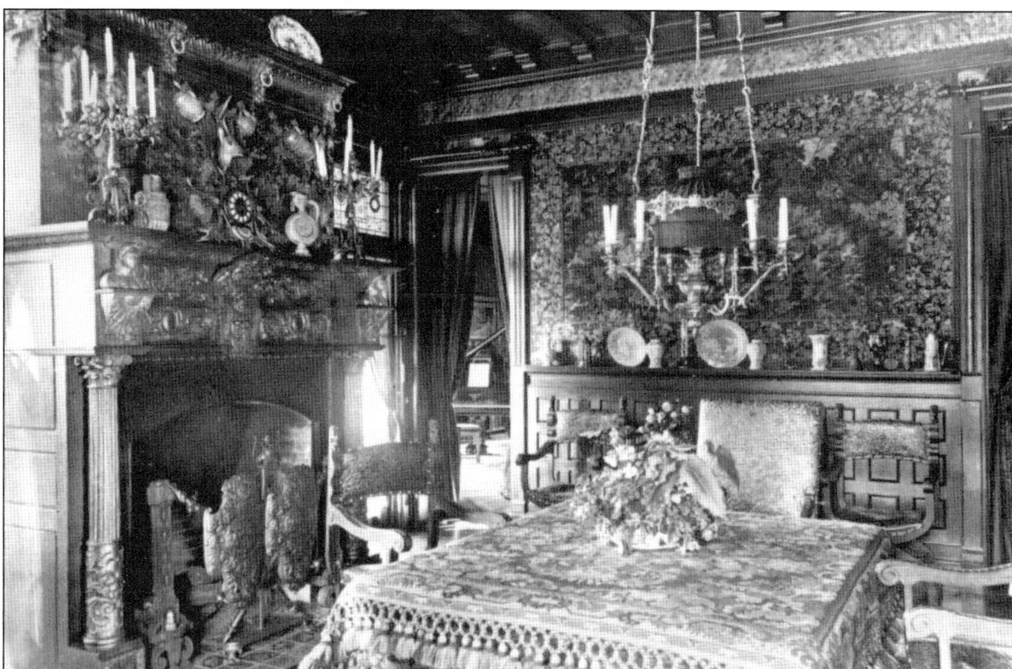

A real estate brochure states that the "dining room [was] finished in old oak and hung with gobelins, and a beautiful carved mantle piece, being a copy of one of the most famous 15th century exhibits in the Cluny at Paris, a very large and artistic colored glass window representing the legend of Lohengrin was secured by the owner in Europe." (Deerpark Historian's Office, Myers Collection.)

"The first floor contains a very large hall (ornamented with a fine collection of moose heads) running through two-stories high with gallery, sitting room, with an especially grand view," according to a real estate brochure. The house also had five bedrooms with dressing rooms, a butler's pantry, a large kitchen, and servants' rooms in a wing by themselves. (Deerpark Historian's Office, Myers Collection.)

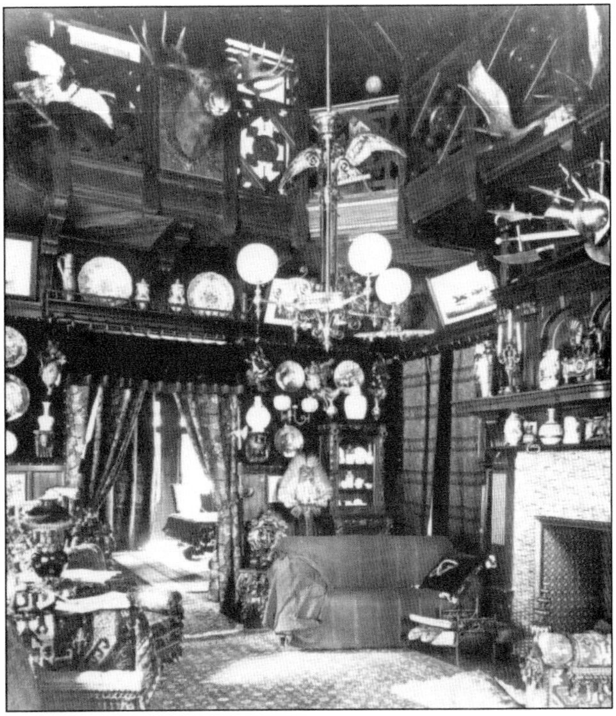

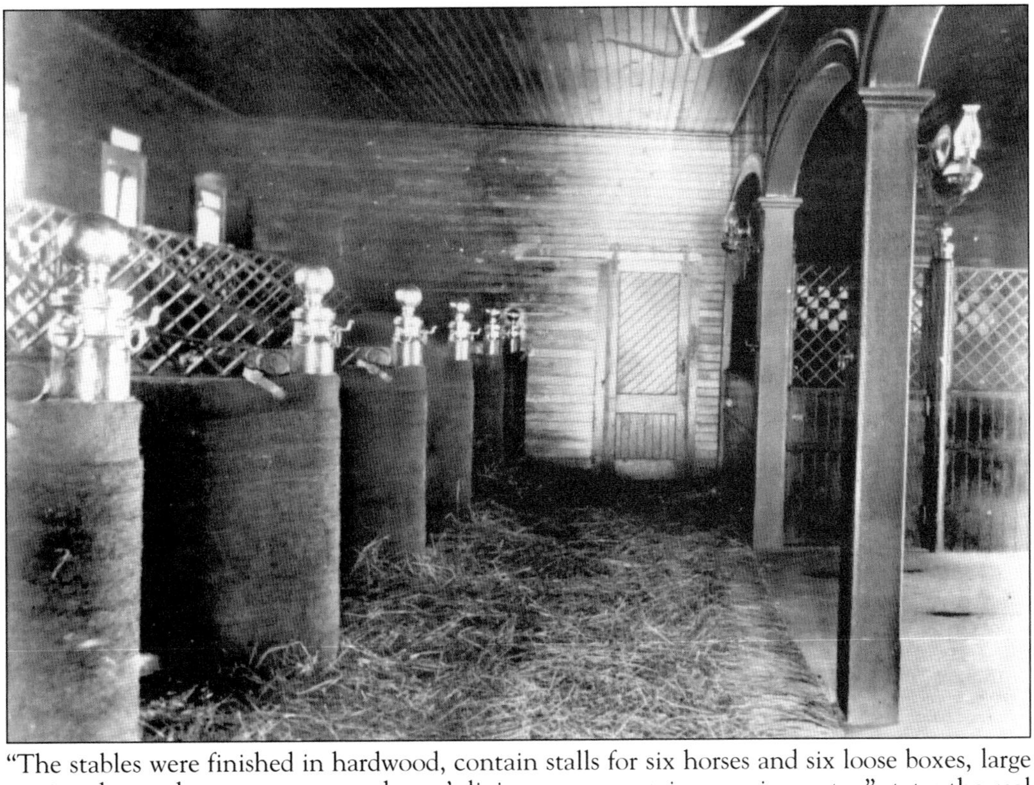

"The stables were finished in hardwood, contain stalls for six horses and six loose boxes, large carriage house, harness room, coachman's living rooms upstairs, running water," states the real estate brochure. (Deerpark Historian's Office, Myers Collection.)

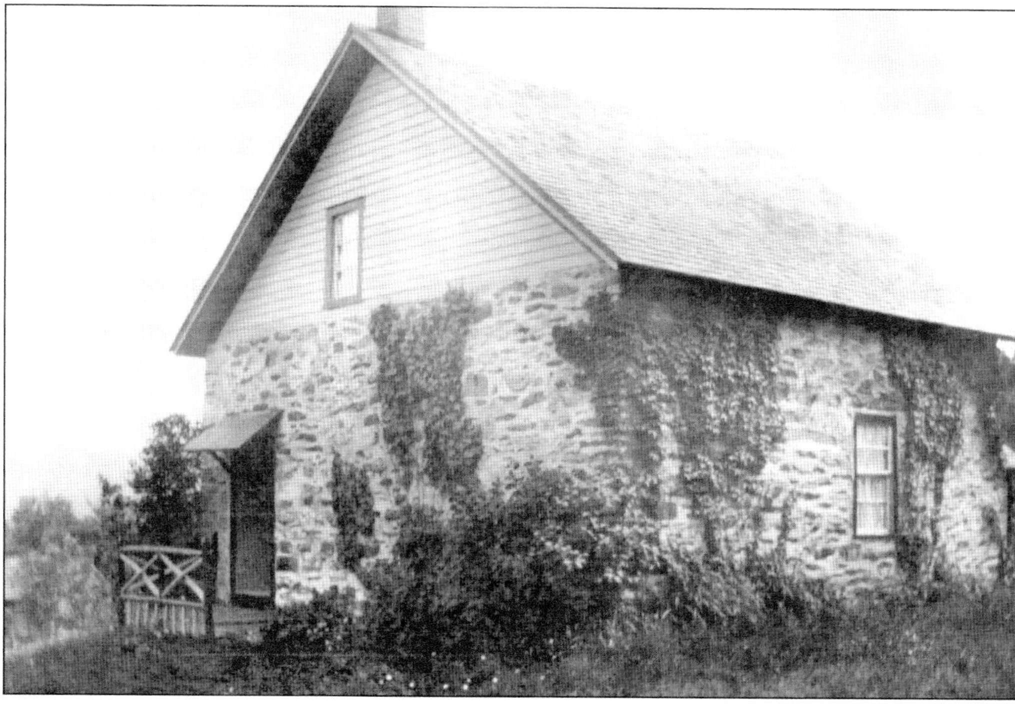

Jacques Caudebec was born in 1666 and died *c.* 1766. Caudebec, who was the builder of the first gristmill in the Peenpack area (Godeffroy), built his small stone fort *c.* 1740s. Fortunately, when Joseph Brant's raiders swept through the valley in October 1778, burning and looting, this building was left intact. Still standing, the stone house can be seen on Route 209 in Godeffroy. (Neversink Valley Area Museum.)

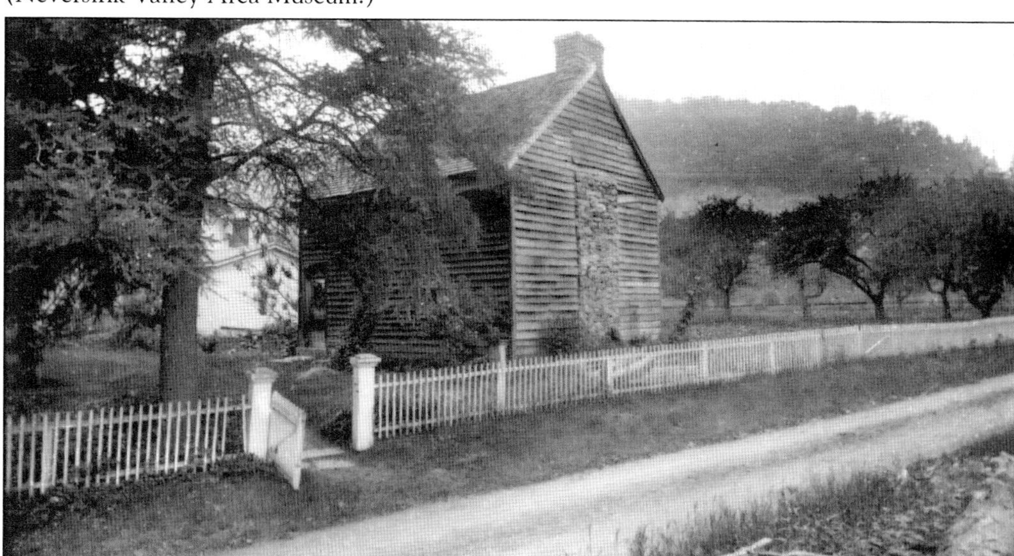

The birthplace of DeWitt Clinton still stands near the Neversink bridge at Roses Point. It was part of the Capt. Jacob Rutsen DeWitt Fort. During Brant's raid, this fort is said to have sheltered about 100 people. In the 1940s, the fort was owned and used by Marcus Stamp as a magistrate's office and a court. (Minisink Valley Historical Society.)

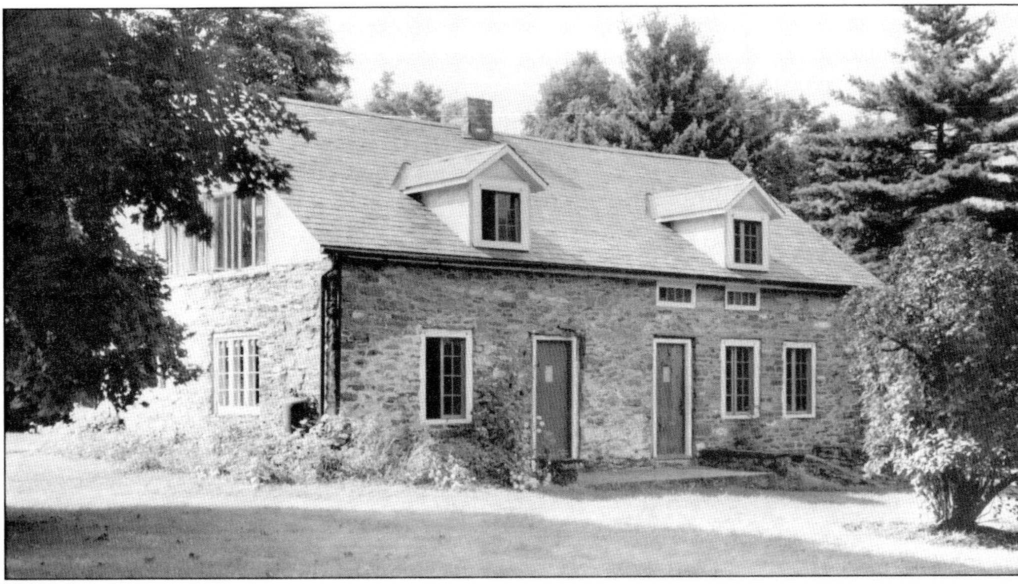

This stone house was built by Benjamin DePuy after the original fort and outbuildings were destroyed during Brant's raid of October 1778. The property was sold to Peter E. Gumaer in 1803, after the DePuys moved upstate. The stone house later belonged to the Godeffroy estate but is still known as the "old Gumaer stone house." (Minisink Valley Historical Society.)

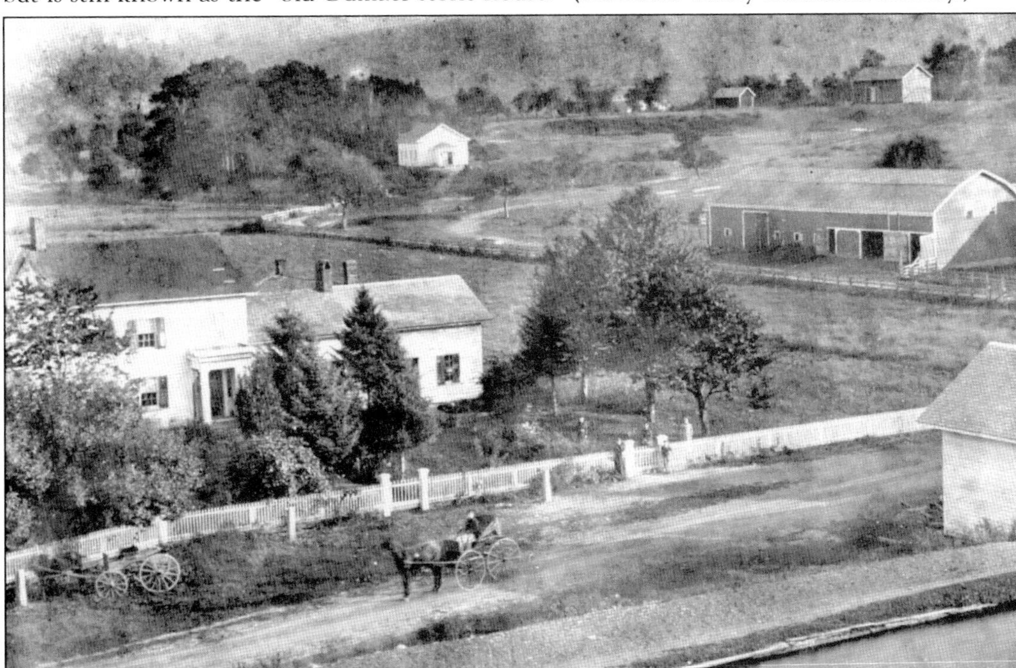

The Peter E. Gumaer homestead, built *c.* 1814, stands near the corner of Guymard Turnpike and Canal Drive (Old Route 209), in Godeffroy. It later became the Myers farm. In the forefront of the picture, the Delaware and Hudson Canal can be seen flowing past the farmhouse. The small white building in the background is the Godeffroy schoolhouse. (Minisink Valley Historical Society.)

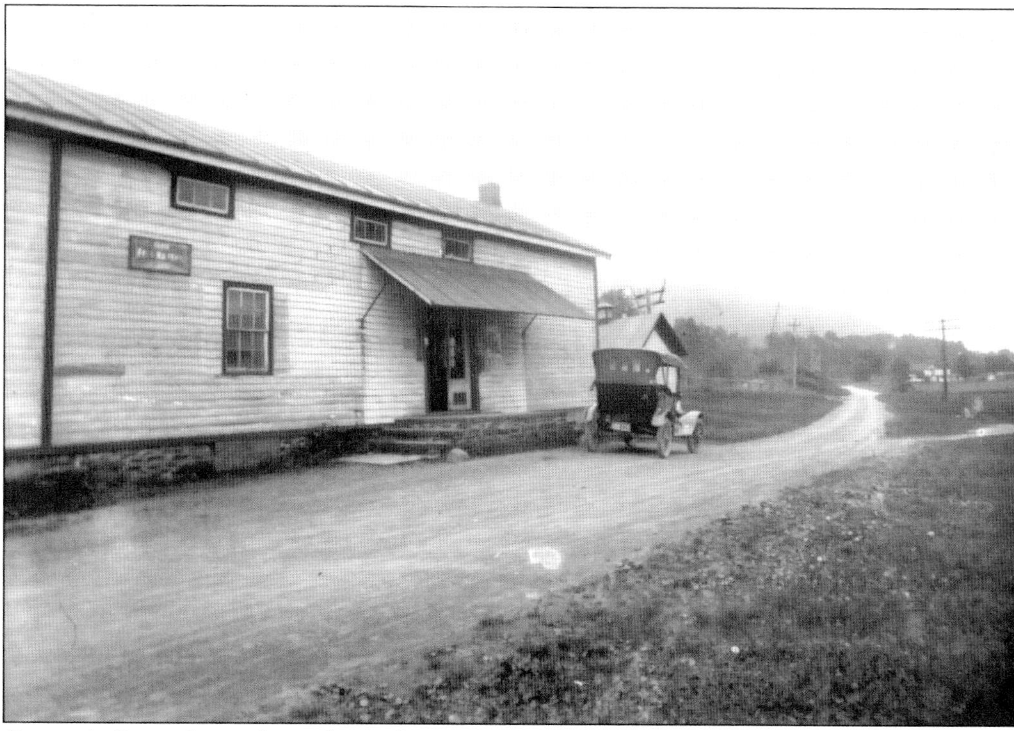

Gumaer's Store, located on the Delaware and Hudson Canal, served Canawlers as well as townspeople and housed the post office. This photograph was taken *c.* 1910. Today, the building is a private residence. (Minisink Valley Historical Society.)

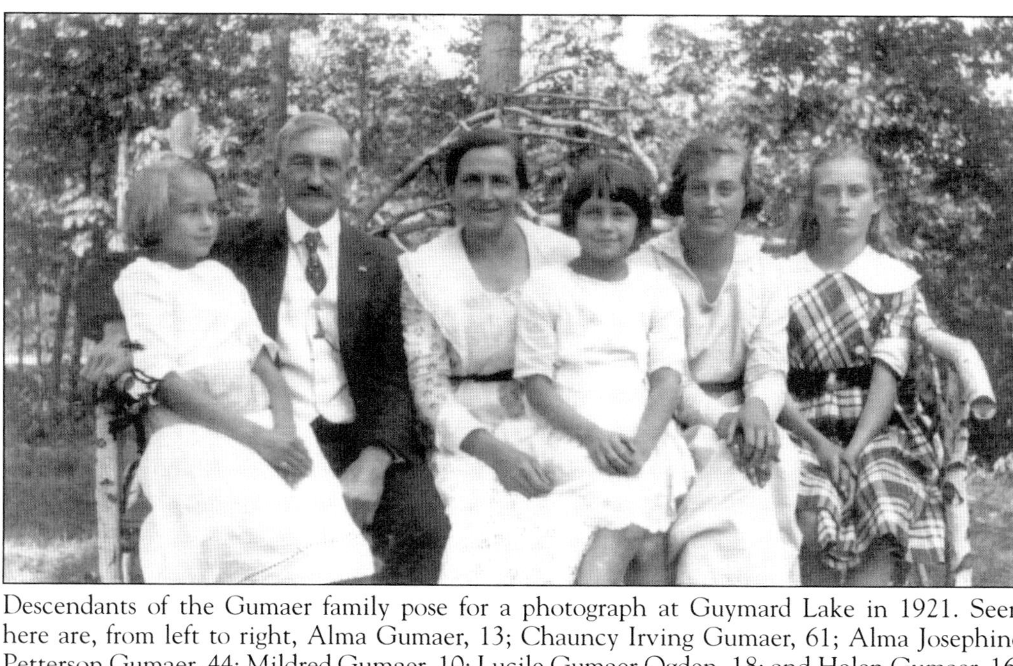

Descendants of the Gumaer family pose for a photograph at Guymard Lake in 1921. Seen here are, from left to right, Alma Gumaer, 13; Chauncy Irving Gumaer, 61; Alma Josephine Petterson Gumaer, 44; Mildred Gumaer, 10; Lucile Gumaer Ogden, 18; and Helen Gumaer, 16. (Deerpark Historian's Office, Gumaer Collection.)

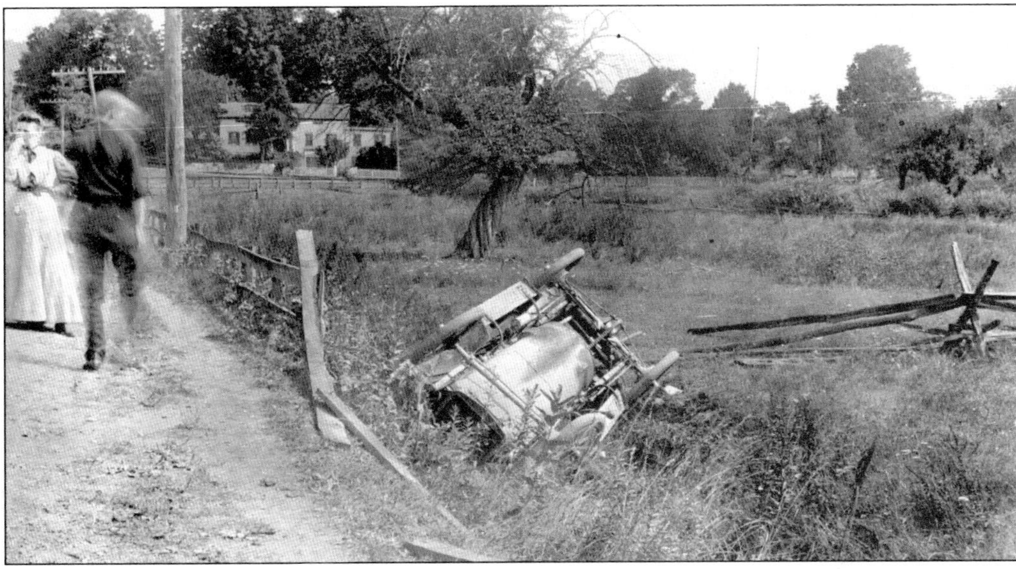

August 31, 1907, marks the day of the first major car accident in the area. Andrew Maxwell of Wurtsboro lost control of his Buick car, overturning on the Benjamin Cuddeback farm in Cuddebackville. Andrew Maxwell and John S. Fields were killed. Katherine Eglinger and her two children were severely injured. This accident was so unusual and newsworthy that a number of photographic-postcard views were made. (Author's collection.)

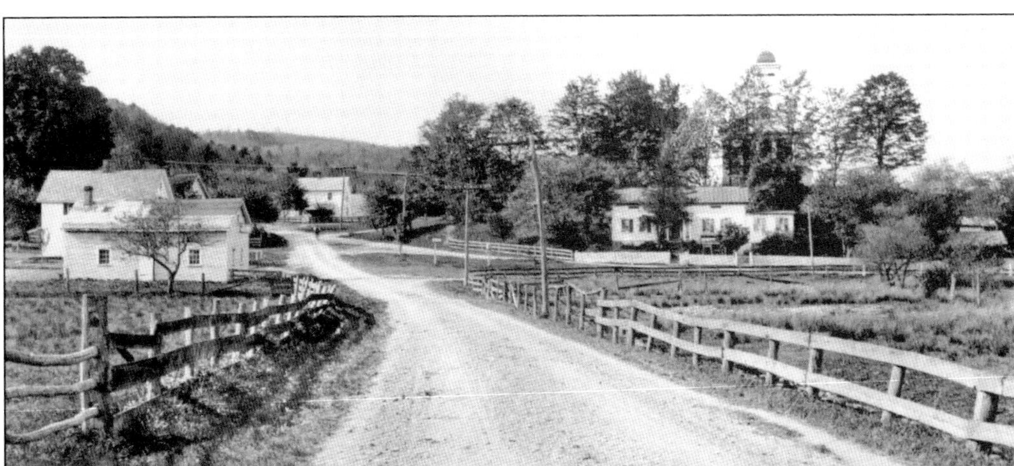

The former Lewis Cuddeback house overlooks the intersection of present-day Routes 209 and 211. The building in the left foreground of this photograph, which was taken in the 1890s or early 1900s, is no longer there. (Author's collection.)

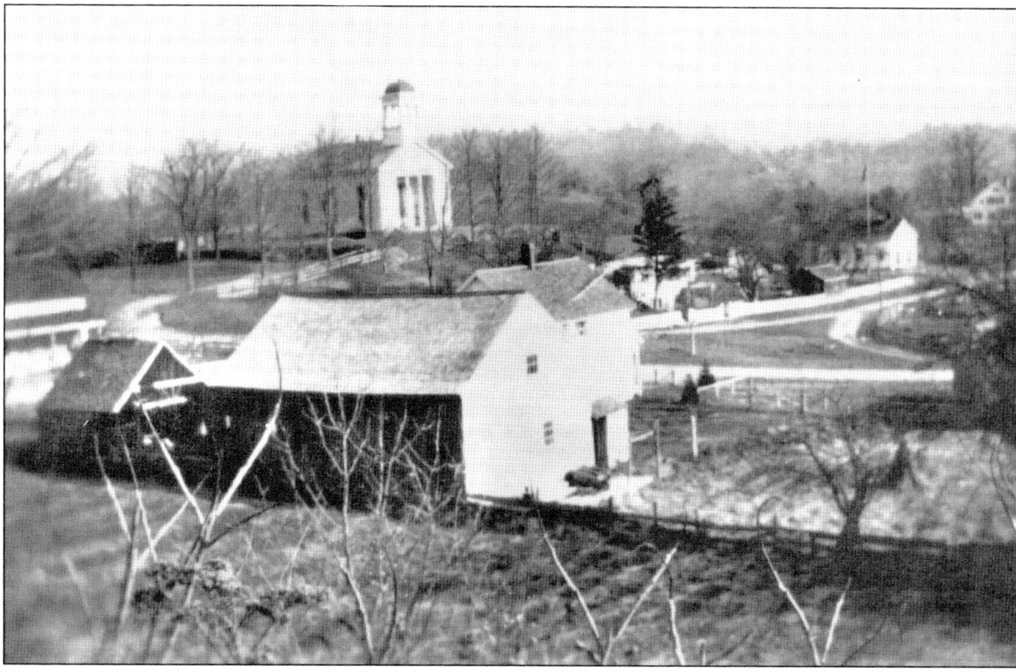

This *c.* 1900 view of Cuddebackville shows the intersection from the Delaware and Hudson Canal towpath. In the foreground is the Feibiger Egg Farm. A number of Cuddeback houses can be seen, and the Cuddebackville Dutch Reformed Church is on the hill. (Jerry and Margaret Peill.)

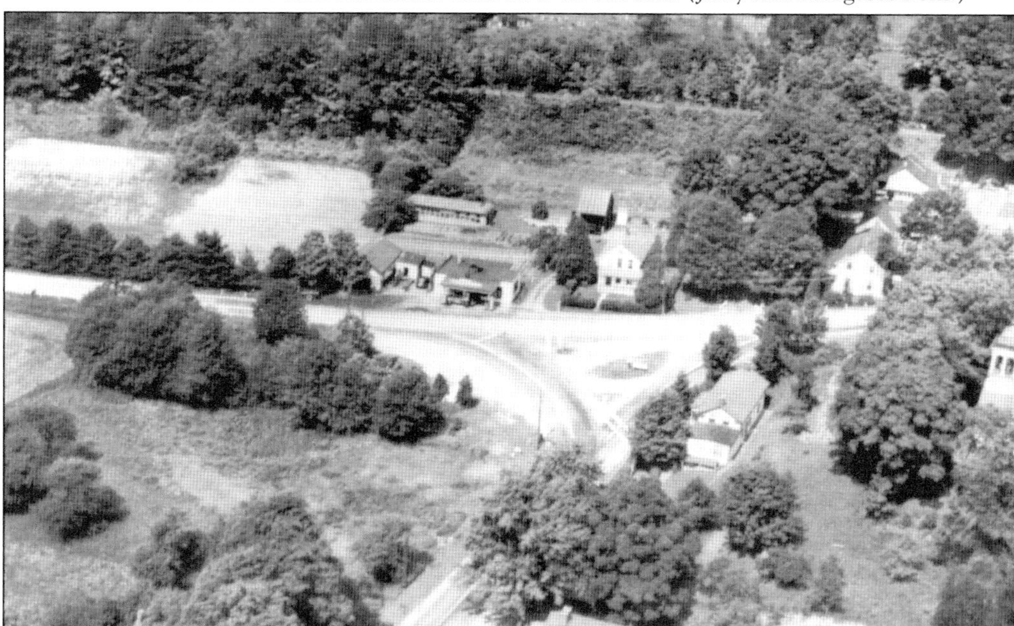

In this 1940s photograph, Cuddebackville has not changed a great deal from the previous photograph. The intersection, houses, and church are all the same. The Winters family built a garage and general store (later Baker's Store) next to the former Feibiger Egg Farm. The Delaware and Hudson Canal, its towpath, and the old section of the Rural Valley Cemetery can be seen. (Bill Flieger.)

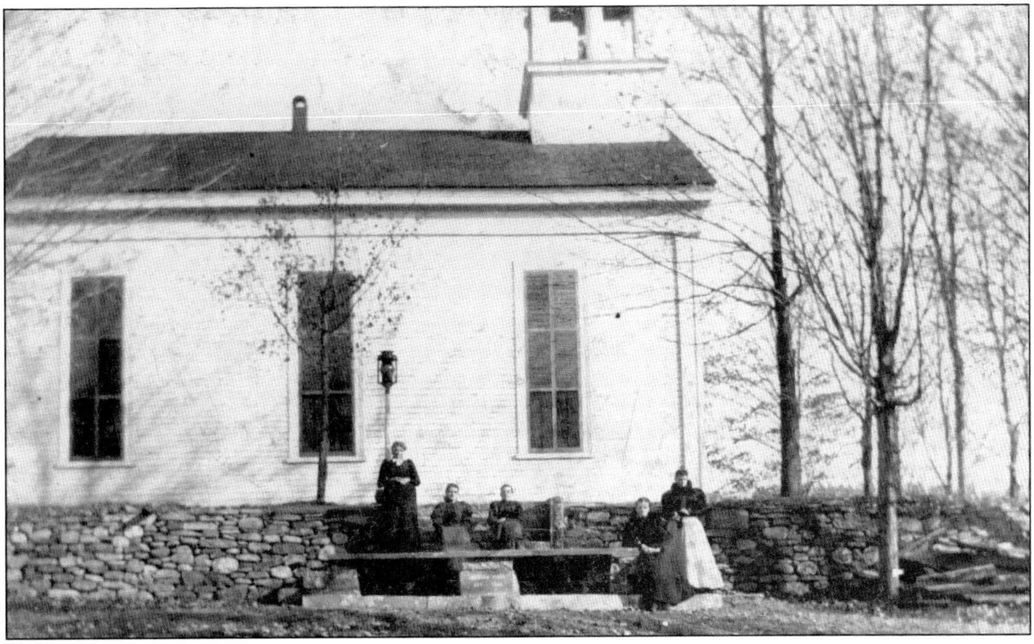

This *c.* 1896 photograph shows the Cuddebackville Reformed Church, built in 1853 by Martin Wheeler in the Greek Revival style on land donated by Lewis Cuddeback. The cost of the church was $3,300. In 1856, the bell was brought by canal boat to the site and was rung continually the last few miles of the trip to announce its arrival. Peter E. Gumaer, the oldest man in town, was honored to ring the bell the first time after it was raised. In 1896, the stone steps and walk were installed by Jackson Brothers, costing $69. The church changed over the years. In the picture, shutters cover the windows. Today, there are stained glass windows. In 1936, the belfry was enclosed and the metal roof was replaced. (Deerpark Historian's Office.)

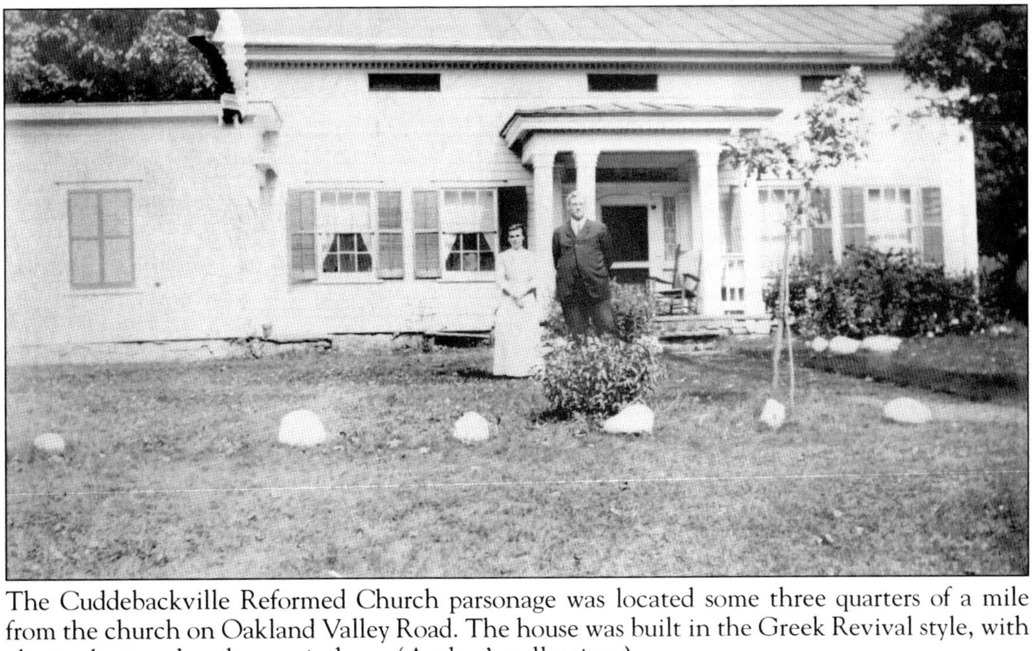

The Cuddebackville Reformed Church parsonage was located some three quarters of a mile from the church on Oakland Valley Road. The house was built in the Greek Revival style, with classic shuttered eyebrow windows. (Author's collection.)

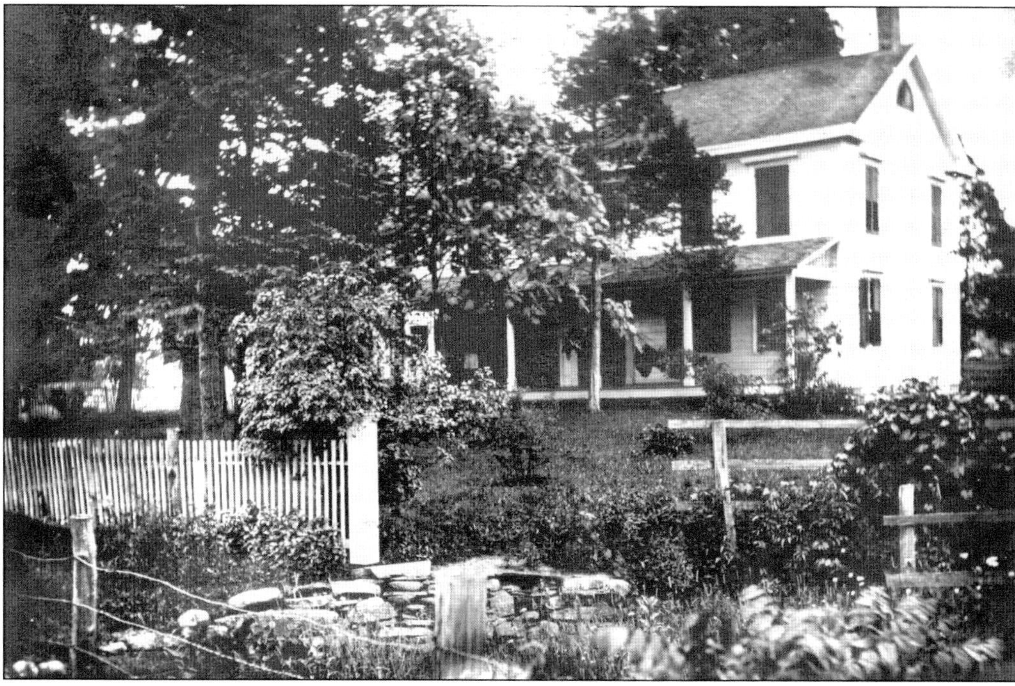

This *c.* 1880 view of the original Benjamin Cuddeback farmhouse, located on what is now Route 209, near the Route 211 intersection, is likely the only photograph showing the building as a house. The building was later moved to the back of the property and made into a chicken coop. The structure still stands. (Deerpark Historian's Office.)

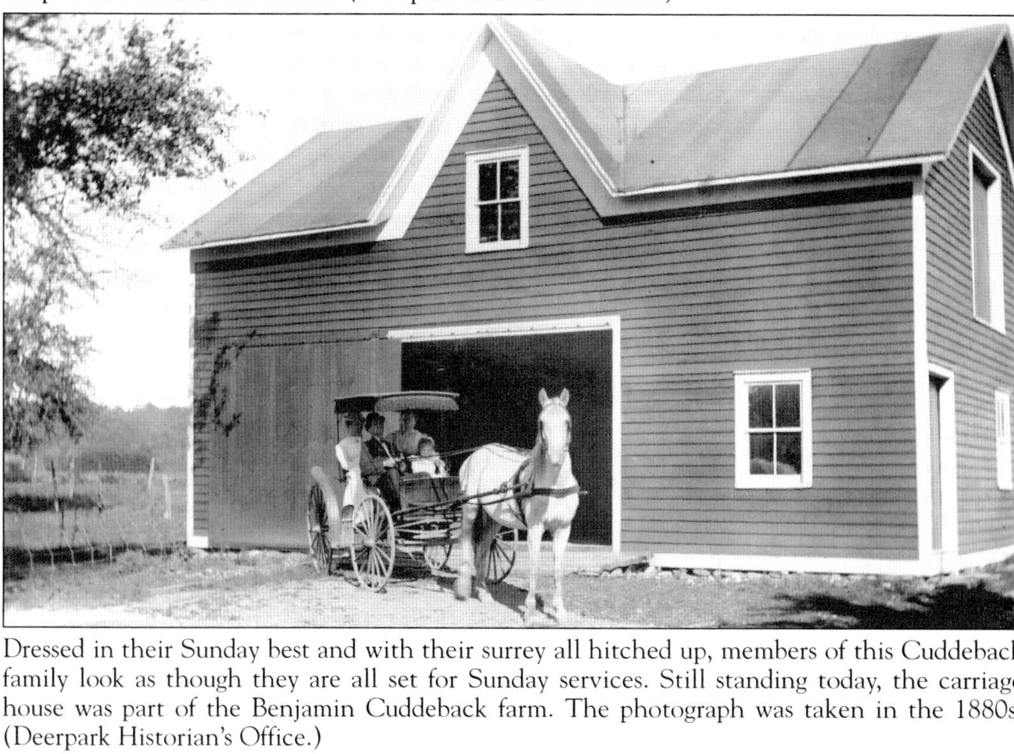

Dressed in their Sunday best and with their surrey all hitched up, members of this Cuddeback family look as though they are all set for Sunday services. Still standing today, the carriage house was part of the Benjamin Cuddeback farm. The photograph was taken in the 1880s. (Deerpark Historian's Office.)

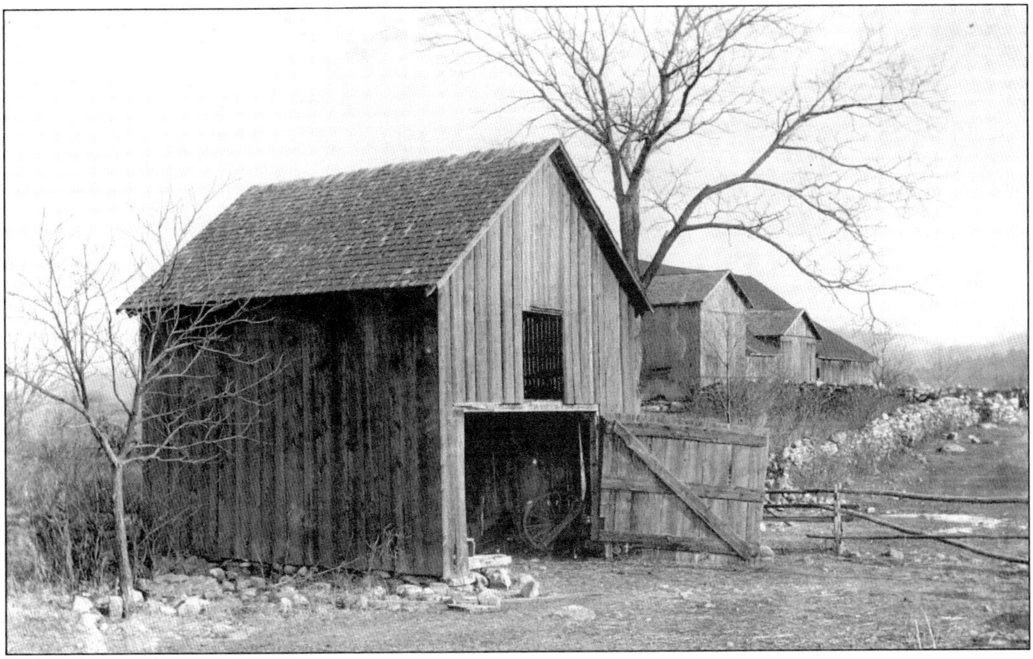

The Benjamin Cuddeback farm had several barns and outbuildings. These two are no longer on the property, but a few remain. This photograph was taken in the 1880s. (Deerpark Historian's Office.)

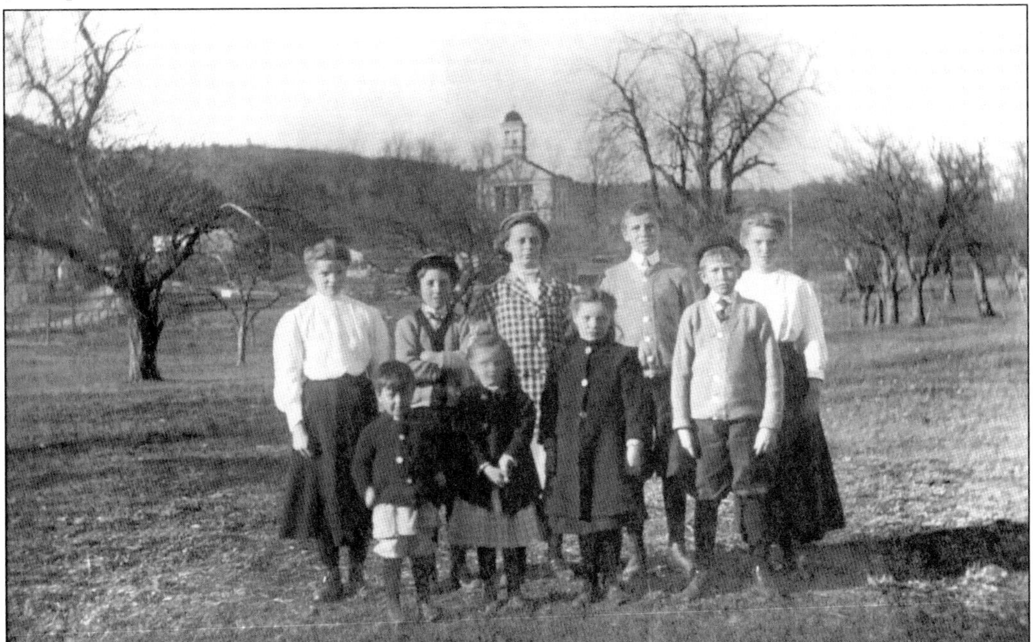

Sunday school students from the Cuddebackville Reformed Church pose on the Benjamin Cuddeback farm in front of the orchard between the 1890s and 1910. Seen here are, from left to right, the following: (front row) Arthur Hoag, Marion Collins, Babe Gould, and Frank Jackson; (back row) Mamie Gould, Elting Cuddeback, Emmaline Cuddeback, Job Jackson, and Anna Gould. (Neversink Valley Area Museum.)

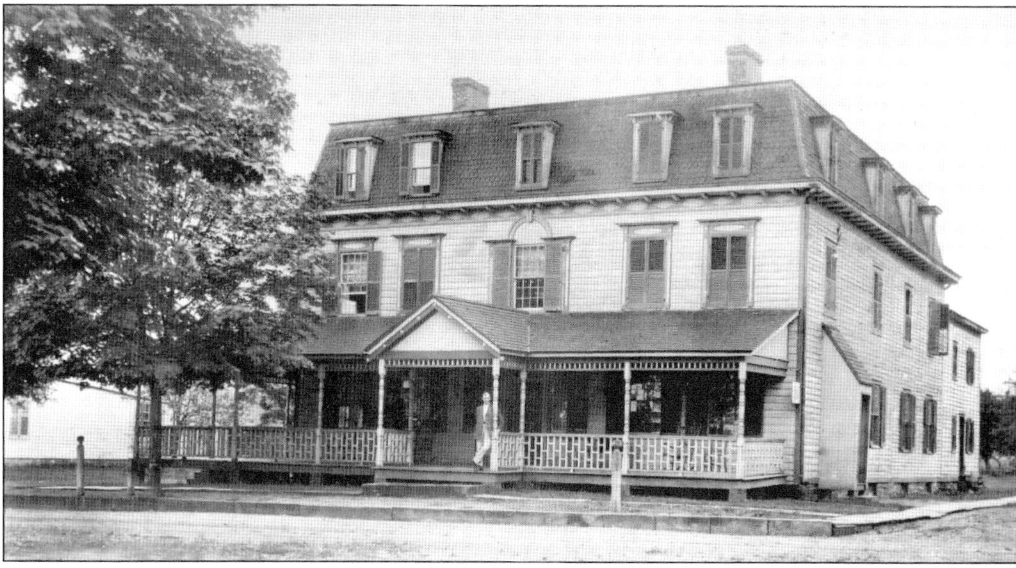

This very rare photograph of the Caudebec Inn, taken *c.* 1905, shows the Second Empire–style Victorian hotel as it once stood on Oakland Valley Road, between the two entrances of the Rural Valley Cemetery. It is said that the hotel could accommodate 80 guests, with some sleeping on cots in the halls, all sharing one bathroom. (Author's collection.)

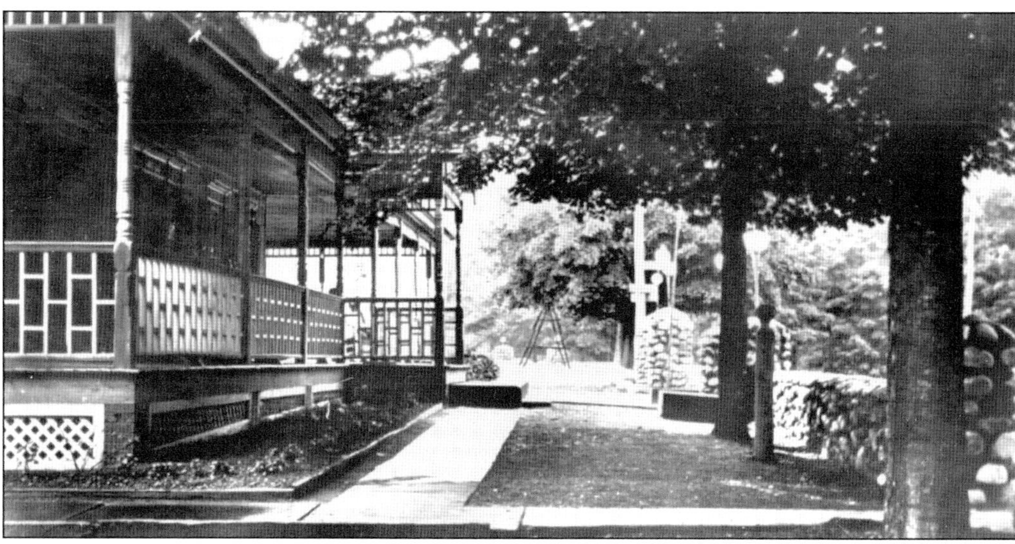

A few years later, the porch was extended around the side of the hotel, and a stone wall and pillars were erected. D.W. Griffith made six trips between 1909 and 1911 to make 20 silent films in Cuddebackville, and it was at this hotel that the stars stayed, including Mary Pickford, Lillian Gish, Florence Lawrence, Mack Sennett, and Henry Walthall. (Deerpark Historian's Office.)

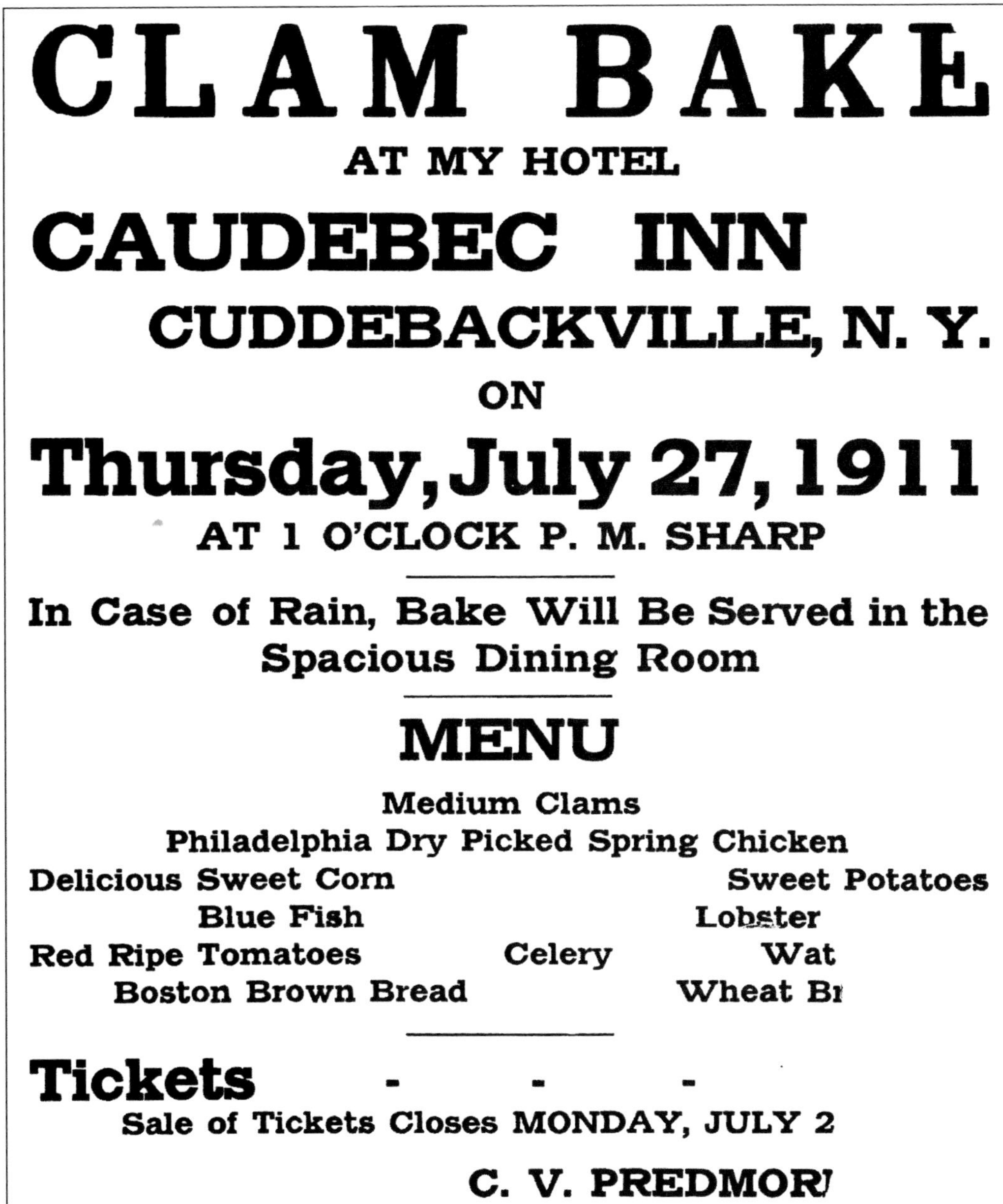

CLAM BAKE

AT MY HOTEL

CAUDEBEC INN

CUDDEBACKVILLE, N. Y.

ON

Thursday, July 27, 1911

AT 1 O'CLOCK P. M. SHARP

In Case of Rain, Bake Will Be Served in the Spacious Dining Room

MENU

Medium Clams
Philadelphia Dry Picked Spring Chicken
Delicious Sweet Corn — Sweet Potatoes
Blue Fish — Lobster
Red Ripe Tomatoes — Celery — Wat
Boston Brown Bread — Wheat B

Tickets - - -

Sale of Tickets Closes MONDAY, JULY 2

C. V. PREDMOR

In 1911, the Predmores owned the Caudebec Inn. This poster was for a clambake, which likely was held for the film stars and crew in 1911. It was found in California on the back of a picture frame by one of the Predmore descendants. (Neversink Valley Area Museum.)

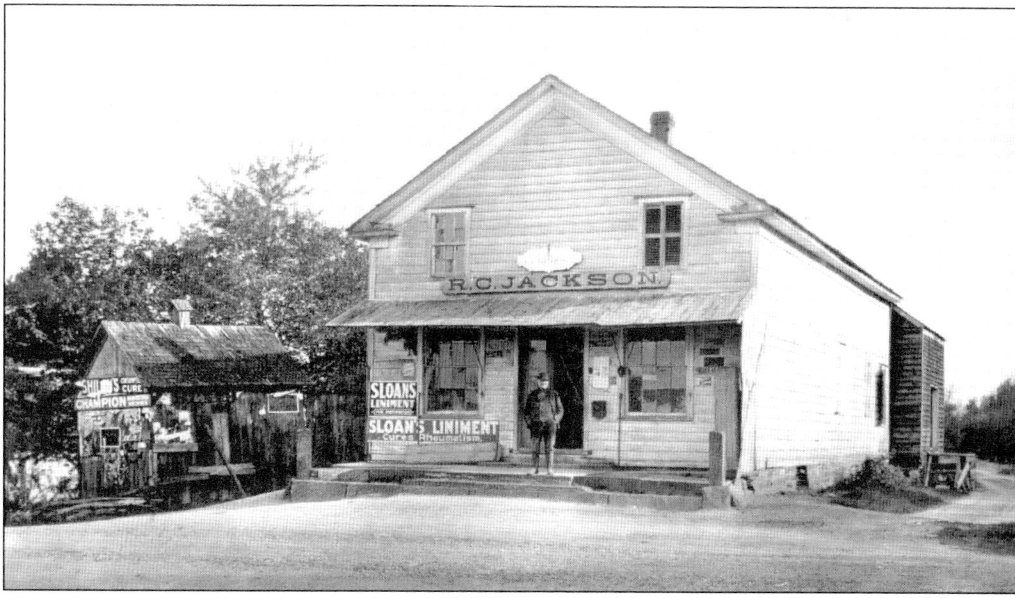

Still standing, R.C. Jackson's store and post office were located next to the canal on Oakland Valley Road. It is still popularly known as the Delaware and Hudson Canal Store. It closed for business in the 1990s. (Neversink Valley Area Museum.)

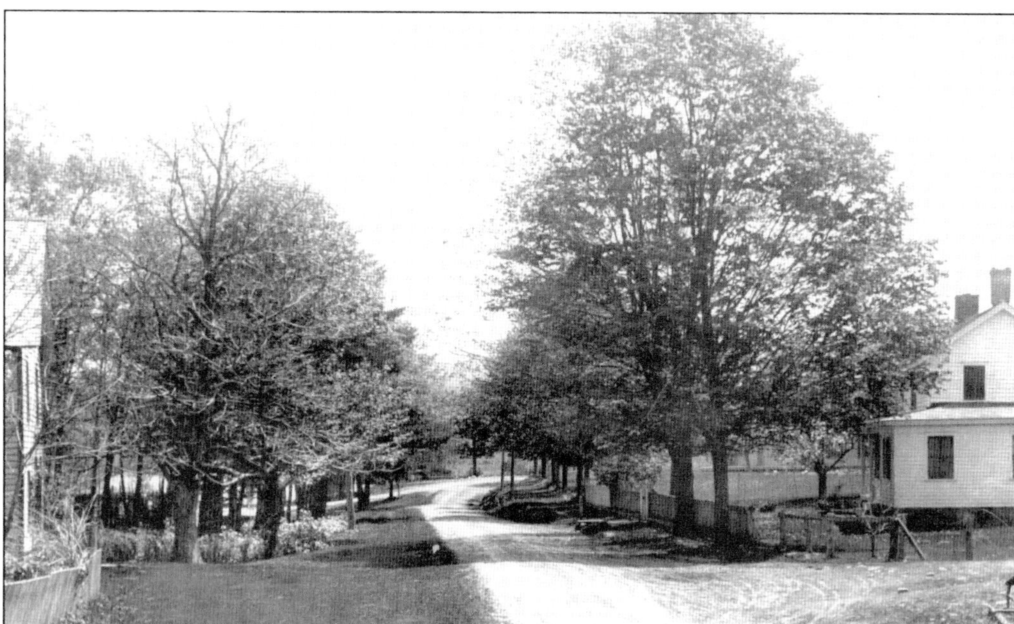

Lover's Lane in Cuddebackville is believed to be Gordon Road. Oakland Valley Road may be the road seen in the distance. The road could not be found on any old maps. (Neversink Valley Area Museum.)

The Cuddebackville firehouse, built in 1944–1945, is located on Route 209. This December 1946 photograph was taken in celebration of the first fire truck. Seen here are, from left to right, the following: (front row) Bill Flieger (chief), Ronnie Flieger (mascot), and Ted O'Hirok; (back row) Ray Lang, Harold Post, Art Morey, Mr. White, Frank VanLewvan, Tommy Conklin (navy uniform), Bill Johnson, Bill Hallock, Ralph Johnson, Charles Post (army uniform), and Floyd Johnson. (Bill Flieger.)

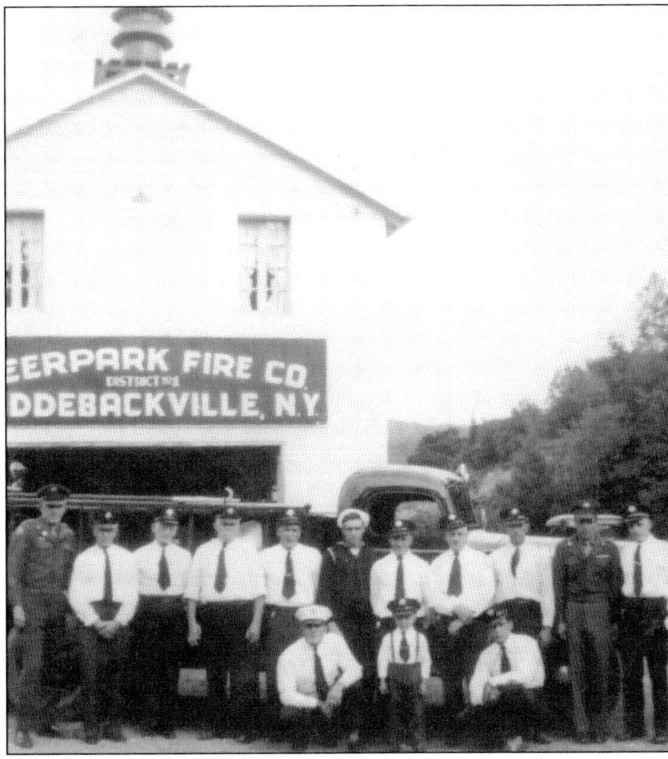

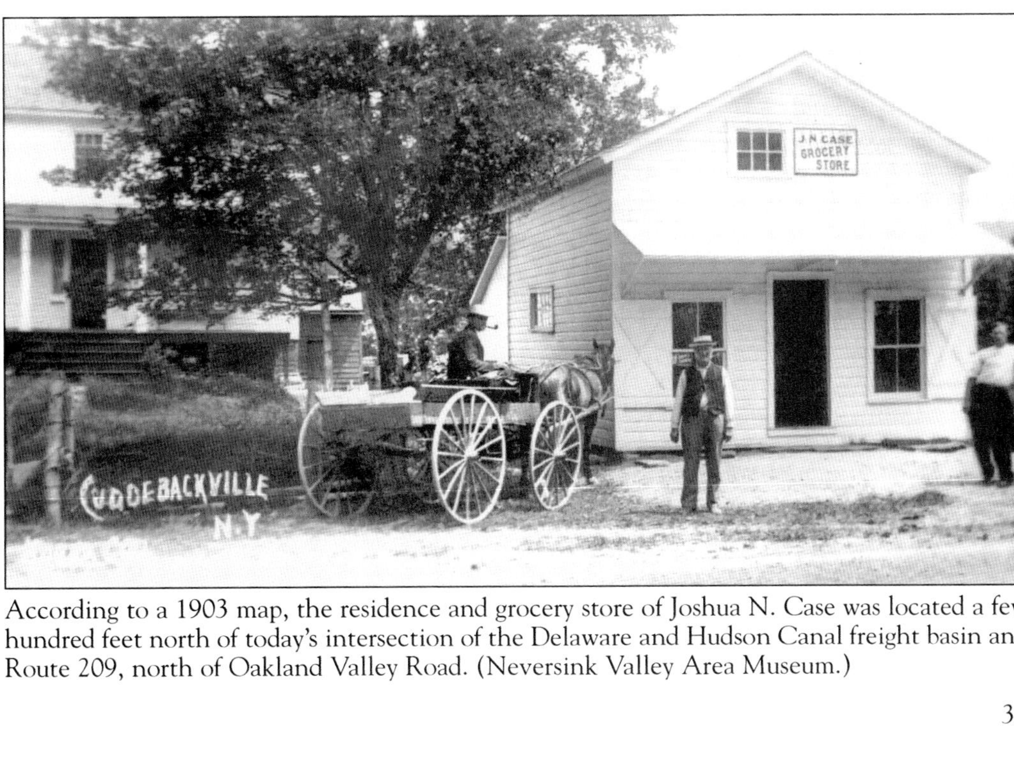

According to a 1903 map, the residence and grocery store of Joshua N. Case was located a few hundred feet north of today's intersection of the Delaware and Hudson Canal freight basin and Route 209, north of Oakland Valley Road. (Neversink Valley Area Museum.)

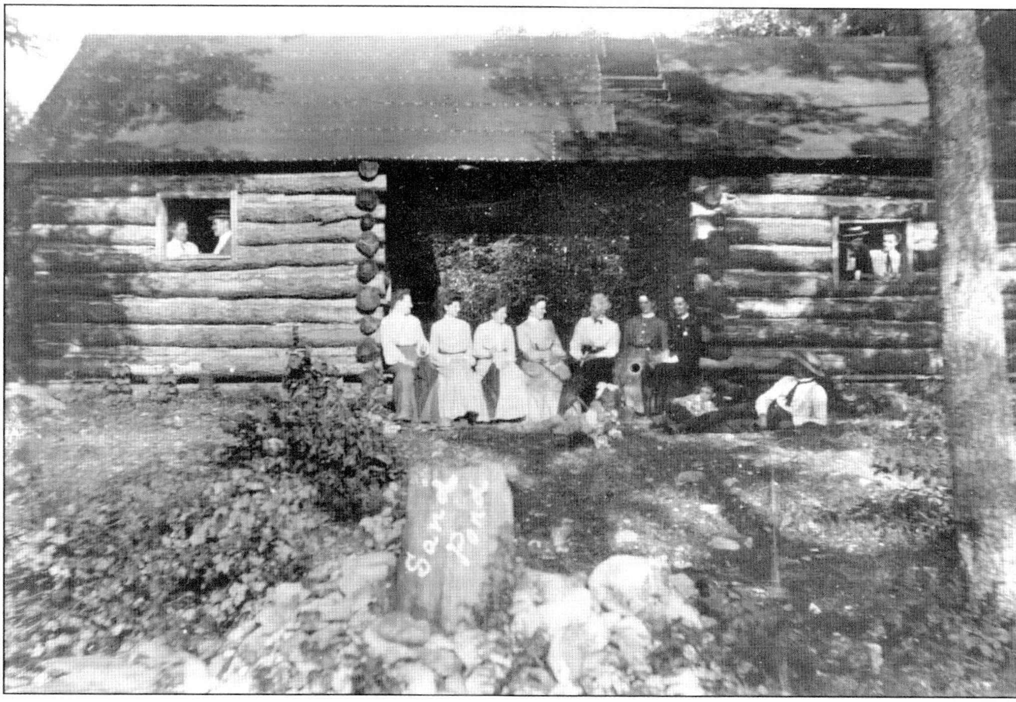

Sand Pond was the name of the lake at Camp Talcott, one of the YMCA camps in Huguenot. When two log cabins share one roof, the resulting structure is called a dogtrot. This photograph was taken in the late 1880s or 1890s. (Deerpark Historian's Office, Hoag Collection.)

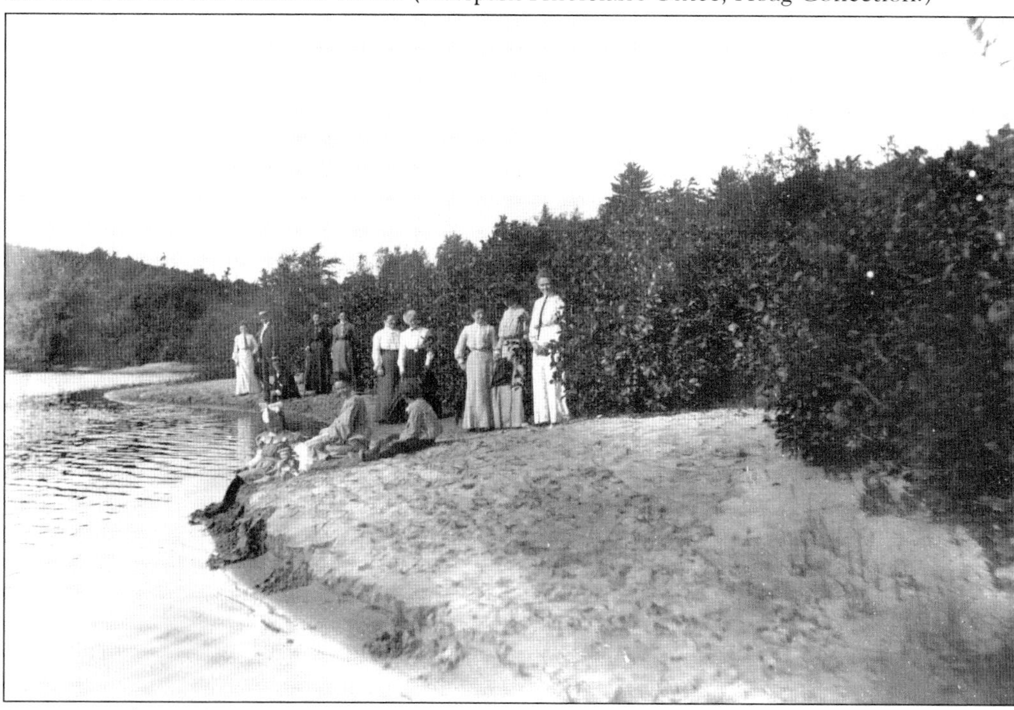

A group of people poses at Sand Pond in the 1880s or 1890s. (Deerpark Historian's Office, Hoag Collection.)

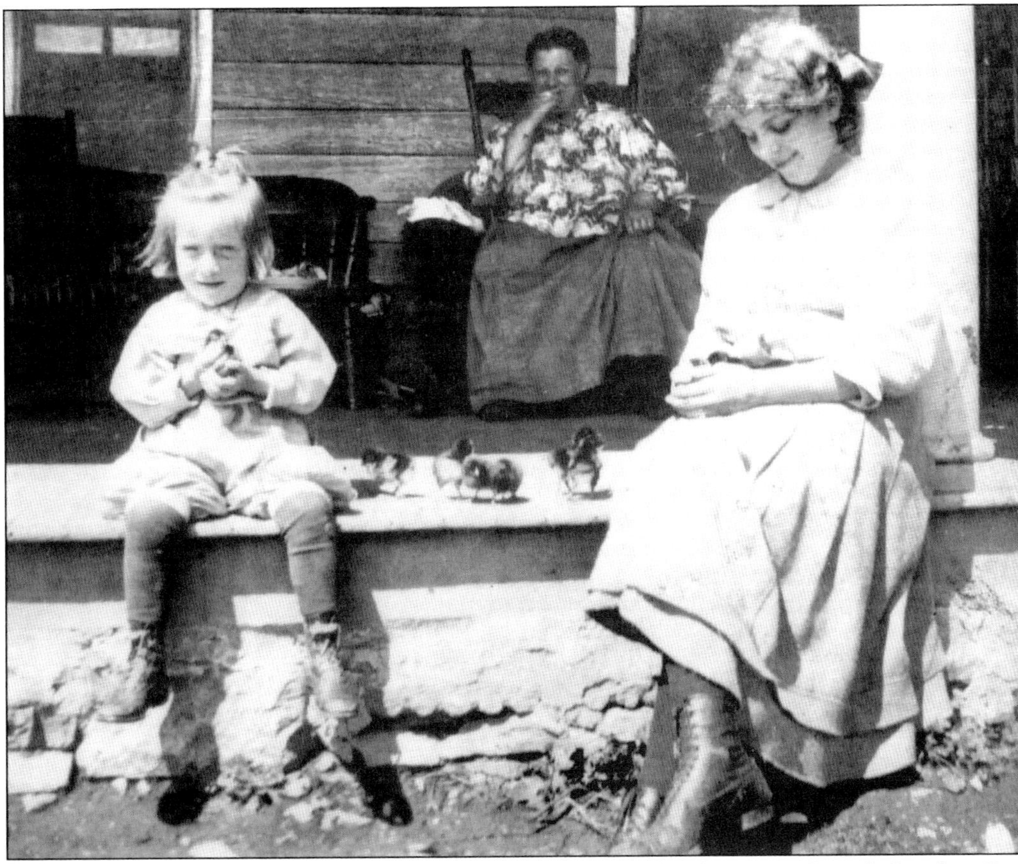

Camp Deerpark was at one time a working farm and boardinghouse on Brandt Road in Port Orange, north of Cuddebackville. Shown in this *c.* 1880 photograph are guests playing with baby chicks. (Deerpark Historian's Office.)

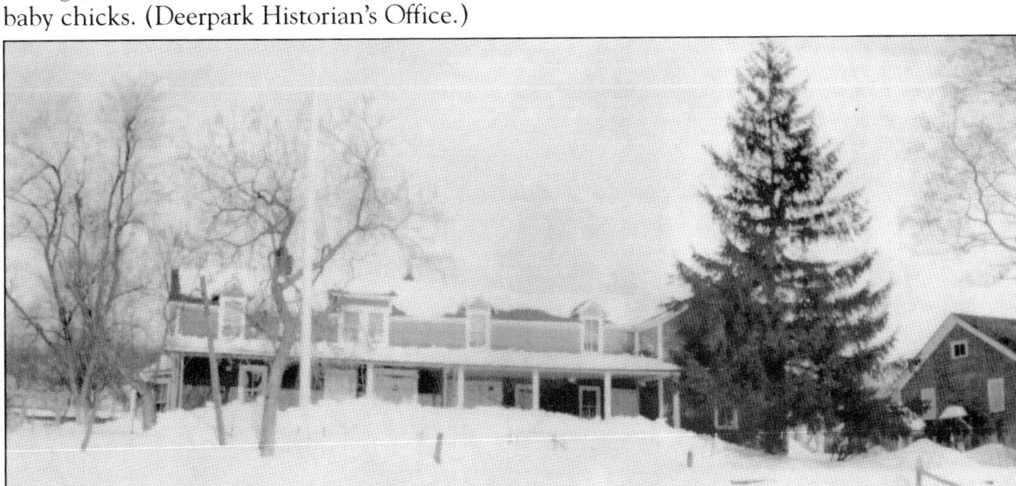

This photograph of Camp Deerpark was taken during a heavy snowstorm in the 1930s. Bill Flieger, an employee at the time, reminisced that it was during this time that electricity was generated from a Delco system. A separate building housed the Delco, a generator that charged a series of batteries connected by wire to power the camp. (Bill Flieger.)

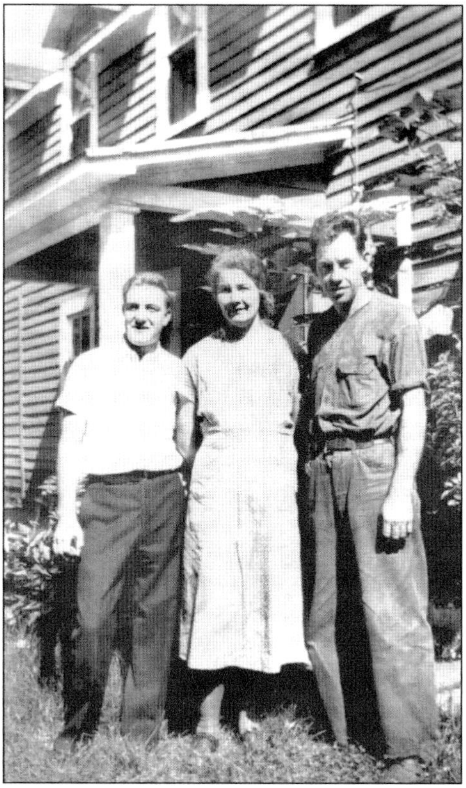

The second half of the 1800s saw as many as 22 boardinghouses and hotels in Deerpark. Foundations are often all that is left of these places. This photograph was taken in front of the main building at Camp Deerpark in the 1930s. Pictured are, from left to right, Bill Fleiger and Lillian and George Brandt, after whom Brandt Drive was named. (Bill Fleiger.)

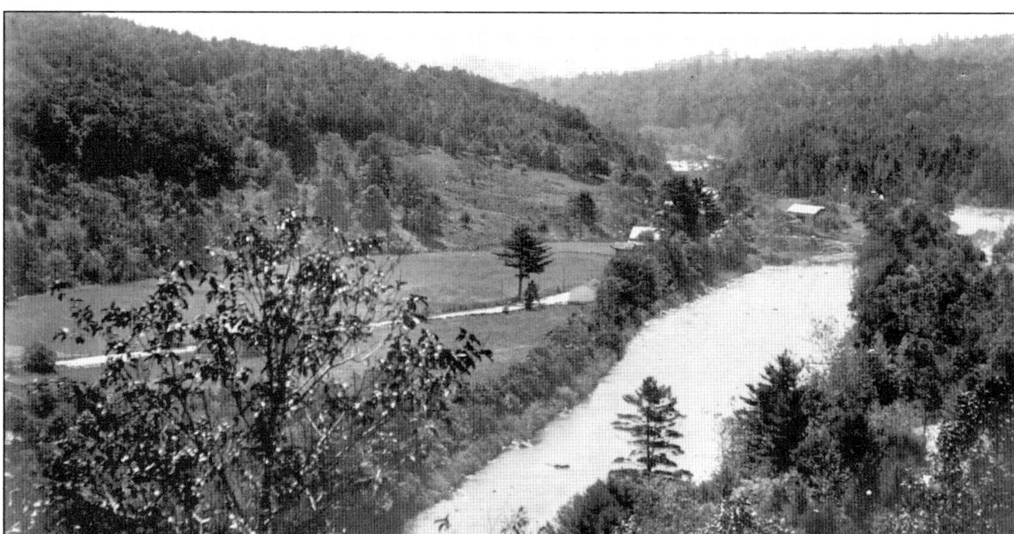

This view was taken looking toward the Neversink River in Oakland Valley in 1908. Oakland Valley Road was a one-lane dirt road until 1932. (Deerpark Historian's Office.)

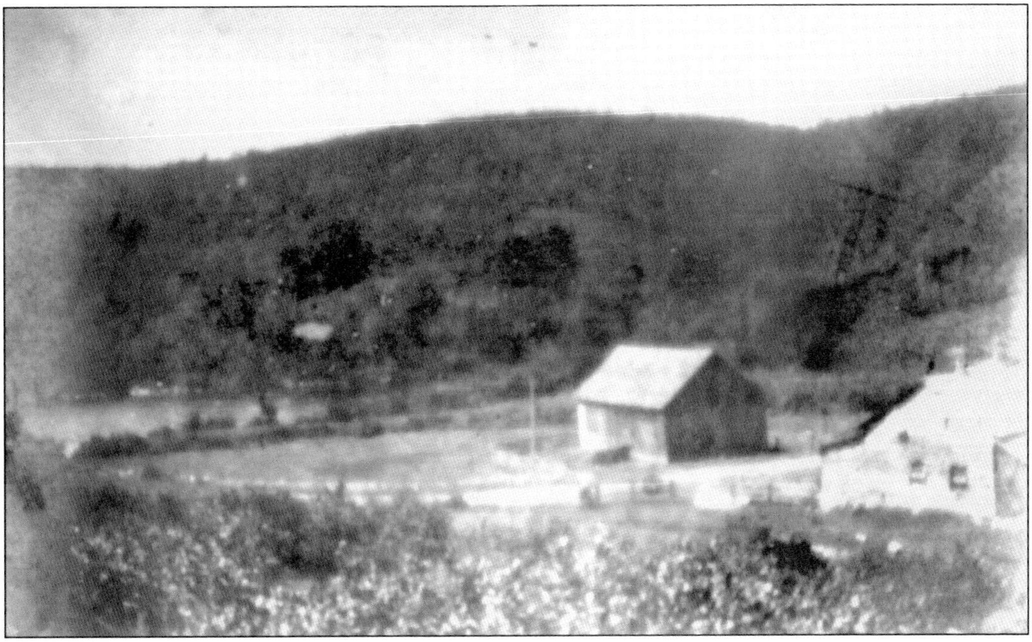

This rare bird's-eye view of the James A. and Anna Decker Lewis homestead in Oakland Valley was taken in the 1890s from above Buttermilk Falls. The Neversink River can be seen on the left, and Oakland Valley Road is visible between the farmhouse and barn. When the road was paved, the barn was in the way and had to be taken down in 1932. The property and waterfall were owned by the Lewis family from 1875 until the mid-1930s. (Author's collection.)

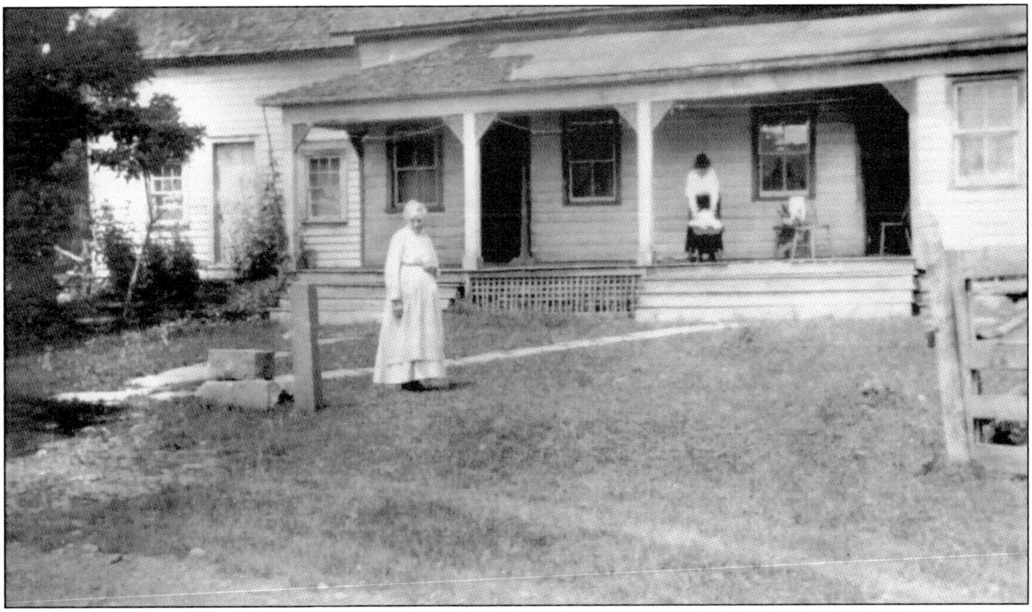

Posing in front of the James Lewis homestead and next to the old hitch post is Anna Decker Lewis. Daughter Lizzie tends to her baby on the porch. Anna's husband, James, was a farmer and cooper. His specialty was making hickory barrel hoops. The barrels were shipped throughout the area via the Delaware and Hudson Canal. The edge of the unpaved Oakland Valley Road can be seen in the lower left corner. The photograph was taken *c.* 1917. (Author's collection.)

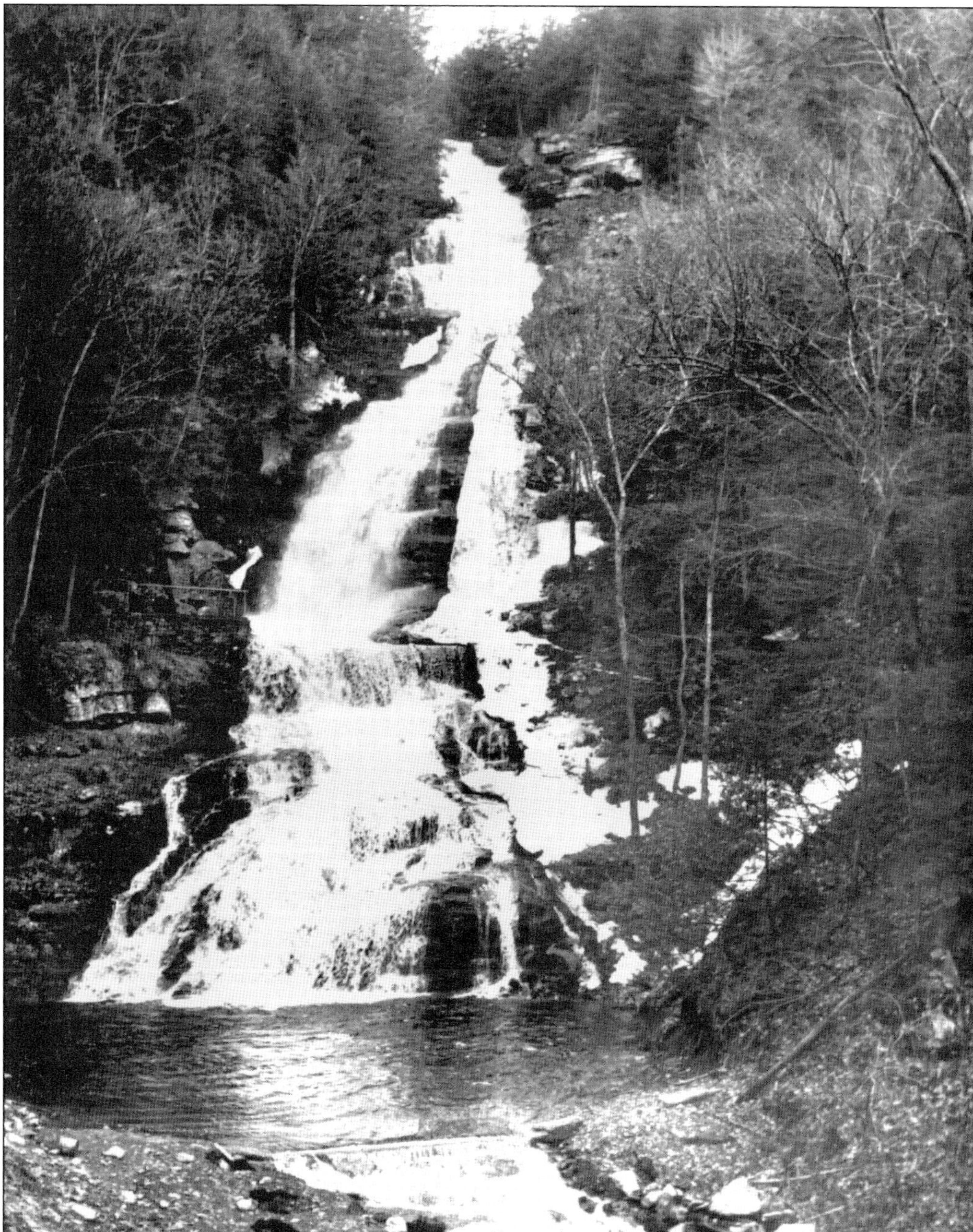

The beautiful cascading Buttermilk Falls is the tallest waterfall in Orange County. A sawmill was built here after the Revolutionary War. (Author's collection.)

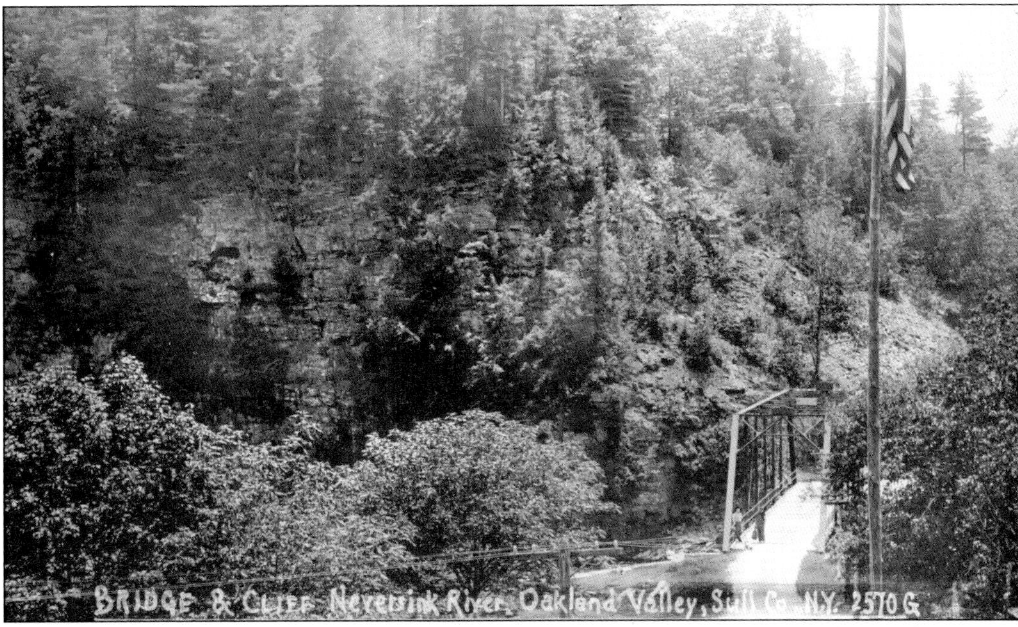

This bridge over the Neversink River was located on Oakland Valley Road near the Orange and Sullivan County line. The flagpole is likely to have been in front of one of many boardinghouses. (Author's collection.)

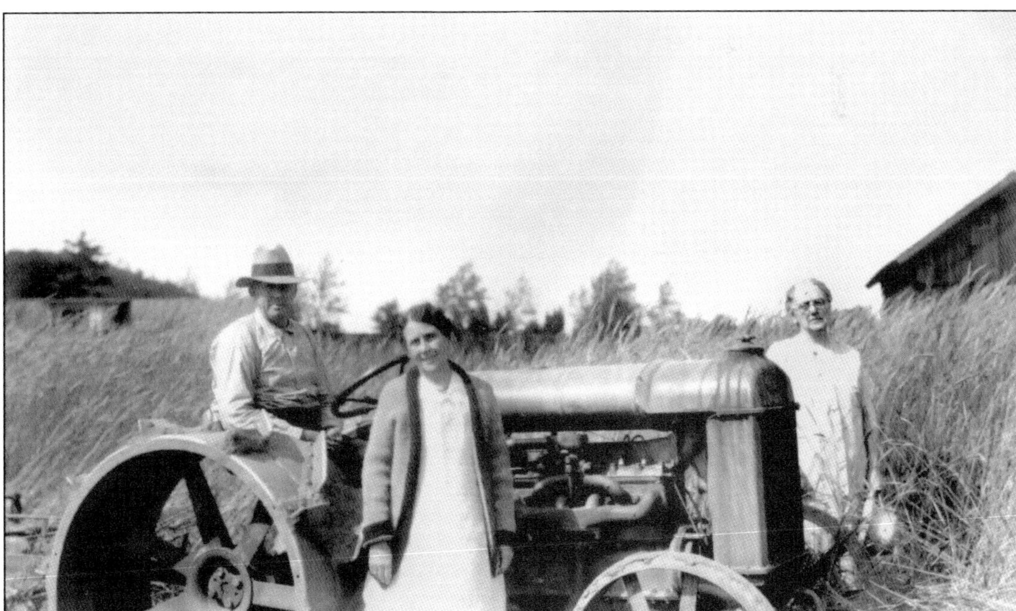

Farming was still important in the 1920s. Joe Lewis's farm was located on the north side of Hoag Road. Seen here are, from left to right, Joe Lewis, Mrs. Hoag (or Mrs. Predmore), and Emaline Case Lewis. (Author's collection.)

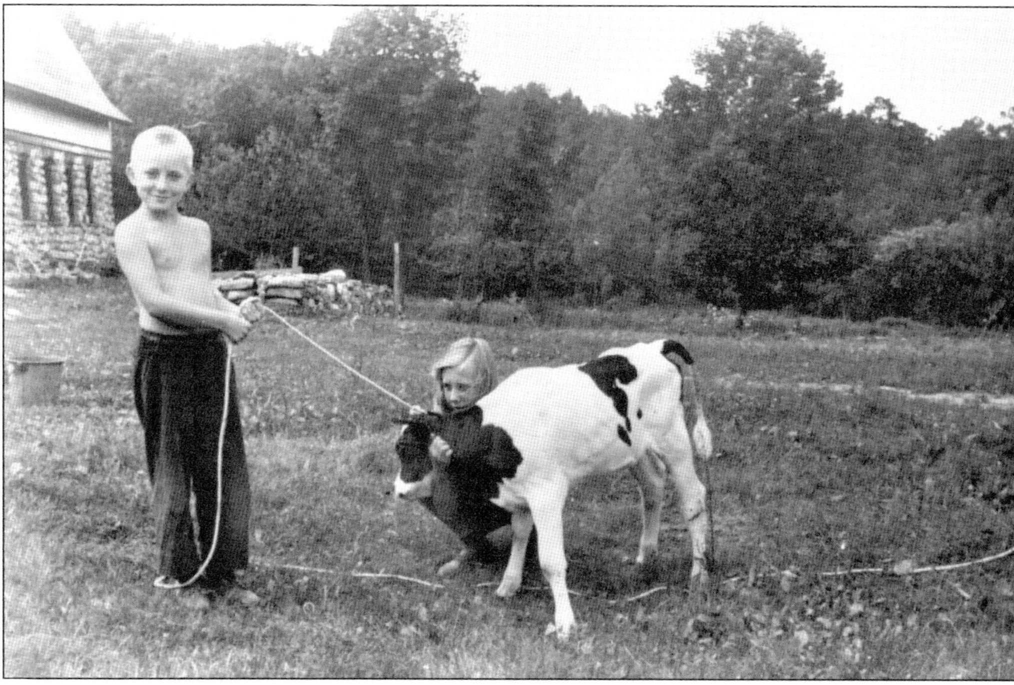

Among the many chores and responsibilities children had on the farm was the job of weaning calves from their mothers. The young animals were fed a mixture of milk and grain, which had the consistency of gruel. They were fed this mixture until they could feed on grain. Tending this calf are Hans Hoefgen and Norma Hoefgen Schadt on their father's farm in 1943. (Norma and Willard Schadt.)

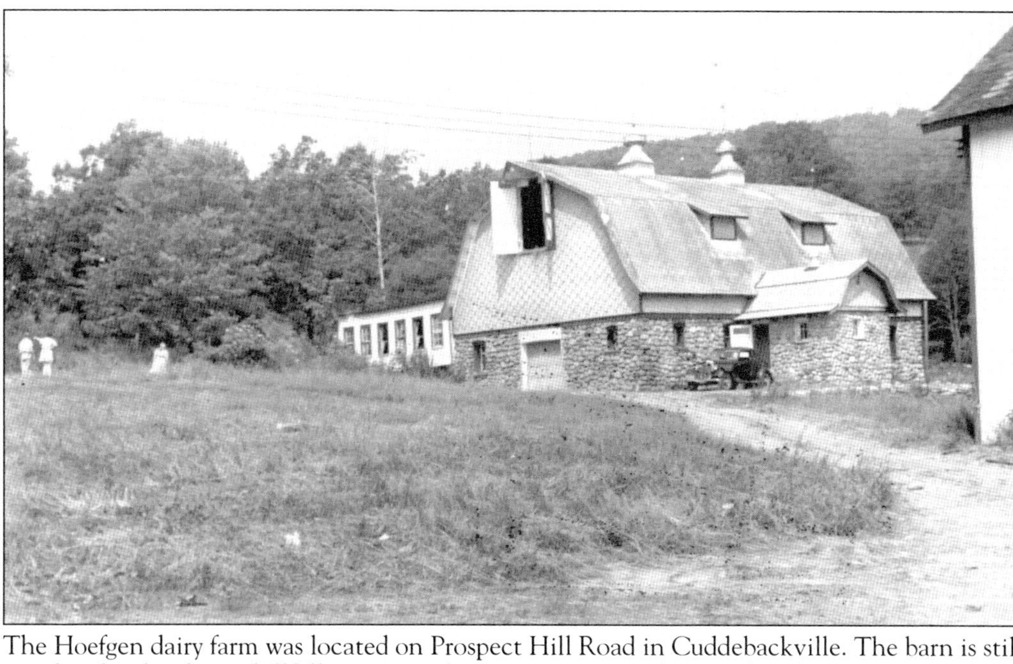

The Hoefgen dairy farm was located on Prospect Hill Road in Cuddebackville. The barn is still standing but has been skillfully converted into a private residence. This photograph was taken on July 4, 1949. (Norma and Willard Schadt.)

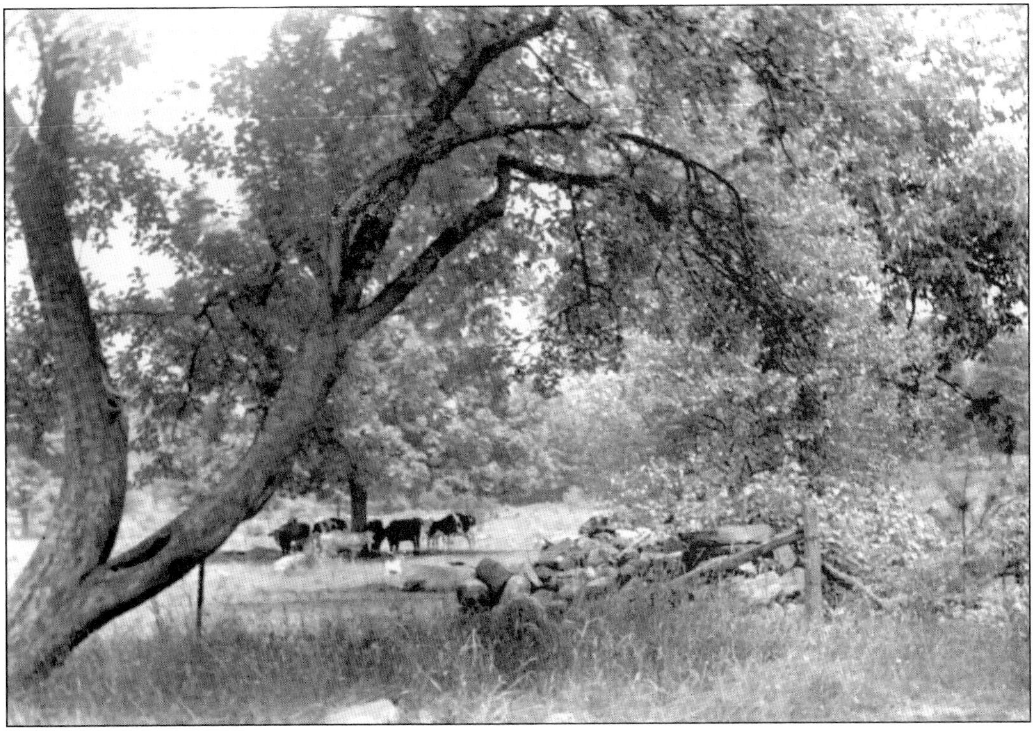

This July 4, 1949 photograph shows the same Hoefgen farm. Taken from the farmhouse, the view looks across the pasture down Prospect Hill toward Oakland Valley. (Norma and Willard Schadt.)

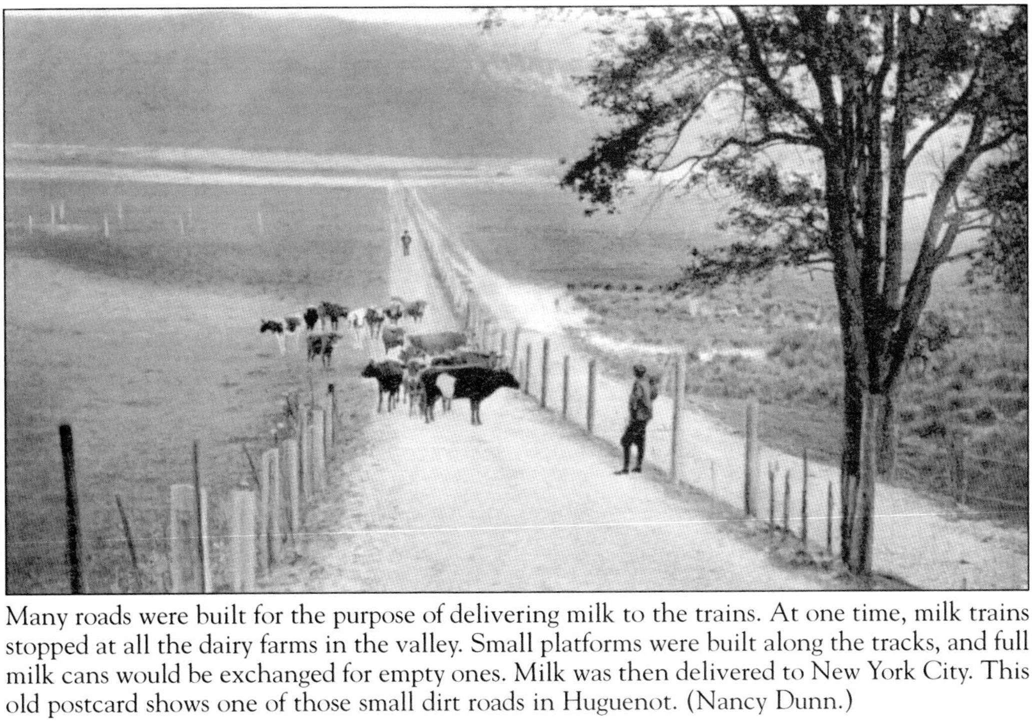

Many roads were built for the purpose of delivering milk to the trains. At one time, milk trains stopped at all the dairy farms in the valley. Small platforms were built along the tracks, and full milk cans would be exchanged for empty ones. Milk was then delivered to New York City. This old postcard shows one of those small dirt roads in Huguenot. (Nancy Dunn.)

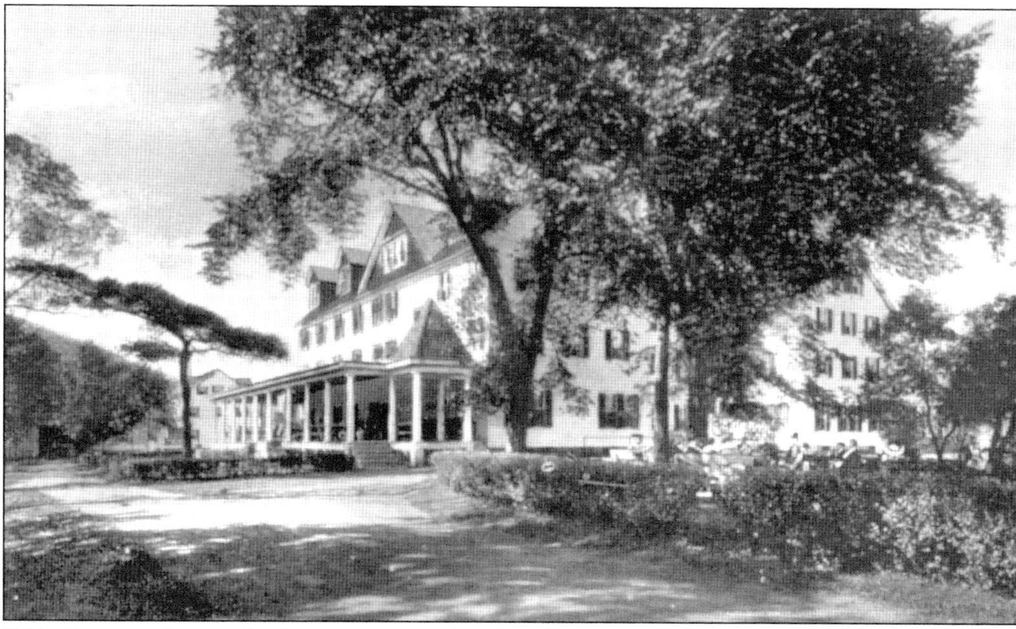

Eddy Farm in Sparrowbush was once a 100-acre farm, situated on the banks of the Delaware River. Named for the eddy in the river, the farm was owned and operated by many generations of the Patterson family, dating back to the early 1870s when John R. Patterson built the town's first boardinghouse on one end of his farm. The postcard shows Eddy Farm as it is today, a resort. (Author's collection.)

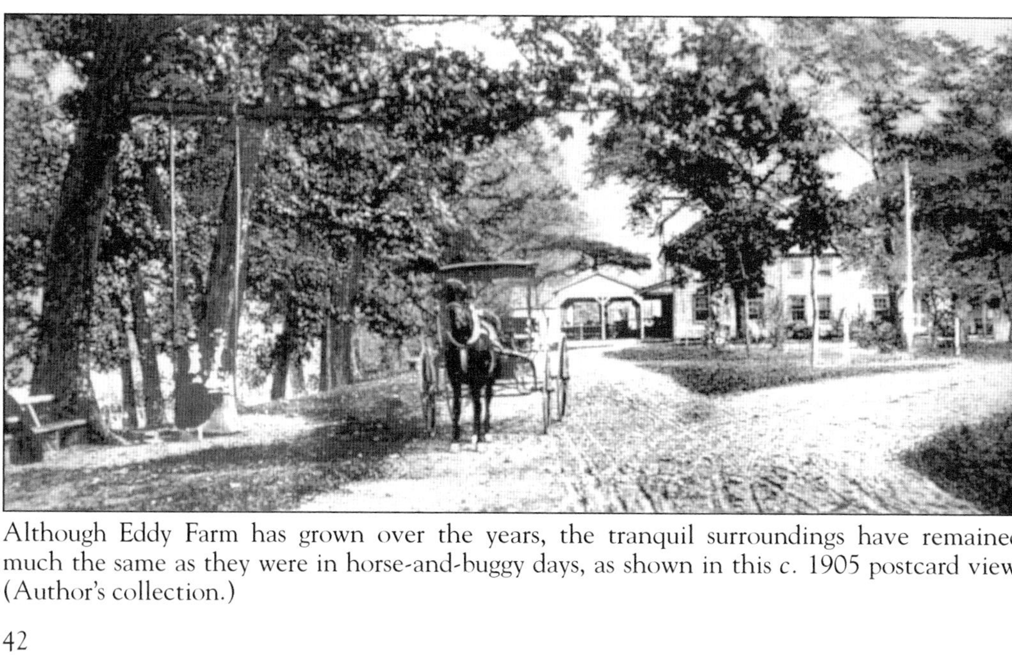

Although Eddy Farm has grown over the years, the tranquil surroundings have remained much the same as they were in horse-and-buggy days, as shown in this *c.* 1905 postcard view. (Author's collection.)

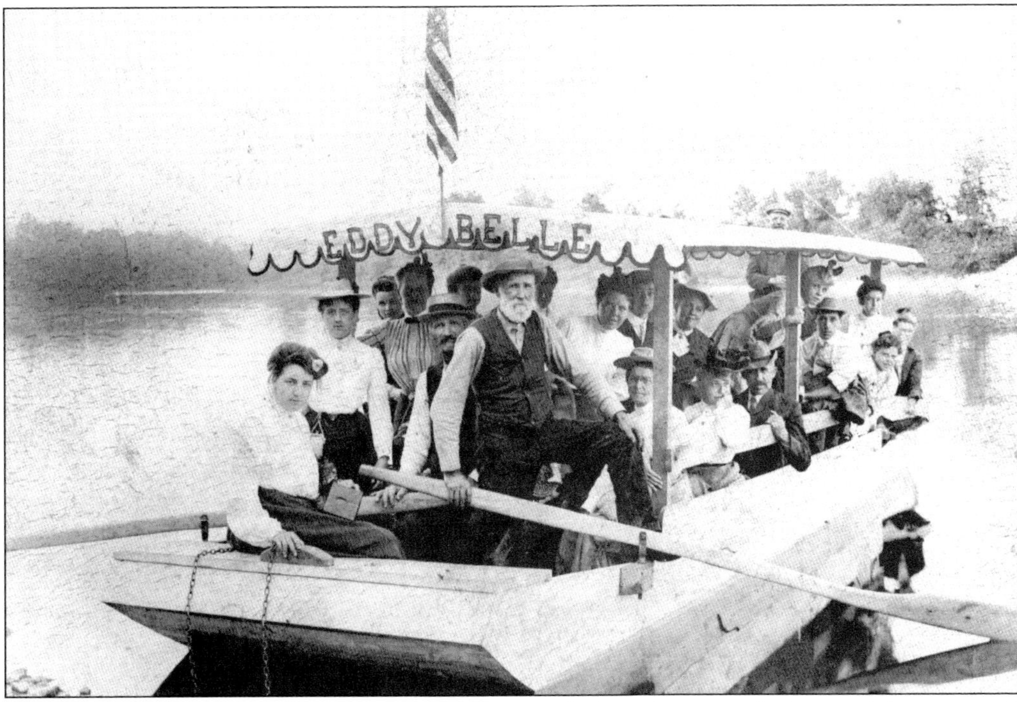

Eddy Farm offered many outdoor activities, including boating, bathing, fishing, tennis, croquet, and baseball. In this late-1800s photograph, the Eddy Belle is ready to launch for a relaxing excursion down the Delaware River. The Eddy Belle was a 24-foot flat-bottomed boat built by John R. Patterson. The boat was manned by two oarsmen, James Van Fredenburg and Mr. Patterson (likely Tom Patterson), and was steered by a large rudder. (Minisink Valley Historical Society.)

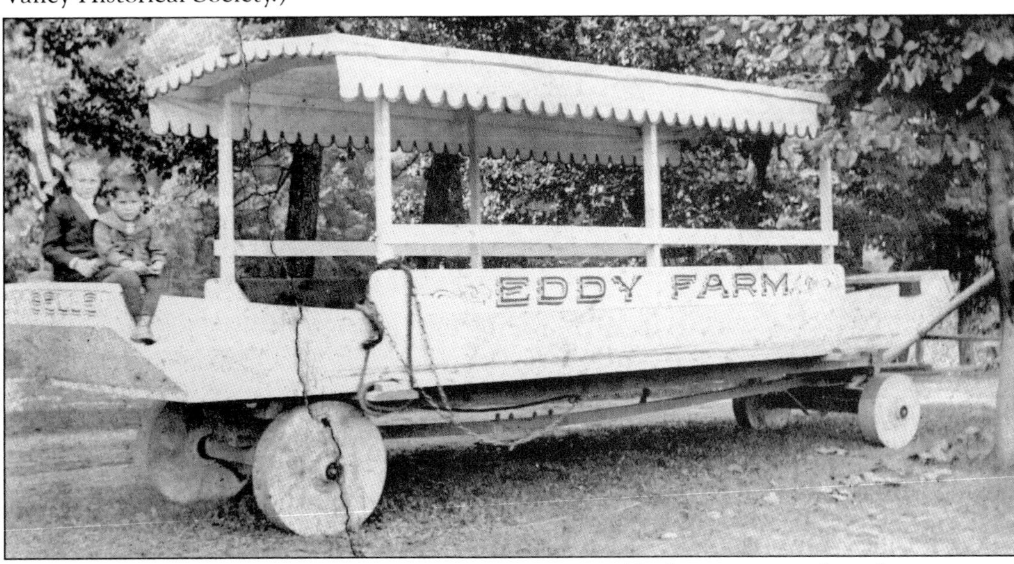

After the excursion down the Delaware River to Milford, a team and trailer were sent to transport the Eddy Belle and the guests back to Eddy Farm. The trailer made the Eddy Belle a perfect stagecoach for the scenic return trip on the Old Milford Road. (Minisink Valley Historical Society.)

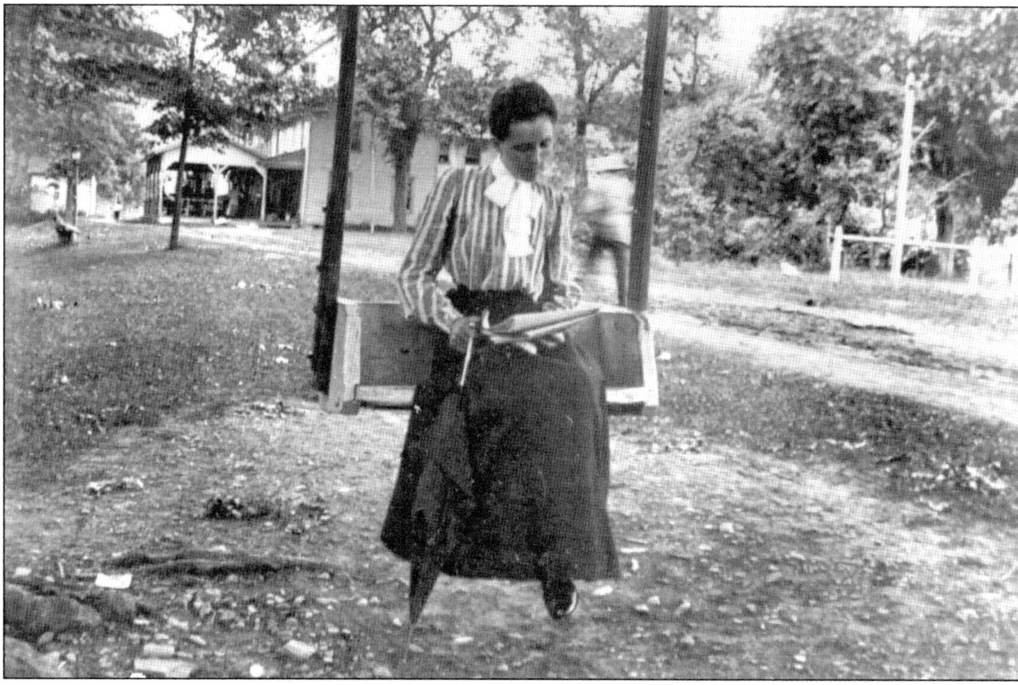

This early-1900s view shows Sarah Chambers Patterson relaxing on the swing by the riverbank at Eddy Farm. (Minisink Valley Historical Society.)

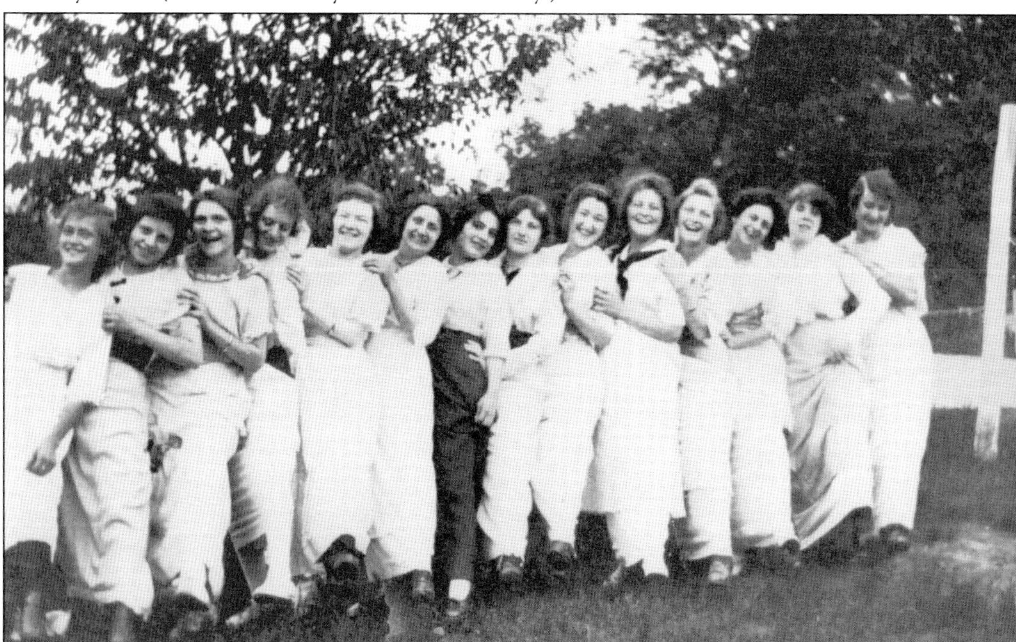

Eddy Farm would never have earned its good reputation or been able to care for all of its guests over the years without the help of many employees. Pictured here are 14 waitresses from 1914. They are, from left to right, ? Ketcham, Helen Hazen, Bessie Burger, Dorothy Eidel, Sarah Robb, Alice Hazen, Rose Schock, Hazel Knight, Margaret Lowrey, Cora Eidel, Carrie Ketcham, Maude Knight, Laura Lamb, and Bertha Tedford. (Minisink Valley Historical Society.)

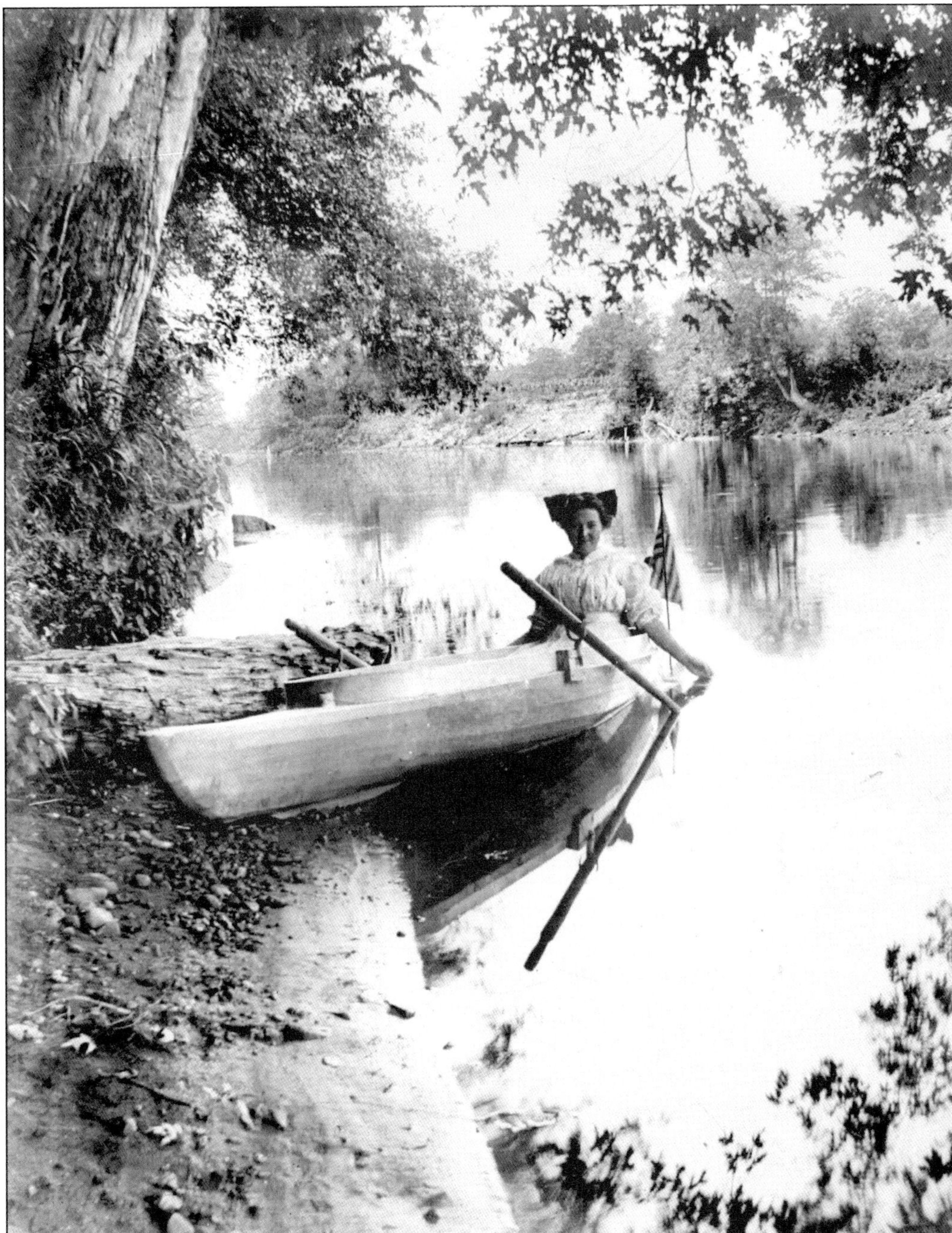

The Delaware River always played an important part in recreation at Eddy Farm. Boating and canoeing were a favorite pastime in the river's eddy as long as one remained in the eddy. Otherwise, one could find oneself in Port Jervis, courtesy of the river current. It was always a big surprise when new unsuspecting guests who were not familiar with the river found themselves floating downstream through rapids and rifts. This photograph was taken in August 1909. (Minisink Valley Historical Society.)

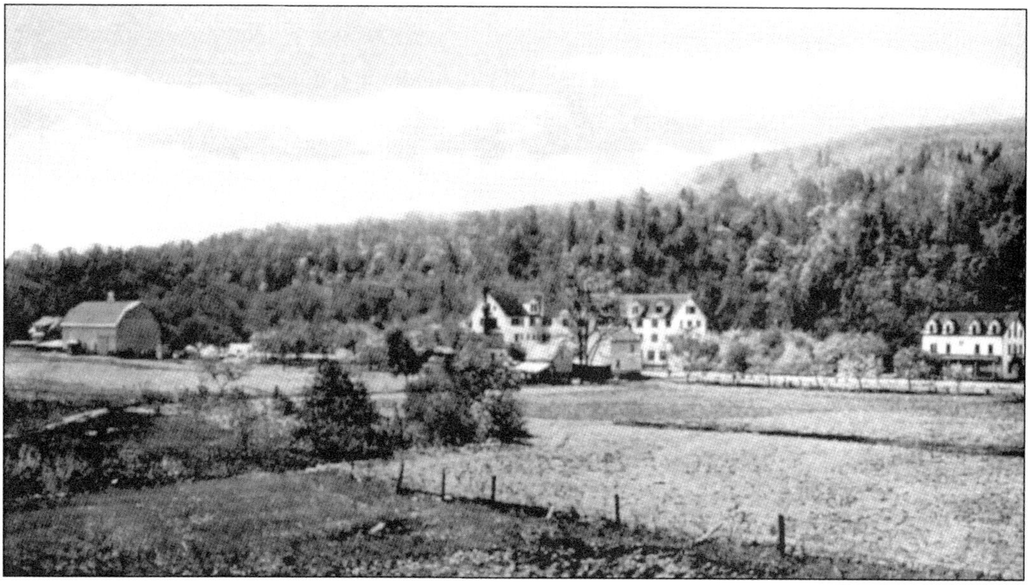

This glimpse of Eddy Farm was taken while it was still operating as a farm. The barn to the left was later converted into lodging by adding a third story and changing the roofline. (Author's collection.)

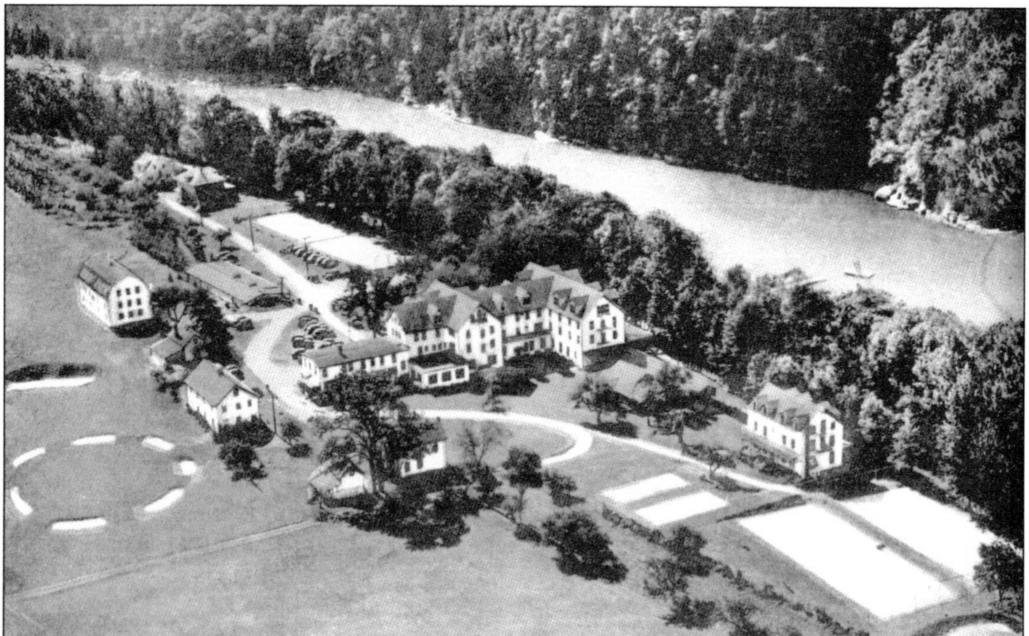

By 1930, Eddy Farm had become a hotel. By 1950, the Pattersons had ended their farming business and added two golf courses, tennis courts, a beach, a large dance hall, and other outdoor facilities to the hotel. (Author's collection.)

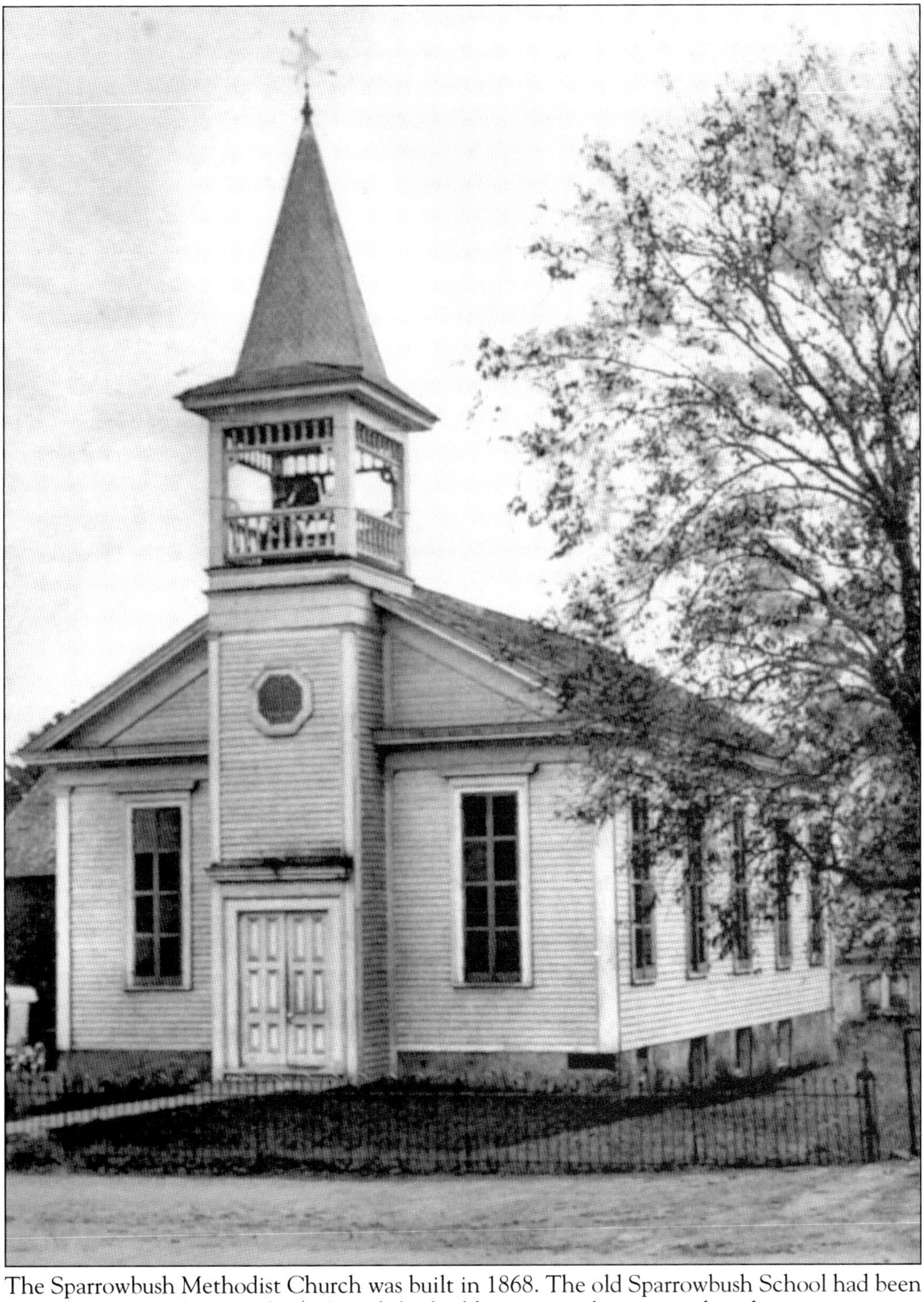

The Sparrowbush Methodist Church was built in 1868. The old Sparrowbush School had been purchased by parishioners for $95, and the building materials were used in the new structure. The final costs were about $2,000. In 1872, the belfry was added. The church still looks the same, except for the stained-glass windows, and has an active congregation on Main Street. (Glenn R. Conklin.)

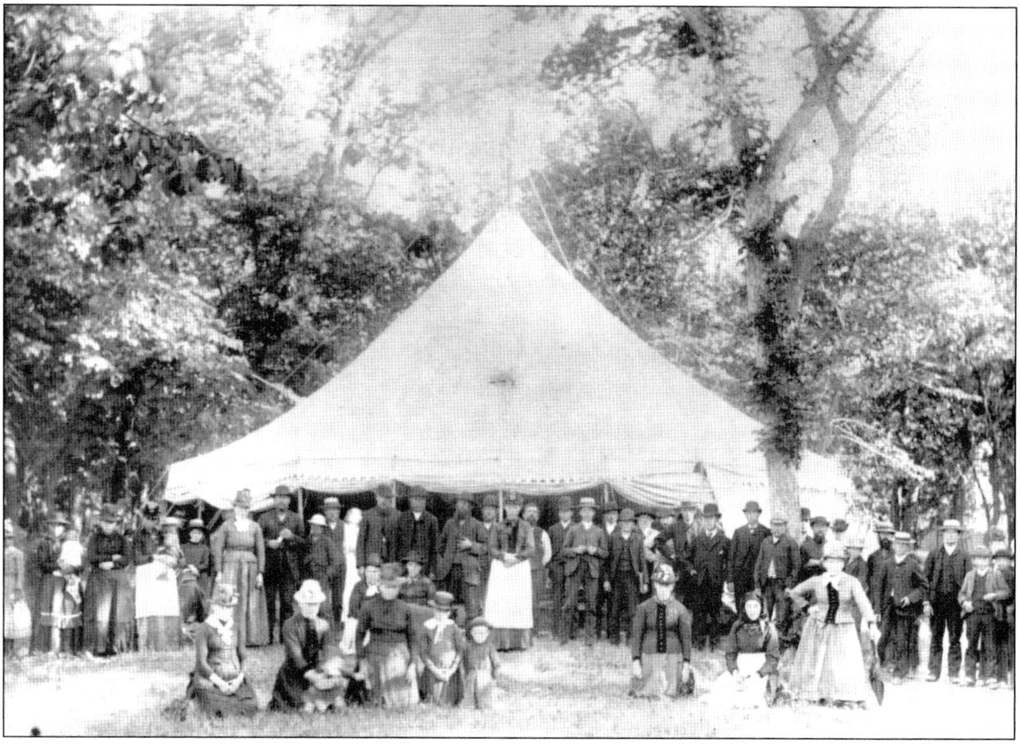

In the 1800s, Methodism exploded across the country with revivals and camp meetings. This 1890s photograph shows a Sparrowbush Methodist Church tent revival. (Minisink Valley Historical Society.)

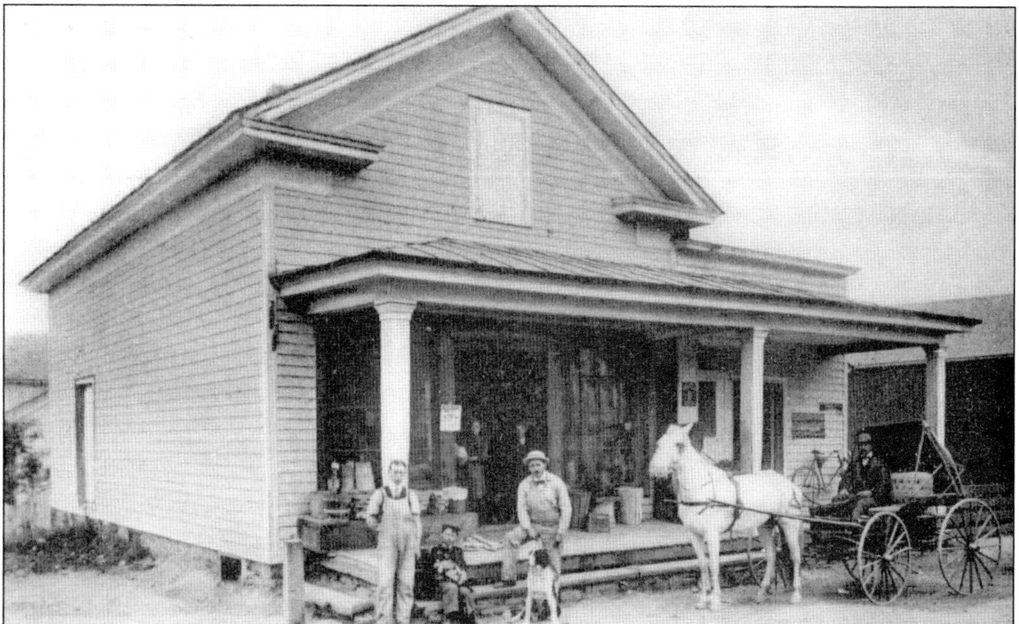

L.A. Johnson's store was a landmark on Main Street for many years. The Sparrowbush Post Office was once located here. (Norma and Willard Schadt.)

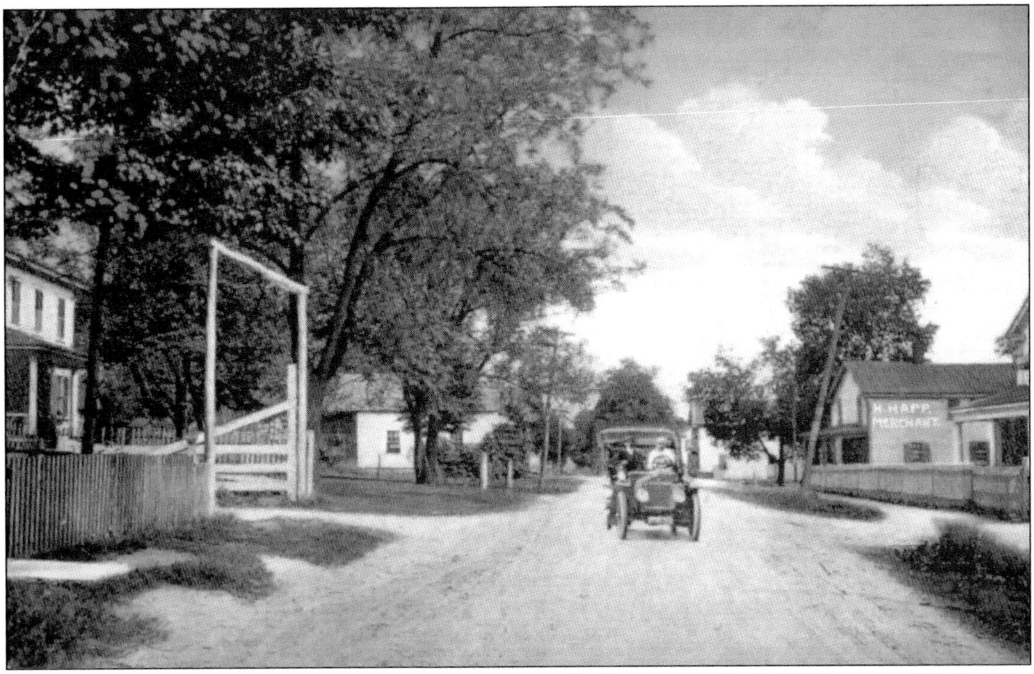

This old postcard view of Main Street in Sparrowbush, postmarked 1910, was published by Henry Happ, merchant and postmaster. The business closed after the 1950s. (Tom Patterson.)

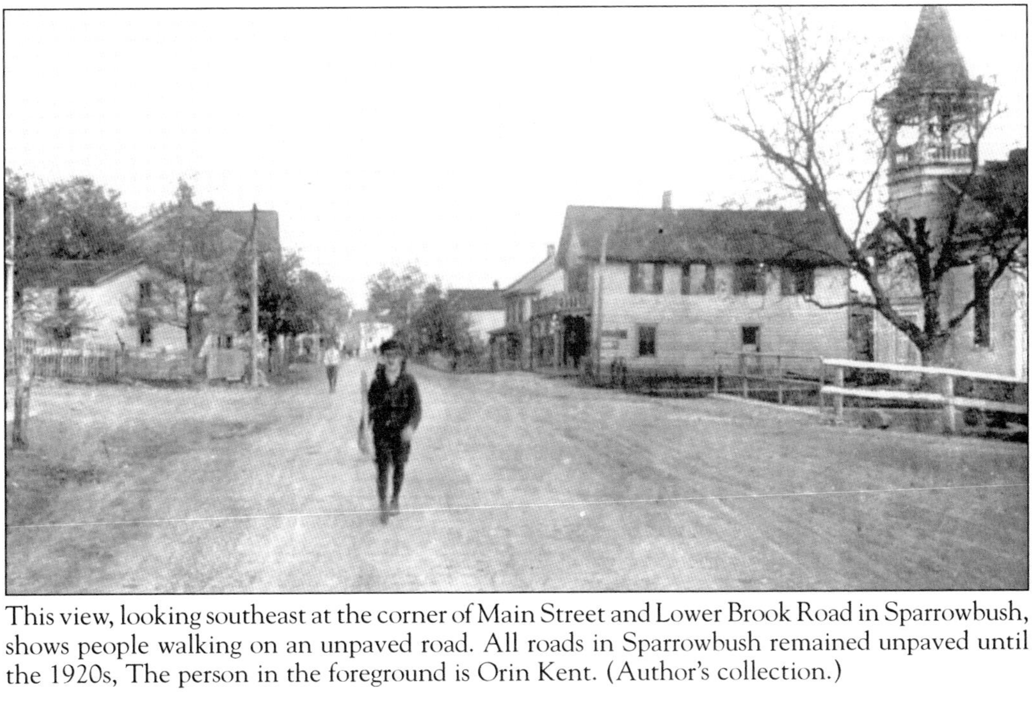

This view, looking southeast at the corner of Main Street and Lower Brook Road in Sparrowbush, shows people walking on an unpaved road. All roads in Sparrowbush remained unpaved until the 1920s, The person in the foreground is Orin Kent. (Author's collection.)

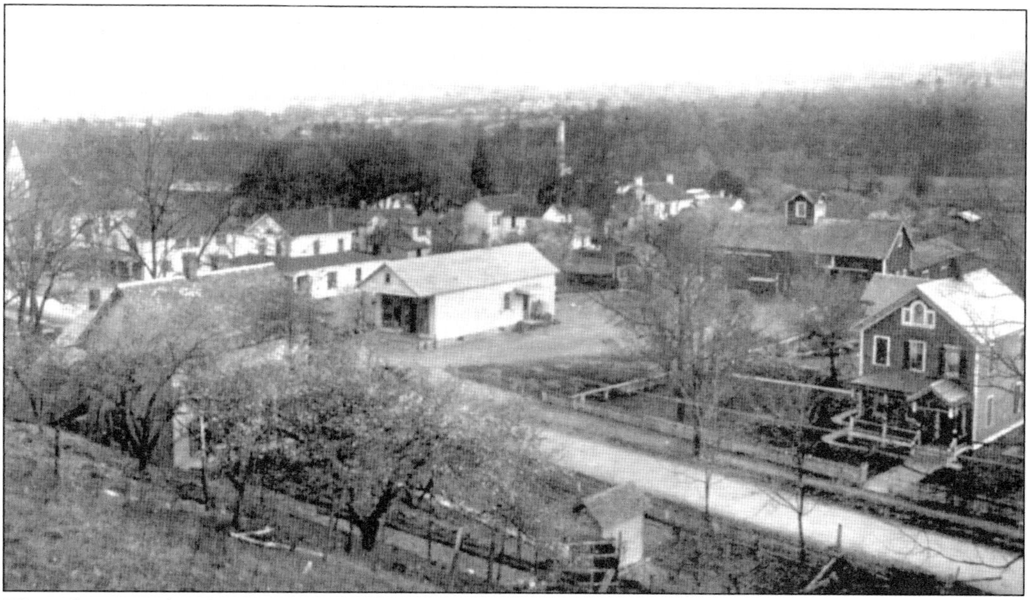

This photograph of Sparrowbush shows that Main Street has been a business center for a long time. The tannery, with a smokestack, is visible in the distance. The Methodist church is on the left. The hardware store, a white building, is in the center. The lumberyard, a dark barn, is to the back right of the store. Many other businesses were also located along Main Street. (Author's collection.)

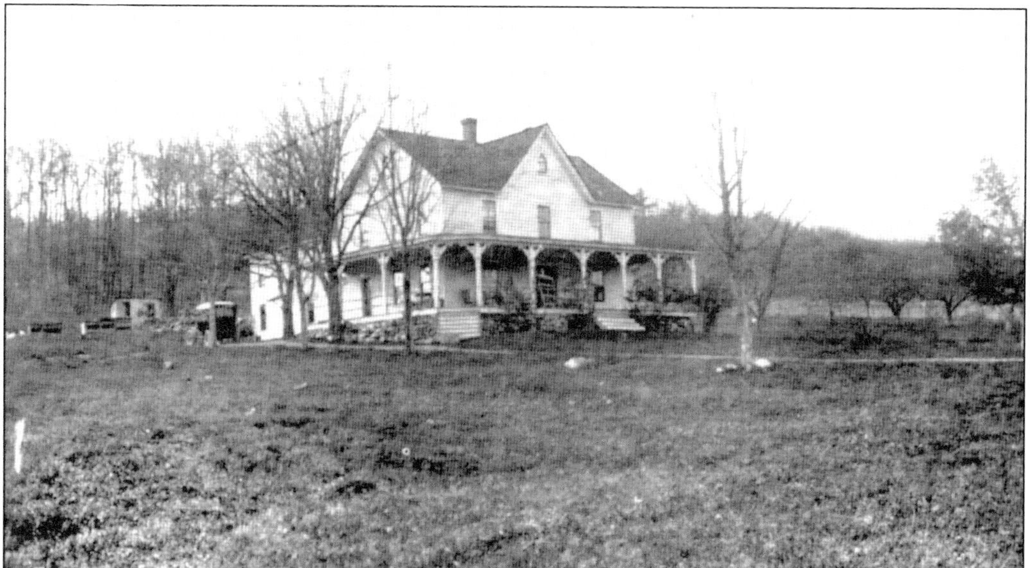

Crystal Spring Farm, in Sparrowbush, was owned by Henry West. In 1902, West's daughter inherited the farm. Because she was married at the time, her husband, L.A. Johnson, became the owner. The first fire department was organized by L.A. Johnson in 1908. It was located on the first floor of Squire Dedrick's hotel. (Author's collection.)

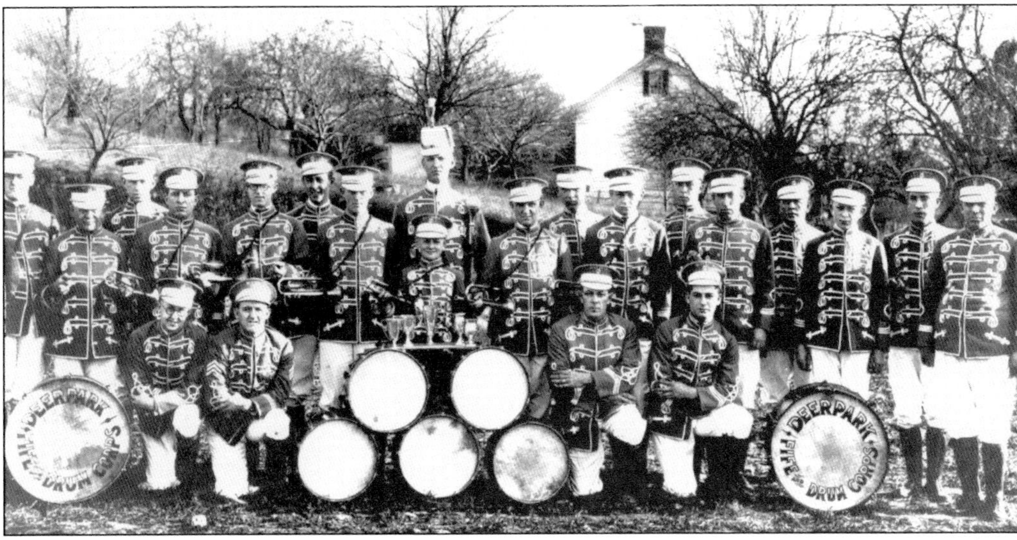

Members of the Deerpark Fife and Drum Corps pose for a photograph 1923. Their uniforms were blue and white. The old farmhouse in the background became the current Scully's Restaurant. Seen here are, from left to right, the following: (front row) Gilbert Weed, George Cabe, Bill Johnson, Jim Kent, and Guss Bamberger; (back row) Julian Johnson, Frank Love, Charles Bodenseick, John Cherry, Vernon Wright, Leland Johnson, Bill Hazen, Percy Osterhoudt, Jim Eidel, Bill Hall, Raymond Slater, Percy Horn, Sammy Gilson, L.A. Johnson, Russ Love, Bert Bowman, and Fred Bowman. (Deerpark Historian's Office.)

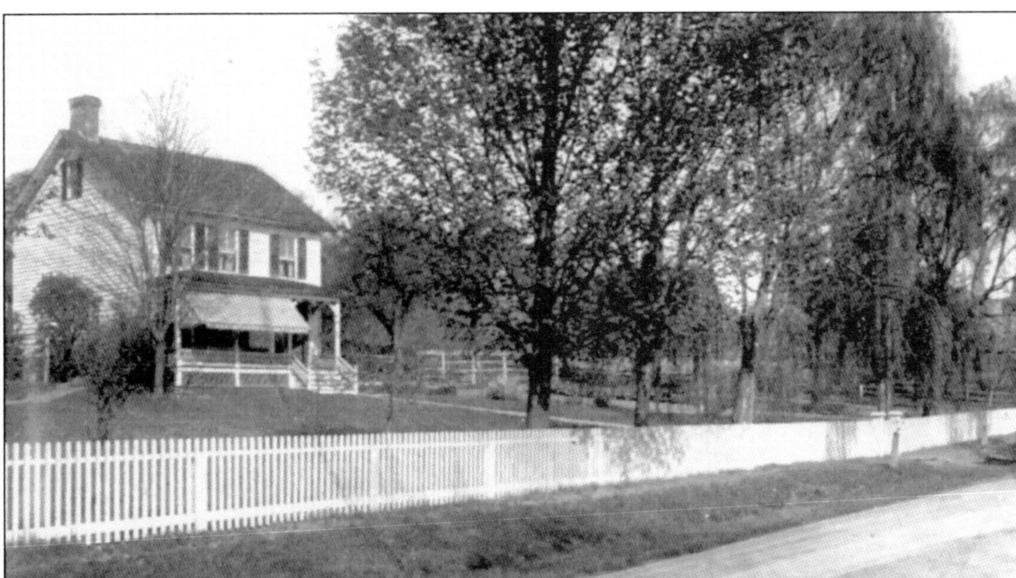

In 1950, C. John Scully bought the late L.A. Johnson's residence, turned it into a restaurant, and built a motel. The place is still located on the west end of Main Street in Sparrowbush. (Author's collection.)

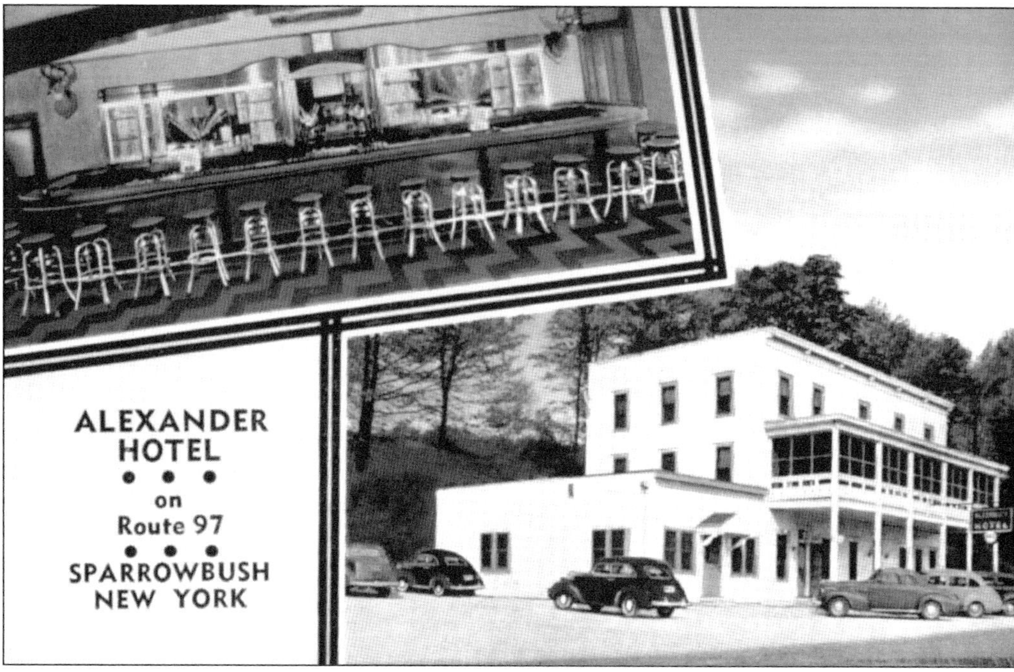

The Raymar Hotel, built in the late 1800s and later named Alexander Hotel, was one of Sparrowbush's most noticeable landmarks. Today, the Alexander Hotel dining room and bar are still intact. The building is now used as an antique shop. (Rosalind Hesleitner.)

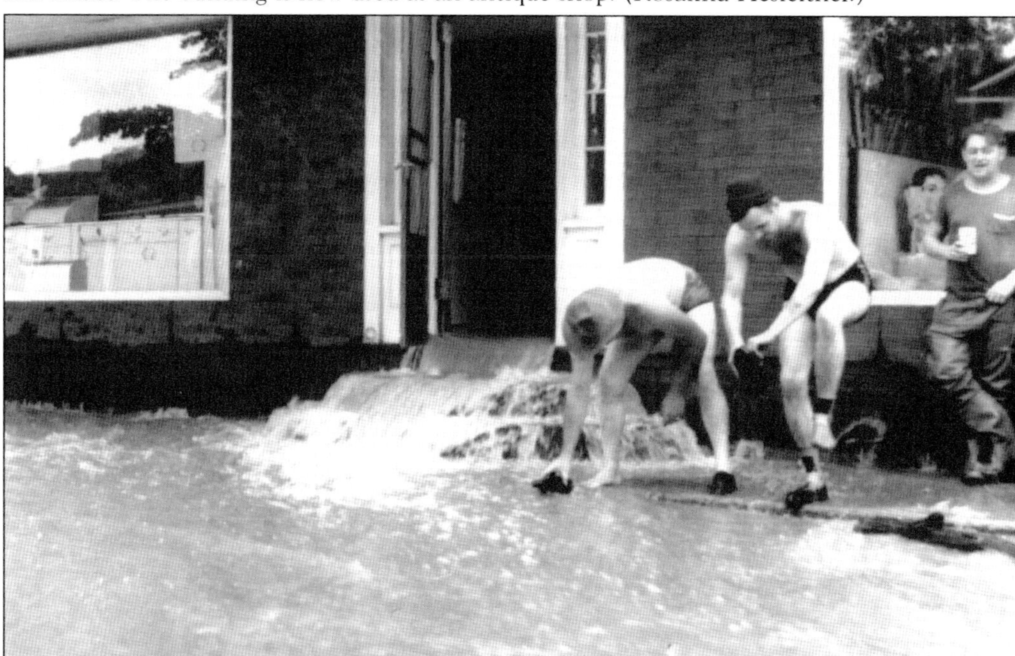

During Hurricane Diane, in 1955, 7.5 inches of rain fell in 36 hours in the tri-state area. Sparrowbush experienced severe damage to roadways and structures as water overflowed the banks of the Delaware River, streams, and runoffs. Floodwaters entered the back door and exited through the front door of John Innella's building-supply store on Main Street. (Bill Flieger.)

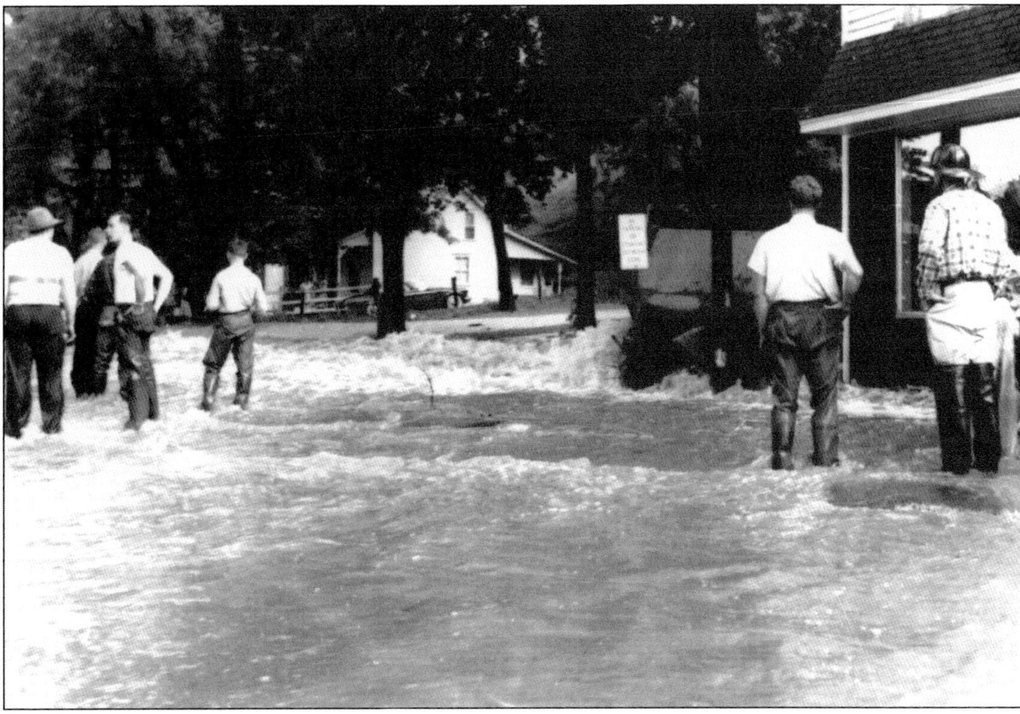

In Sparrowbush, some homes were pushed off their foundations by the rushing floodwaters, and the structures were carried to new locations. This view is looking up Main Street to the left of John Innella's building-supply store. (Bill Flieger.)

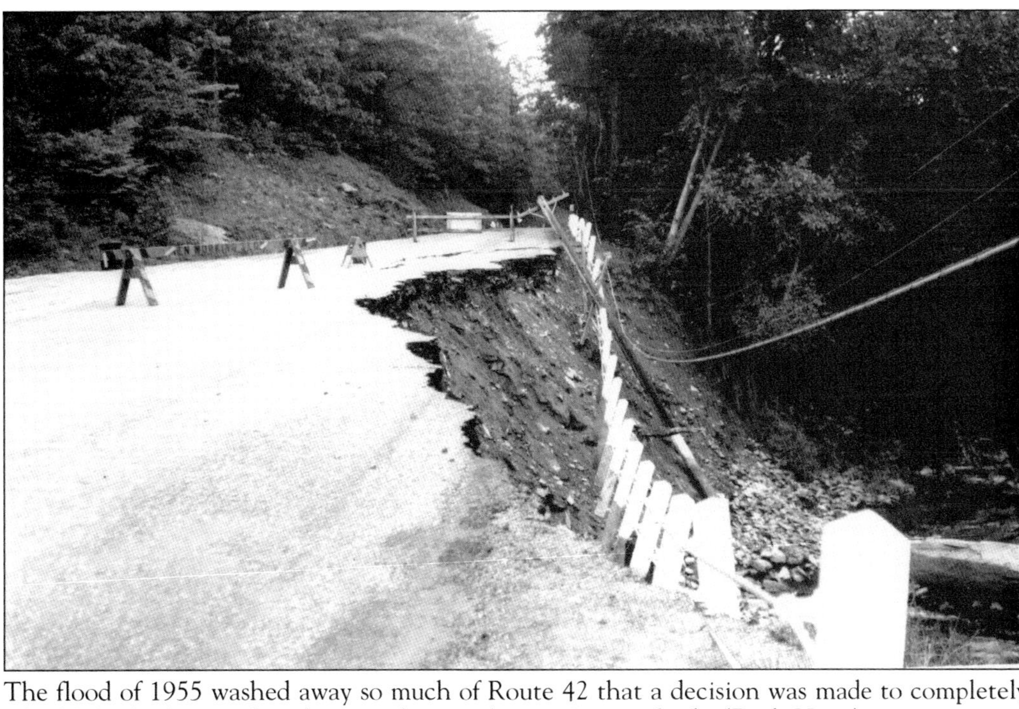

The flood of 1955 washed away so much of Route 42 that a decision was made to completely rebuild the highway. This photograph was taken in Sparrowbush. (Ruth Hurr.)

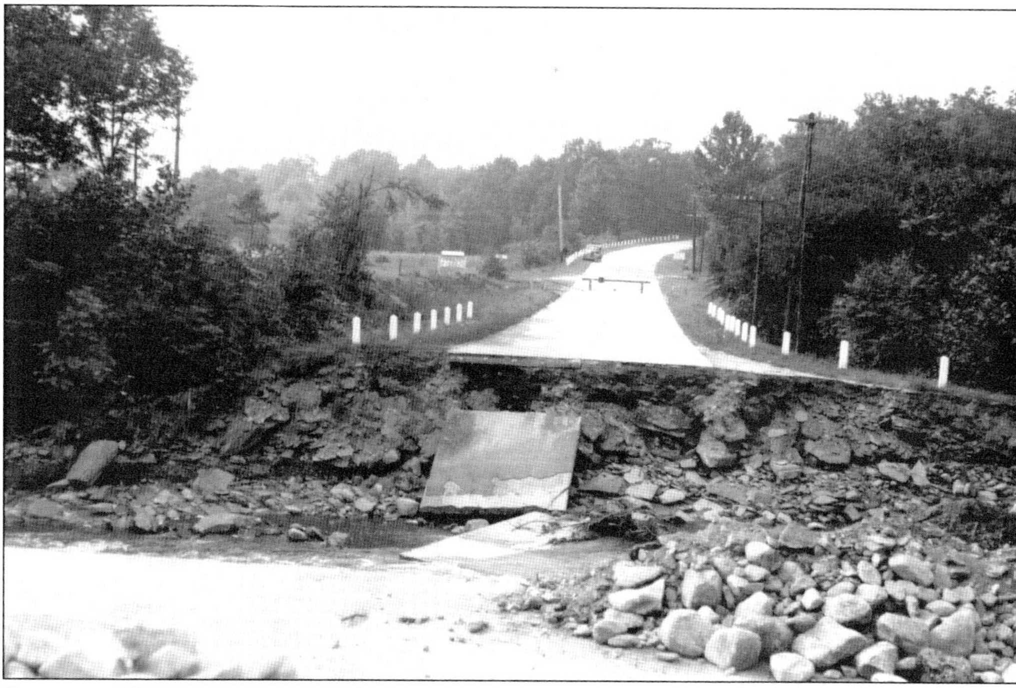

Sections of Route 97 in Sparrowbush were completely washed away during the flood of 1955. (Ruth Hurr.)

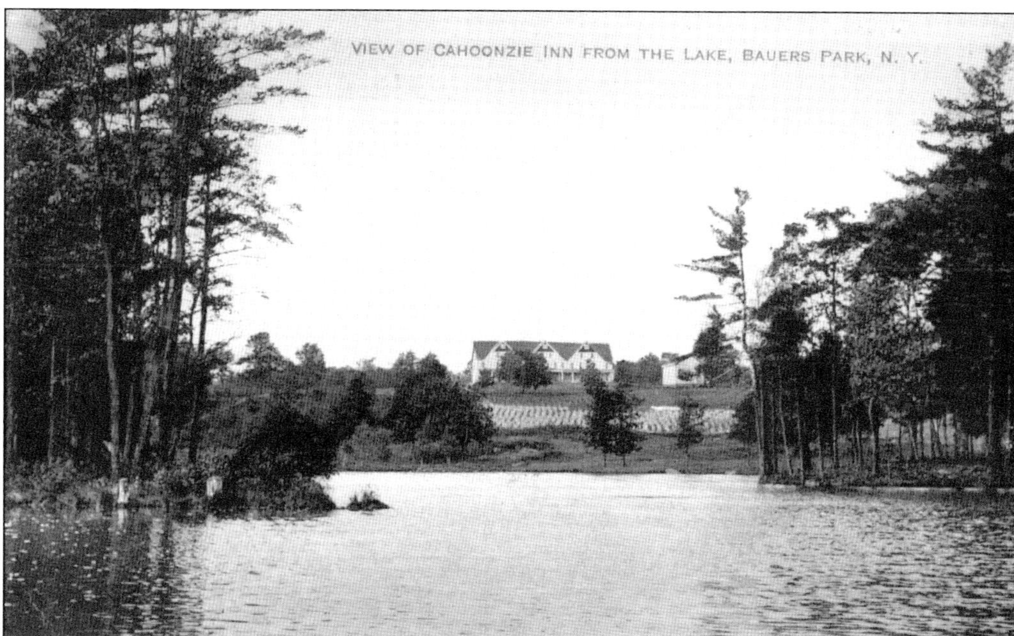

The Cahoonzie Inn was built by Jacob Bauer on a farm that had been owned by J.L. Chase. Bauer built two private lakes on the Steenykill Brook and a park enclosed by a fence. The hotel burned in 1912, after which Bauer built the well-known Bauer Hotel across from the Erie Depot in Port Jervis. It is believed that old Chief Cahoonshe was born and died on the Bauer farmland. (Author's collection.)

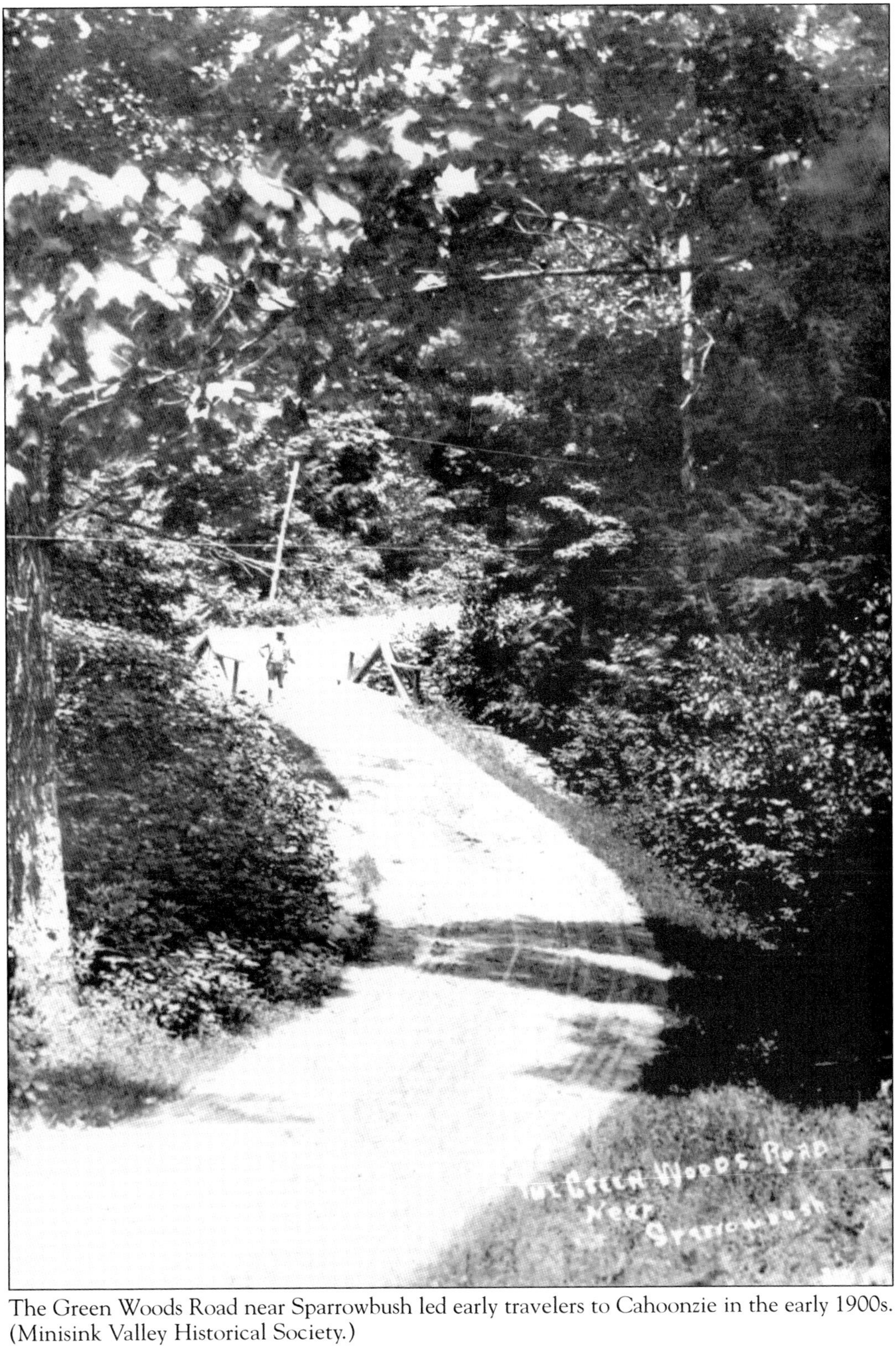

The Green Woods Road near Sparrowbush led early travelers to Cahoonzie in the early 1900s. (Minisink Valley Historical Society.)

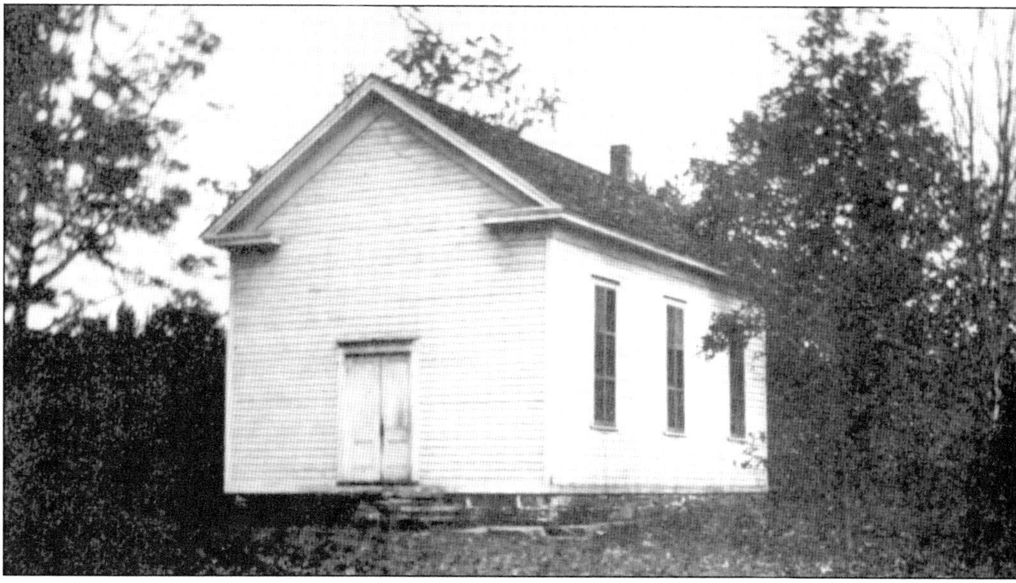

On September 11, 1880, the cornerstone of the Quarry Hill Methodist Church (later known as the Rio United Methodist Church) was laid. Prior to this time, worship services had been held in the Rio schoolhouse. When renovations were being made to the schoolhouse in 1878, services were held in a carriage house loft and, during cold weather, in parishioners' homes. The new building was dedicated on January 18, 1881. (Deerpark Historian's Office.)

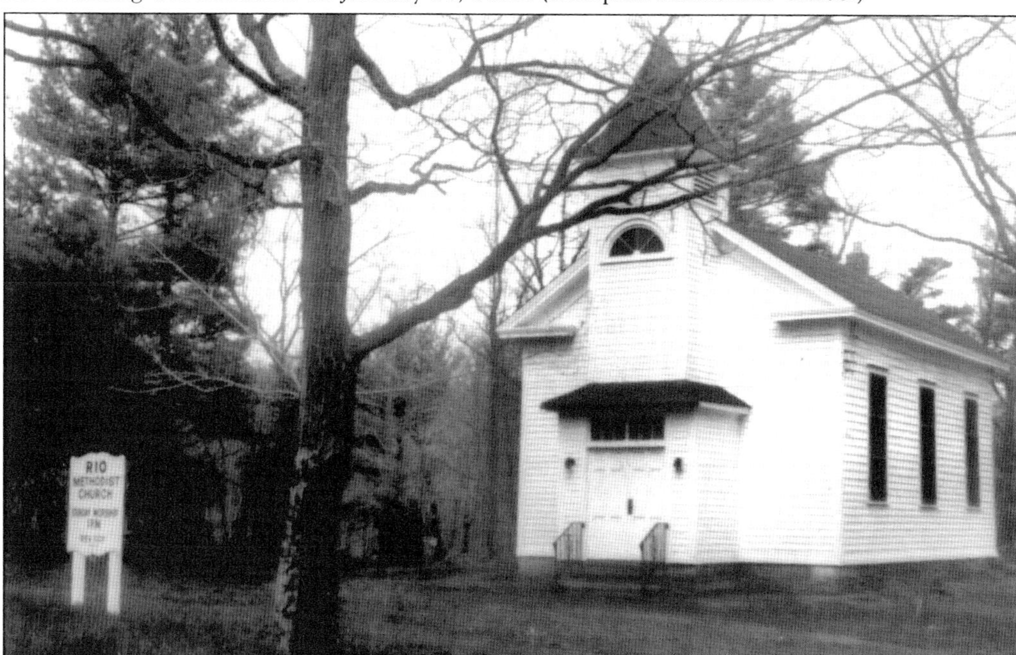

In 1930, a belfry, vestibule, and bell were added to the original Quarry Hill Methodist Church. On May 1, 1966, the church was incorporated as the Rio United Methodist Church. After the Methodists disbanded, the Trinity Evangelical Free Church held services here from March 13, 1983, until September 2, 1983. In 1985, the building was sold and the proceeds were divided between the Greenville and Sparrowbush Methodist Churches. (Rev. Don and Shirley Coy.)

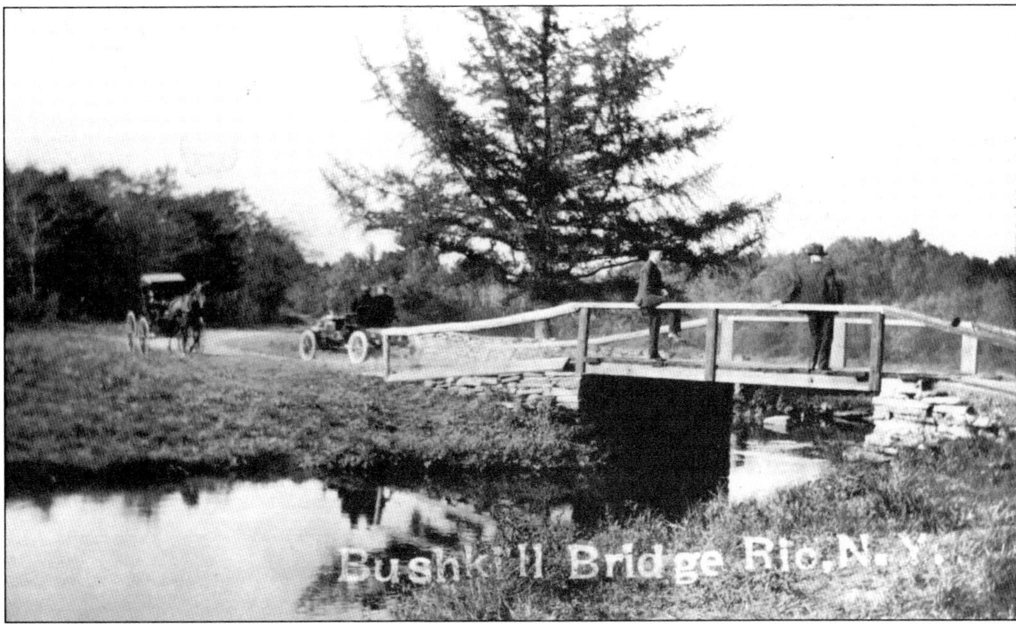

Peter Dunwald (sitting on the bridge railing) and his father take in the scenery from the Bushkill Bridge in Rio. The Dunwalds were a well-known family in the Rio area. (Deerpark Historian's Office.)

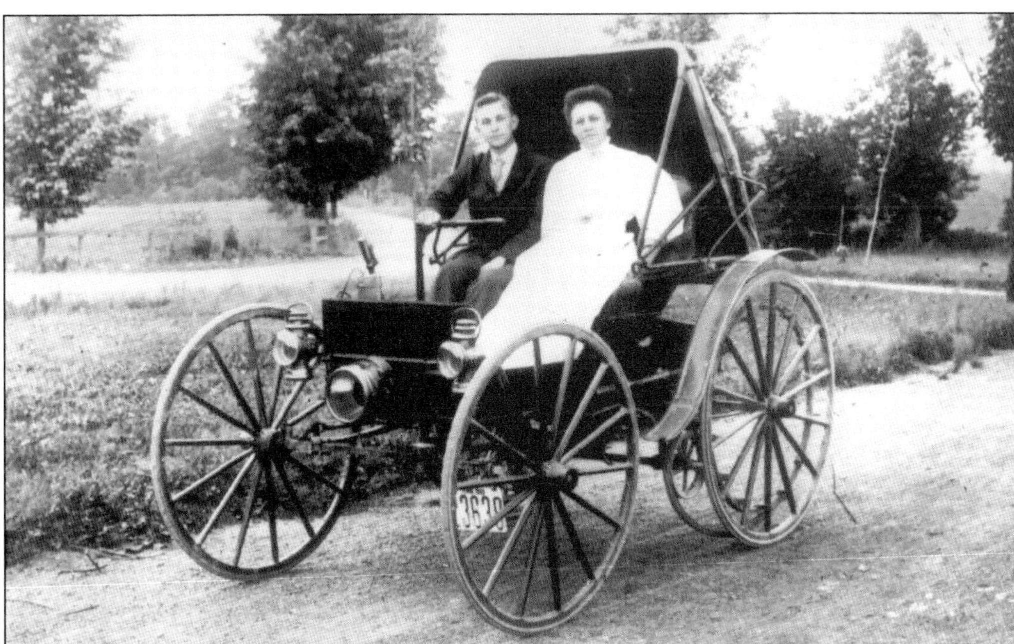

This was one of the early automobiles in the Rio area. The couple is believed to be Peter Dunwald and his wife, out for a drive. Automobiles were novelties in those days. (Deerpark Historian's Office.)

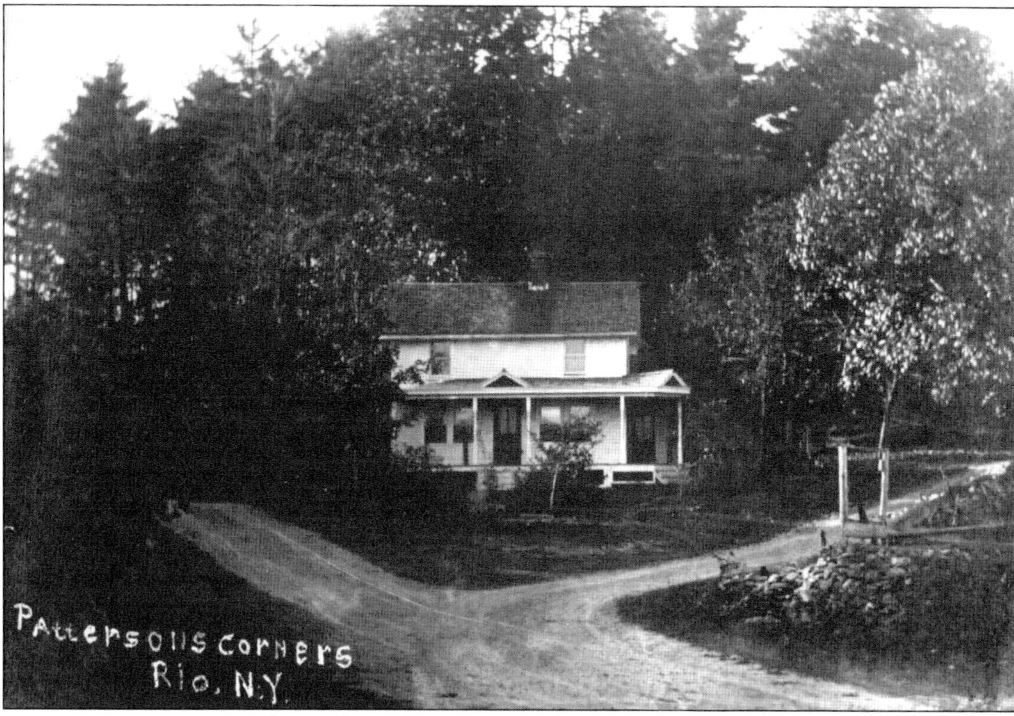

Patterson's Corners was located on the old Route 42 in Rio. This house is still standing on present-day Route 42. (Deerpark Historian's Office.)

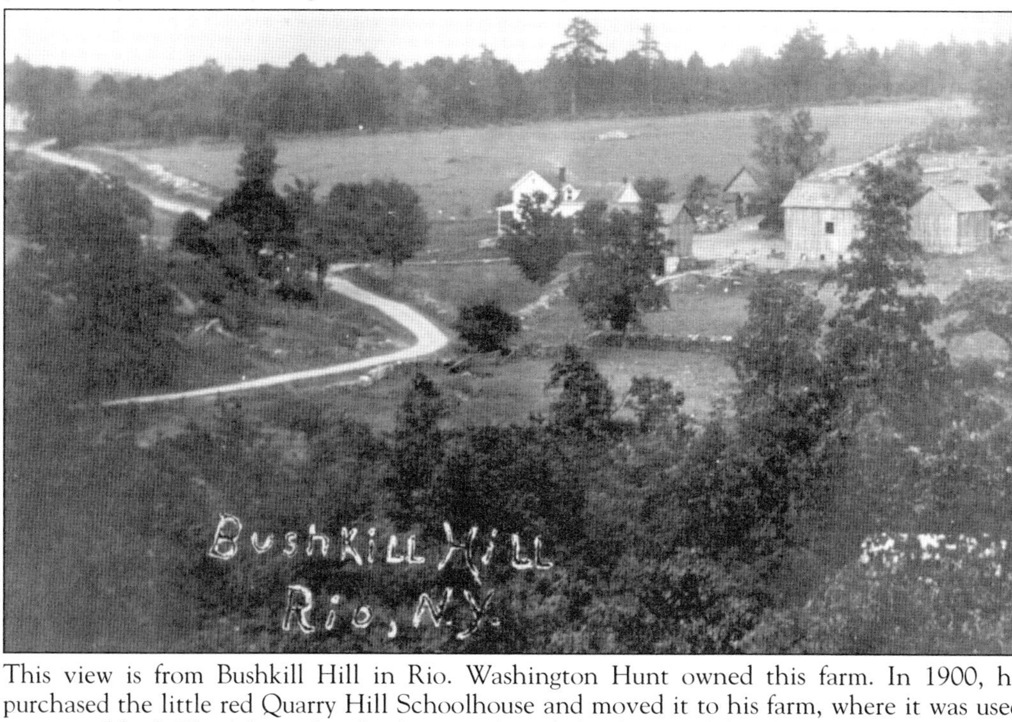

This view is from Bushkill Hill in Rio. Washington Hunt owned this farm. In 1900, he purchased the little red Quarry Hill Schoolhouse and moved it to his farm, where it was used as a woodshed. The Moore family then purchased the farm and lived there for most of the 20th century. (Deerpark Historian's Office.)

Two

EDUCATION

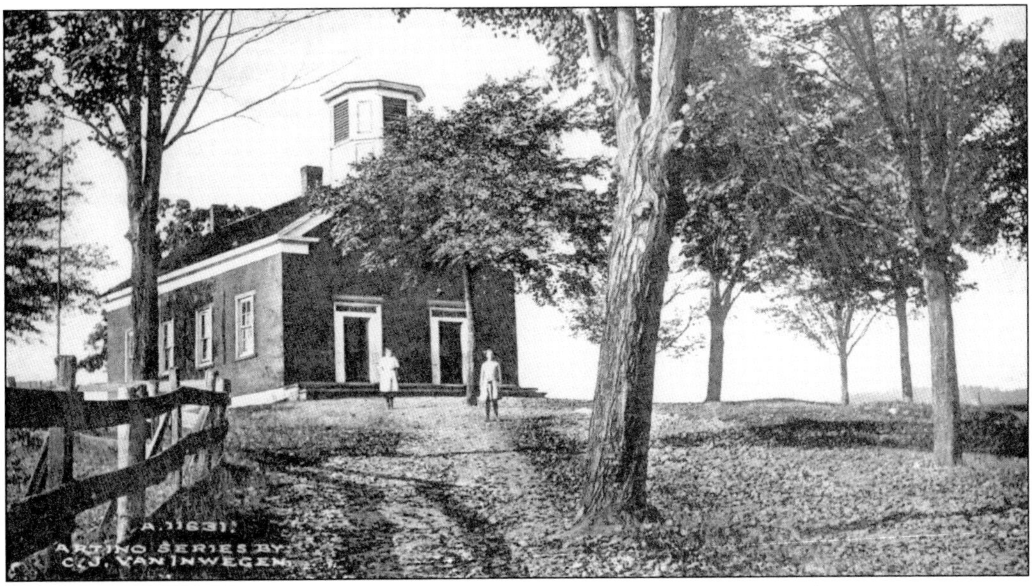

Built in 1863, the Huguenot Schoolhouse, District No. 3, later known as the Upper Huguenot School, was one of the few brick schoolhouses built in Orange County. Local craftsmen made the bricks with clay found along the banks of the nearby Neversink River. On May 4, 1863, William and Mary Cuddeback conveyed the property to the school trustees, Peter G. VanEtten, Henry B. Swartwout, and Peter D. Swartwout. (Author's collection.)

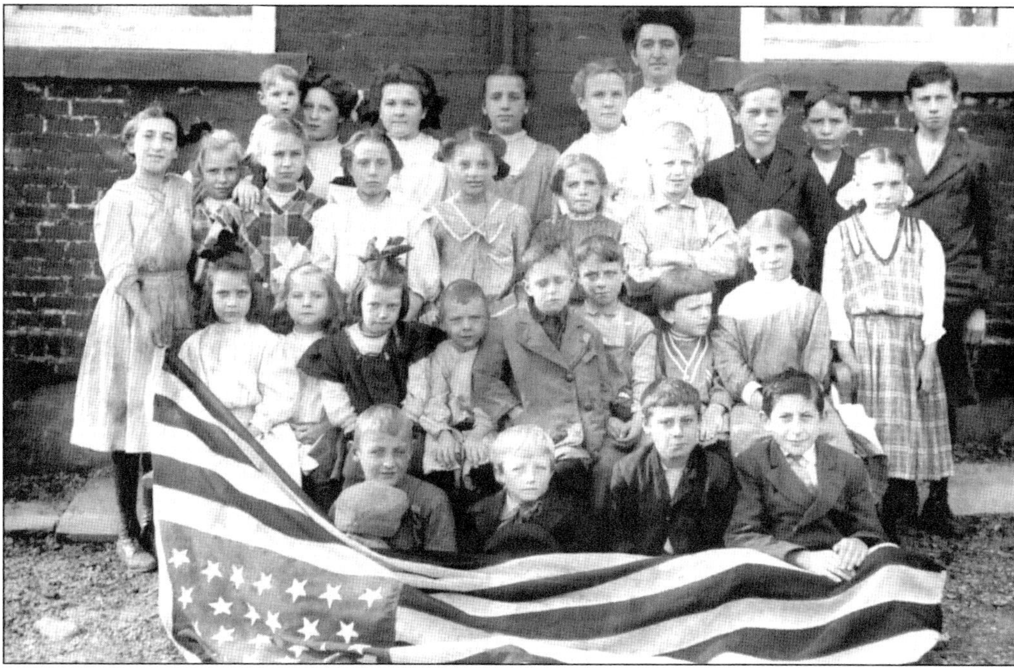

When this *c.* 1880s photograph was taken, 28 students filled the one-room Upper Huguenot School. It is interesting that no one noticed that they were holding the *c.* 1865 flag upside down. During the 19th century, it was common that schoolhouses housed grades one through eight. (Deerpark Historian's Office.)

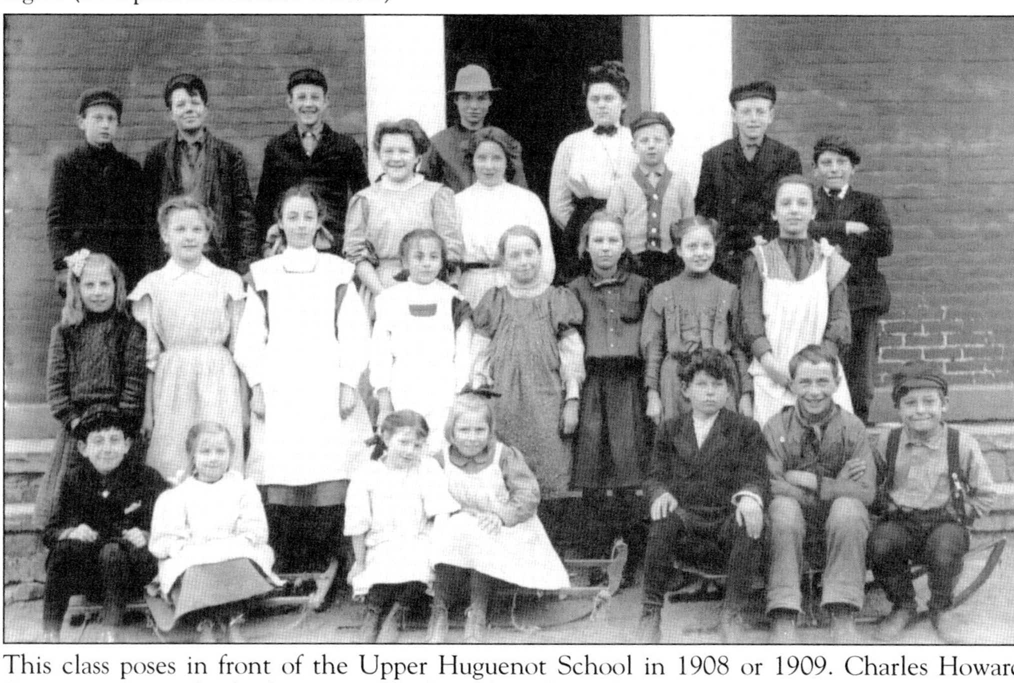

This class poses in front of the Upper Huguenot School in 1908 or 1909. Charles Howard Swartwout is in the back row at the far right. The girl in the middle row at the far left is believed to be Merle Farkett Martin, who later became a teacher in local schools. (Deerpark Historian's Office, Swartwout Collection.)

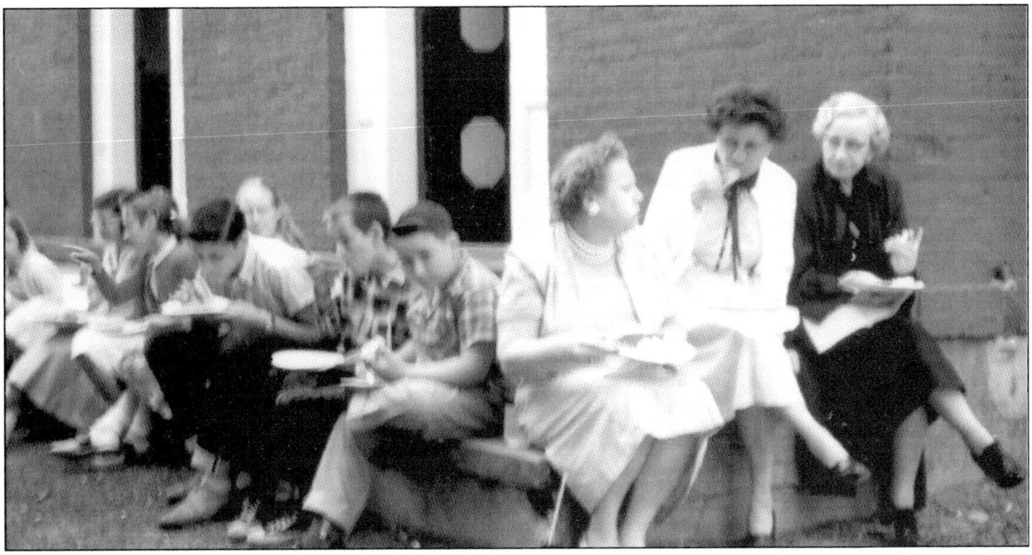

Both the Lower and Upper Huguenot Schools closed in June 1961. This photograph was taken at the Upper Huguenot School during the farewell picnic. Sitting with their students are three teachers. The teacher on the left is probably Miss VonSauer. Teachers Edith Howard (center) and Christine VonSauer are also identified. John J. Lewis is seated seventh from the left, and the fifth student from the left is believed to be Sammy Vicchiariello. (Author's collection.)

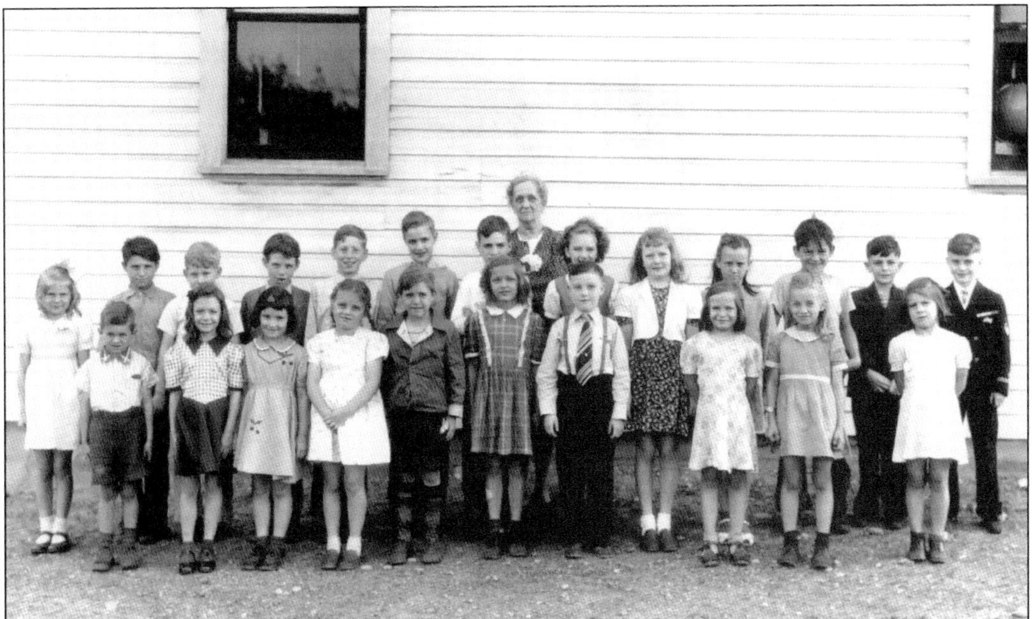

This 1945 picture shows grades 1 through 4 at the Lower Huguenot School. The teacher was Sarah Cuddeback (back). The students seen here are, from left to right, as follows: (front row) Gerald Ward, Shirley Burrows, Barbara Decker, Julie Messinger, Raymond Hale, Gail Caskey, Donald Coy, Philis Conklin, Joan Ward, and Barbara Conklin; (back row) Carol Stoll, Christopher Conklin, Richard Riser, Earnist Conklin, Allan Knapp, Kenneth Williams, Edward Williams, Dorothy Williams, Mary Nolan, Barbara Ward, Lester Taylor, Harry Cuddeback, and Ross Decker (present mayor of Port Jervis, 2000). (Rev. Don and Shirley Coy.)

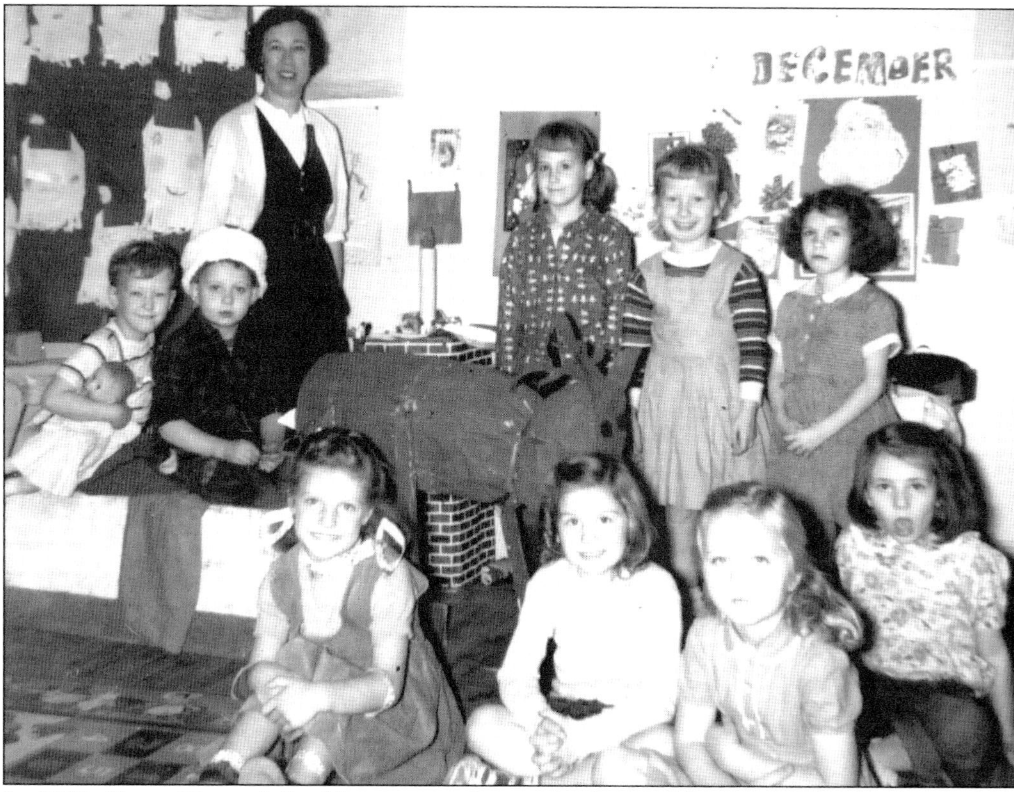

In 1960, Electa Howard (back) was a teacher at the Lower Huguenot School. The students here are, from left to right, as follows: (front row) Beverly Silson, Elaine Frederickson, Anila Naubered, and Nancy Rose; (back row) Harold Zeman, David Drake, Paula Mestek, Sue Piatt, and Joann Conklin. (Deerpark Historian's Office, Howard Collection.)

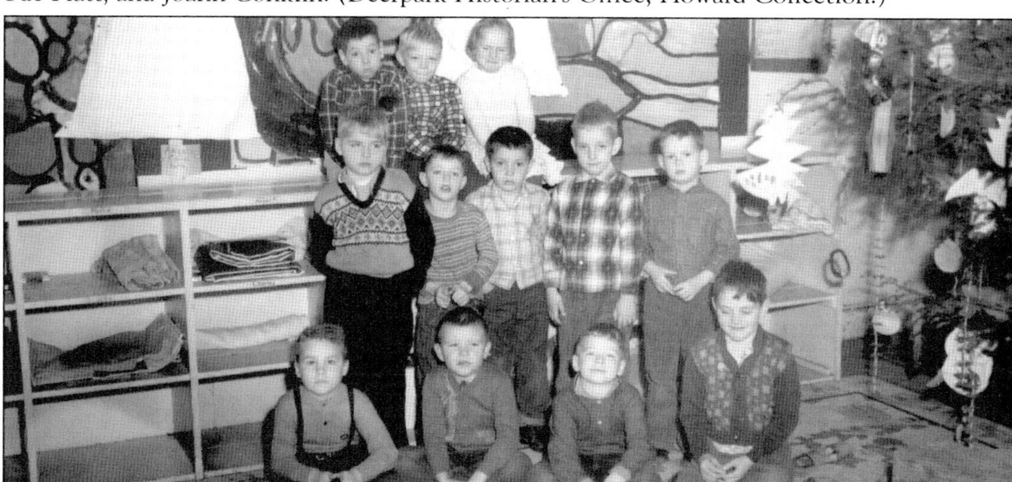

Students at the Lower Huguenot School pose for this picture at Christmastime in 1960. They are the ones who made the church windows and angels. Seen here are, from left to right, the following: (front row) David Lewis, Opart Bansky, Dennis Riordan, and unidentified; (middle row) unidentified, Kenny Eveleth, Mike Vicchiariello, Harry Space, and unidentified; (back row) unidentified, John Conklin, and Ruth Scholtz. (Deerpark Historian's Office, Howard Collection.)

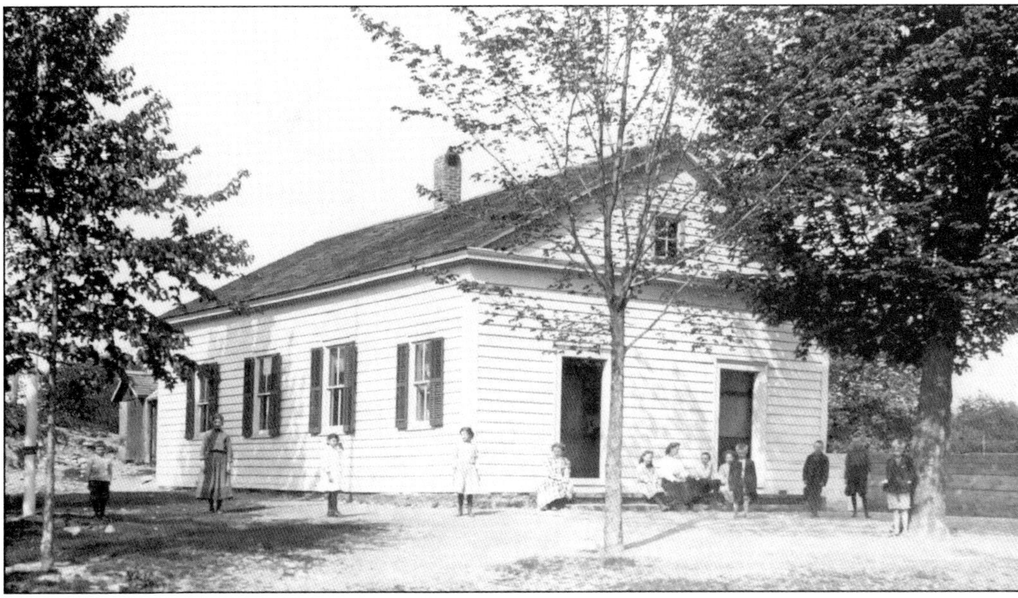

The Cuddebackville School, over 200 years old, now stands on Route 211 on its third site. This building may have been a village meetinghouse at one time. It originally stood somewhere near the present site of the Cuddebackville Reformed Church. It was moved to the second site, Route 211, *c*. 1850. In 1984, to create a building lot for a new Cuddebackville firehouse, Jerry Peill and volunteers moved the school onto his property next to the former site, where it can be seen today. (Deerpark Historian's Office.)

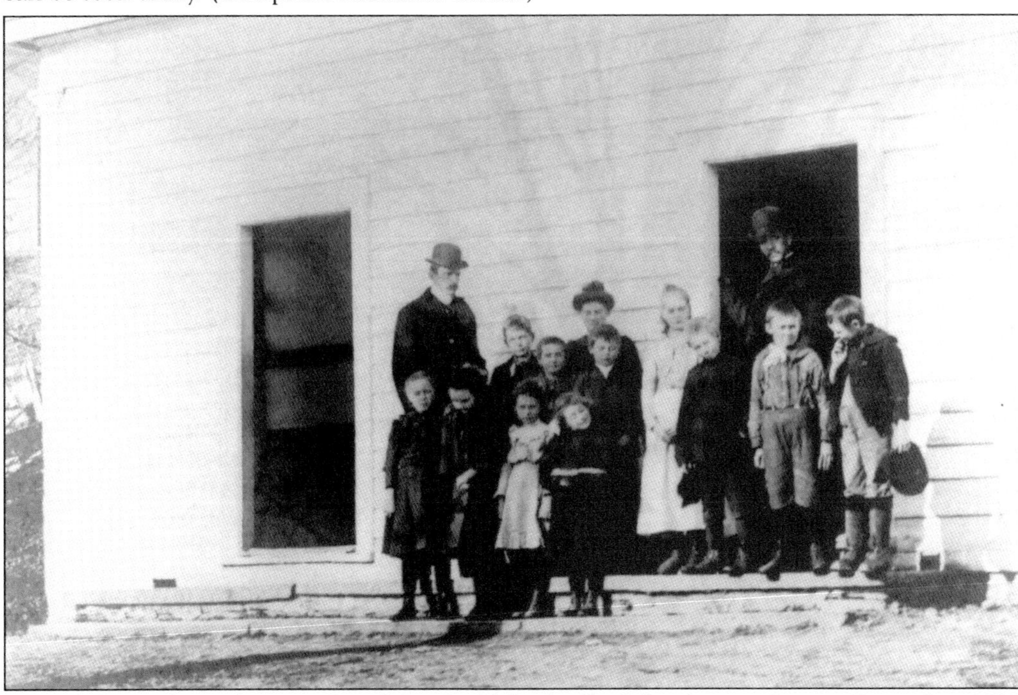

One of the earliest photographs of the Cuddebackville School was taken in December 1902. At this time, the Cuddebackville Reformed Church was located on the hill behind the school. (Jerry and Margaret Peill.)

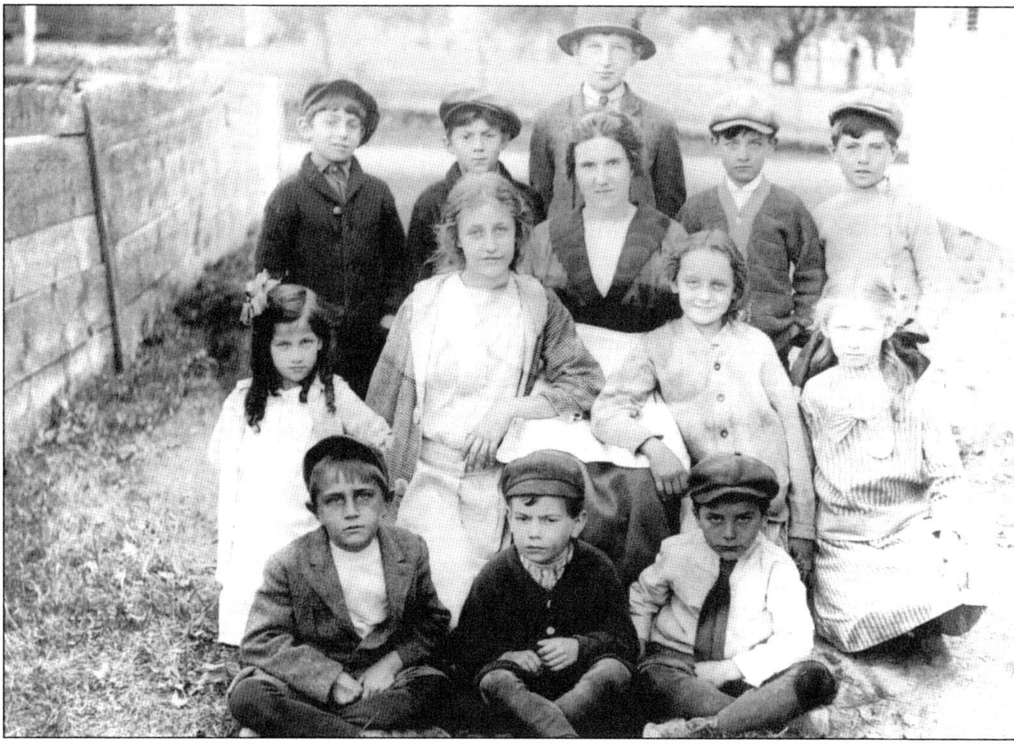

A class from the early 1900s poses for its annual photograph at the Cuddebackville School. Seen here are, from left to right, the following: (front row) Bill Lang, Clifford Gorden, and Hubert Schmitz; (middle row) Harriet Darby, Isabel Swartwout, Miss Worley (teacher), Marion Cuddeback, and Mildred Case; (back row) Percy Marceus, Nathan Marceus, George Lang, Art Hoag, and Frank Cuddeback. (Jerry and Margaret Peill.)

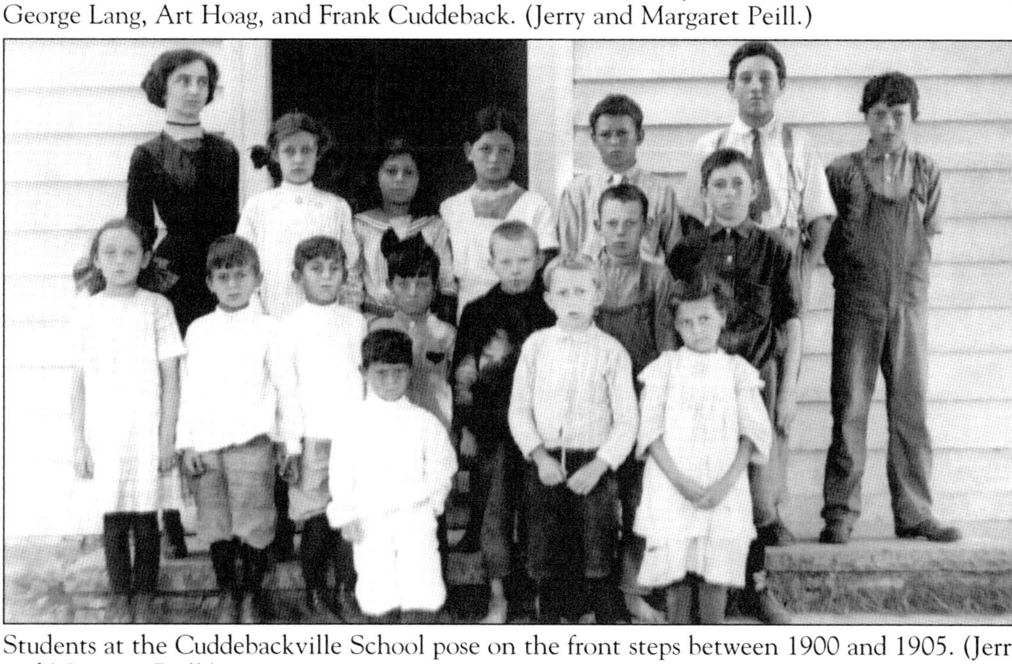

Students at the Cuddebackville School pose on the front steps between 1900 and 1905. (Jerry and Margaret Peill.)

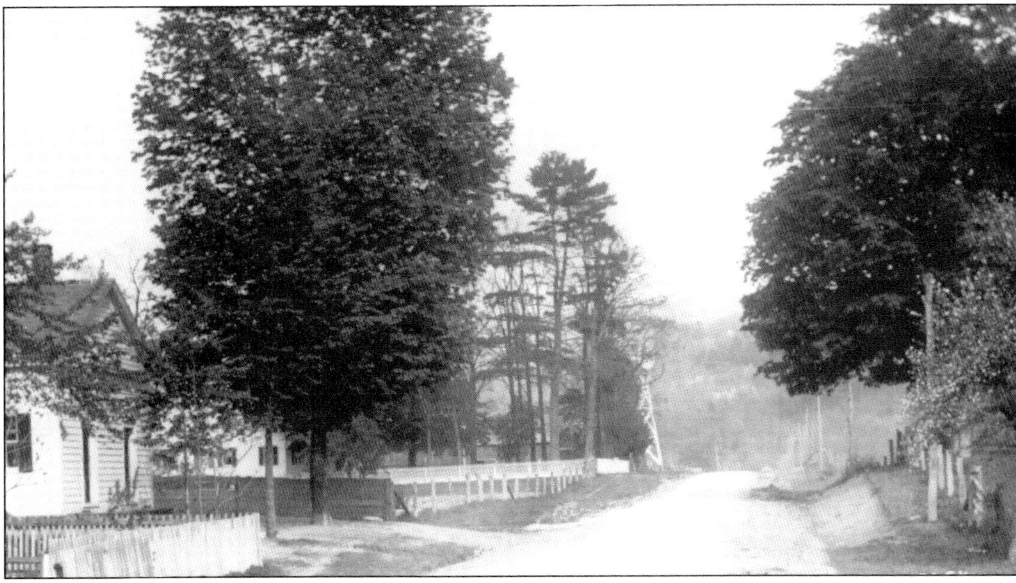

This *c.* 1905 view shows present-day Route 211. On the left are the Cuddebackville School and the William Cuddeback farm, with a working windmill. (Jerry and Margaret Peill.)

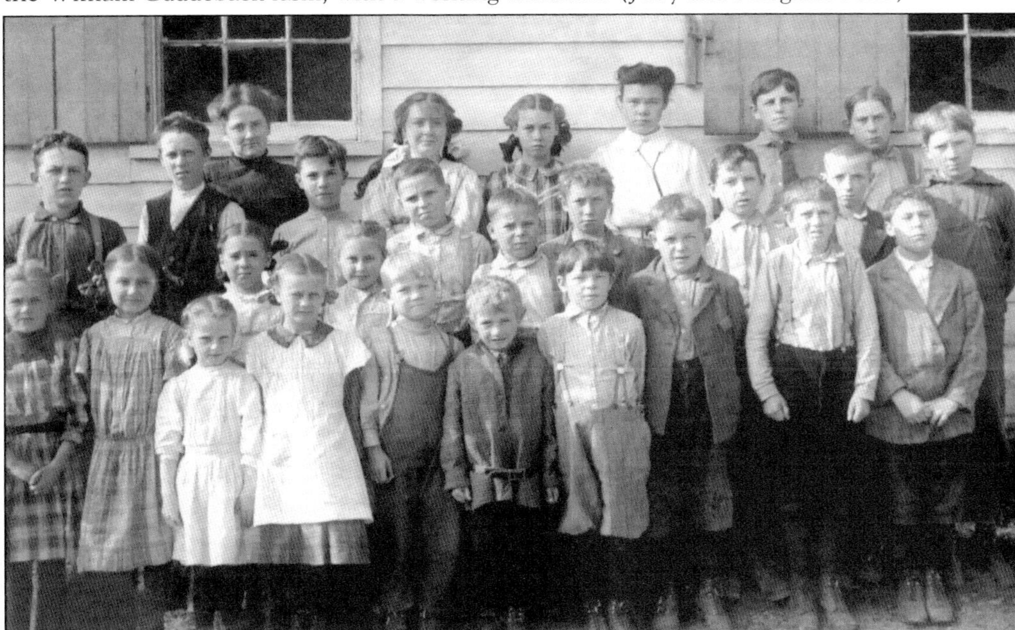

Students at the Oakland Valley School pose for this *c.* 1890s photograph. They are, from left to right, as follows: (front row) Ruth Griffin, Mildred Worden, J. Bassett Case, Edson Worden, and Leroy Ogden; (second row) Sadie Runnals, Lila E. Case, Margaret Galligan, Marjorie Burns, Hubert Arthurs, Jesse Runnals, Louis Worden, and Barney Lewis; (third row) Charles Runnals, Edward Galligan, J. Walter Decker, Millard Arthurs, Donald Decker, Harold G. Case, unidentified, and Wallace Ogden; (fourth row) Florence L. Case (teacher), Leverne Decker, Mary Worden, Nellie Ogden, Fred Lewis, and Russell Johnson. Although the Oakland Valley School District was a Deerpark district, the school was located in Sullivan County just across the Orange-Sullivan County line. (Neversink Valley Area Museum.)

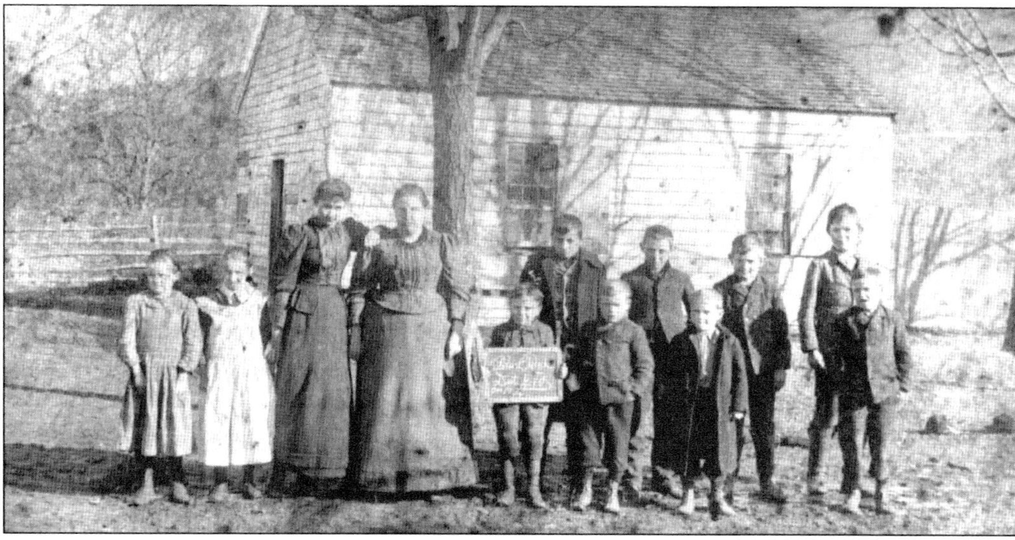

The Black Rock School, located on Neversink Drive, is the source of one of Deerpark's favorite tales, the "Painted Apron Story." During the American Revolution, Mohawk chief Col. Joseph Brant and his raiders, who were fighting for the British, swept through the valley. On July 20, 1779, they attacked the Black Rock School. Teacher Jeremiah Van Auken was killed and scalped, and some boys were injured as others fled into the woods. Stricken with fear, the girls stayed with their teacher. Suddenly, an Indian appeared and marked the girls' aprons. The Indian, who was Brant, told the girls to show the mark when they saw an Indian, saying that it would spare them. When the boys returned, the girls stamped the impression of the mark onto the boys' clothes, thereby saving the children's lives. This photograph was taken c. 1894. (Minisink Valley Historical Society.)

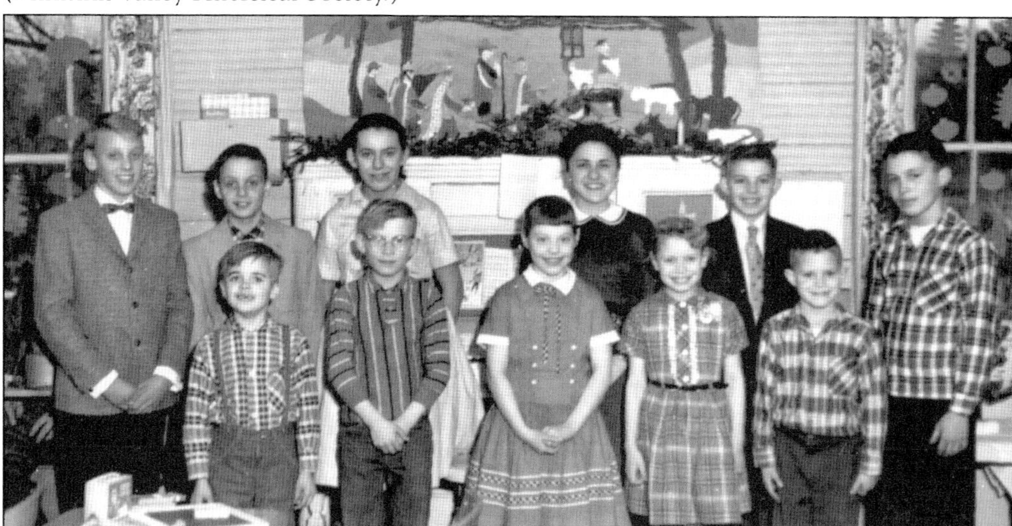

The following three photographs were taken at the Black Rock School Christmas Program on December 17, 1959. The classroom teacher was Sadie Bateman Reagen (not shown). Seen here are, from left to right, the following: (front row) Michael Lane, Albert Johnson, Norinne Lane, Ann Sarine, and Gary Flieger; (back row) John Eagan, Billy Eagan, Diane Pierson, Gloria Calaiaco Celletti (assistant district music supervisor and teacher), Wayne Pierson, and Jack Flieger. (Deerpark Historian's Office, Celletti Collection.)

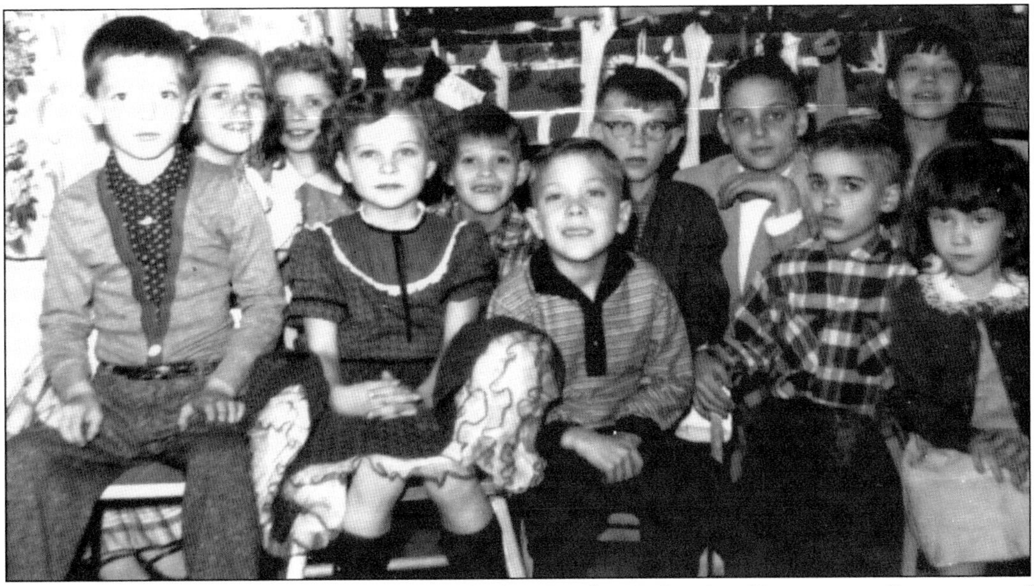

These are participants in the Black Rock School Christmas Program of December 17, 1959. Seen here are, from left to right, the following: (front row) Robert Zeller, Connie Johnson (Eagan), Gary Flieger, Mike Lane, and unidentified; (back row) Linda Heal, Ann Sarine, unidentified, Albert Johnson, Billy Eagon, and Norinne Lane. (Deerpark Historian's Office, Celletti Collection.)

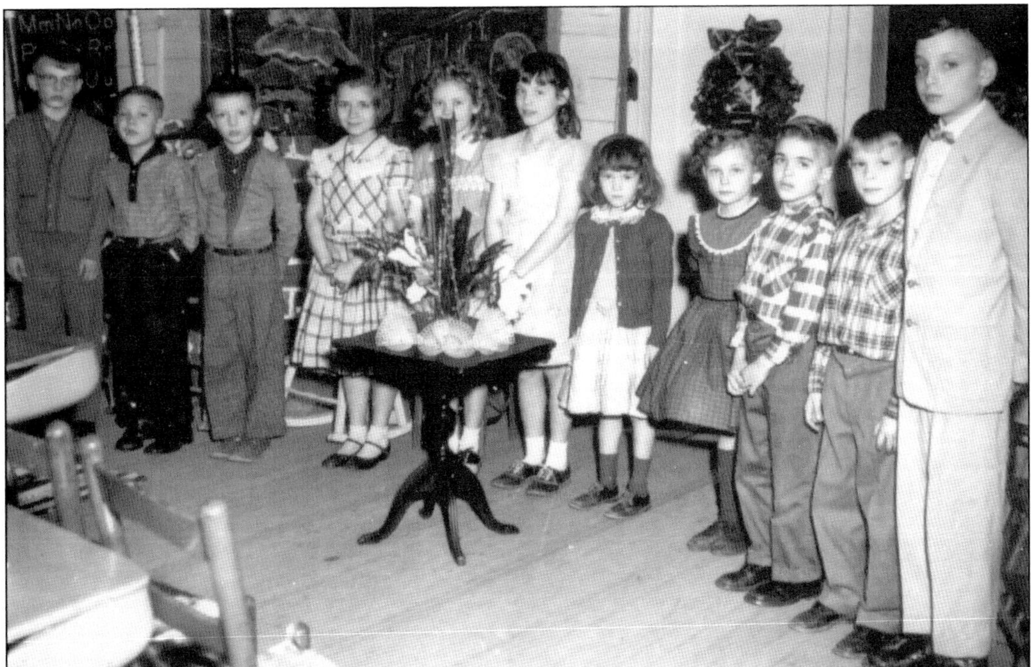

Another photograph of the Black Rock School Christmas Program of December 17, 1959, shows, from left to right, Albert Johnson, unidentified, Robert Zeller, Linda Heal, Ann Sarine, Norinne Lane, unidentified, Connie Johnson (Eagan), Mike Lane, Gary Flieger, and Billy Eagan. (Deerpark Historian's Office, Celletti Collection.)

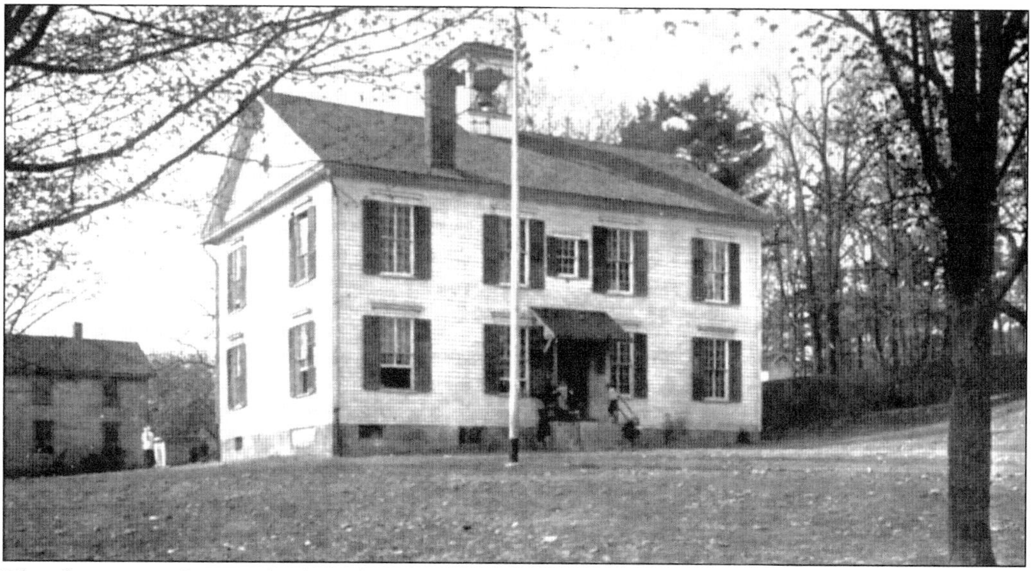

The four-room Sparrowbush School served its community for nearly 100 years, until the centralization of the Port Jervis School District. The structure was built on Academy Avenue just after the Civil War, in 1868. It was remodeled sometime in the early 1900s. The auditorium was added as a Works Progress Administration project in the 1930s. At one time, the building was an elementary and junior high school. The school was taken down to make room for a private residence. (Author's collection.)

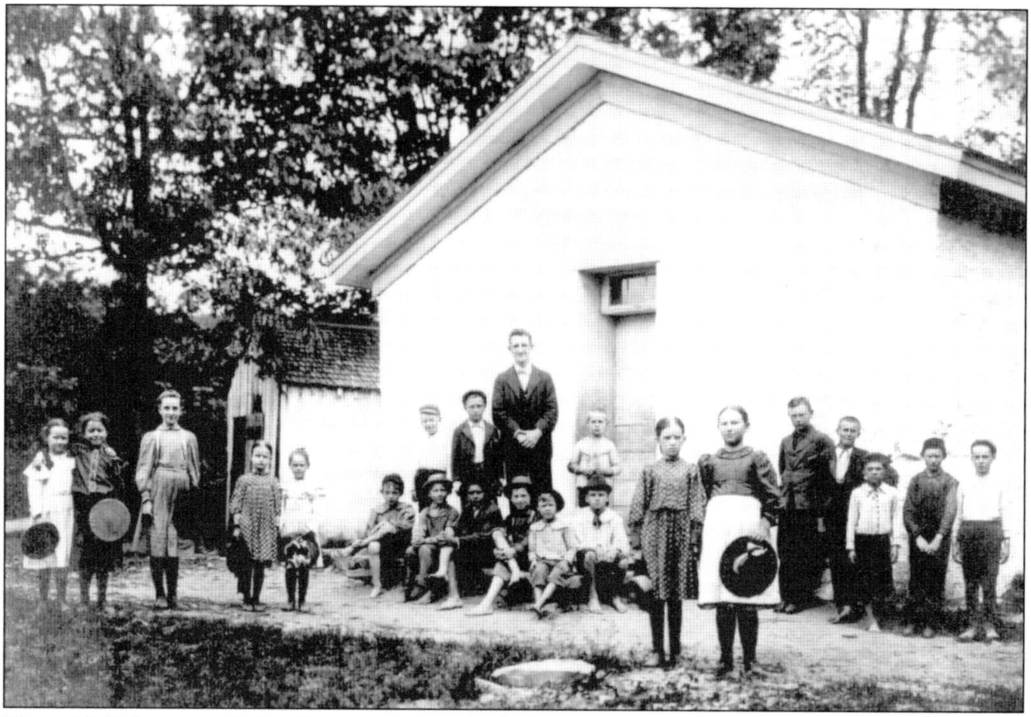

The old Cahoonzie Schoolhouse was an Indian fort that was later used as a school. This photograph was taken in 1898. The teacher was Warren Heidenthaw, and the boy seen standing in the doorway is William Boehmler. (Deerpark Historian's Office.)

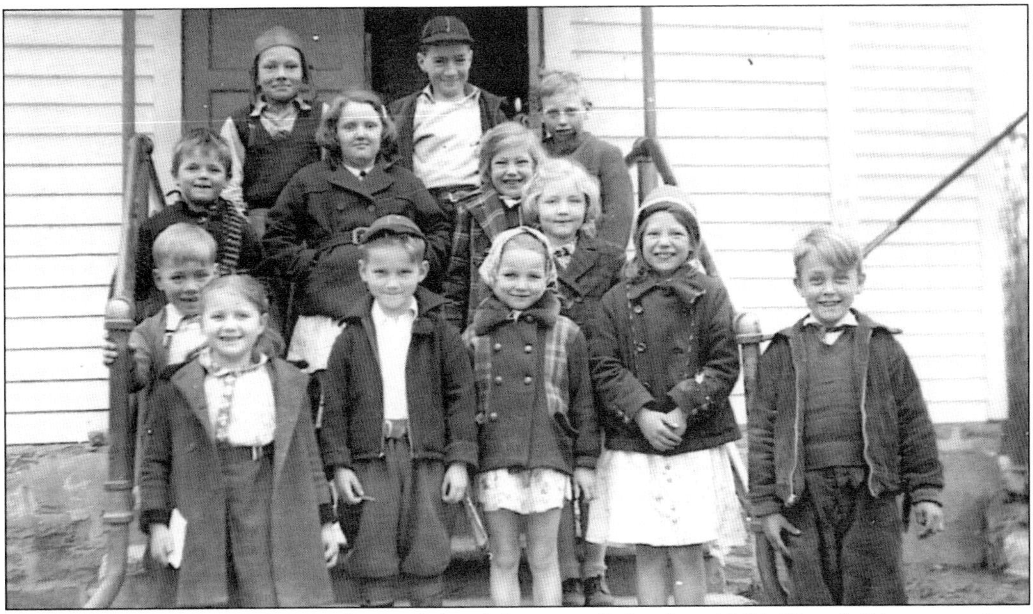

This photograph was taken in front of the Cahoonzie School in 1937. The children seen here are, from left to right, as follows: (front row) August Brown, George Hammond, Mary Packer, Olive Hulse, and Richard Freytag; (second row) Alden Schock and Gertrude Akt (Aber) (first grade); (third row) Lowell Hulse, Frances Heater, Dorothy Schock, and Leonard Hulse; (fourth row) Conrad "Ronny" Schock and Robert Aber (third grade). (Deerpark Historian's Office, Hammond Collection.)

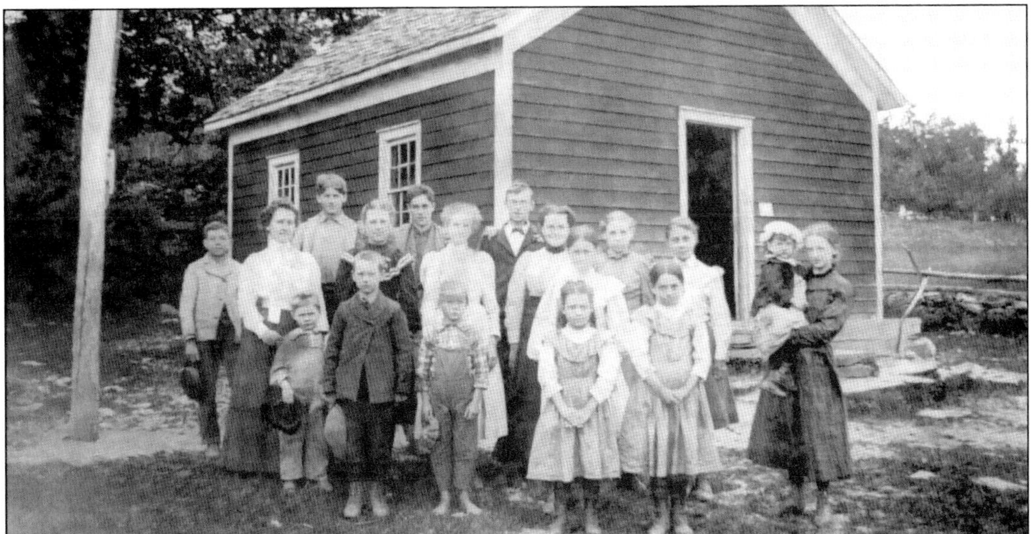

In this schoolhouse, the Quarry Hill Methodist Church held its first services. Therefore, according to an old newspaper clipping, this school had to have been built prior to 1850. Church services continued to be held there until 1878. Seen here are, from left to right, the following: (front row) three unidentified people, Florence Sturdevant, Ann Sturdevant, and Nan Whitaker holding Florian Greenleaf; (back row) unidentified, Gertrude Quackenbush, Harry Howlett Sr., unidentified, Horace Patterson, Laura Reed, Chester Whitaker, Sarah Boyd, unidentified, Pearl Hunt, and Sarah Gordon. (Harold Moore.)

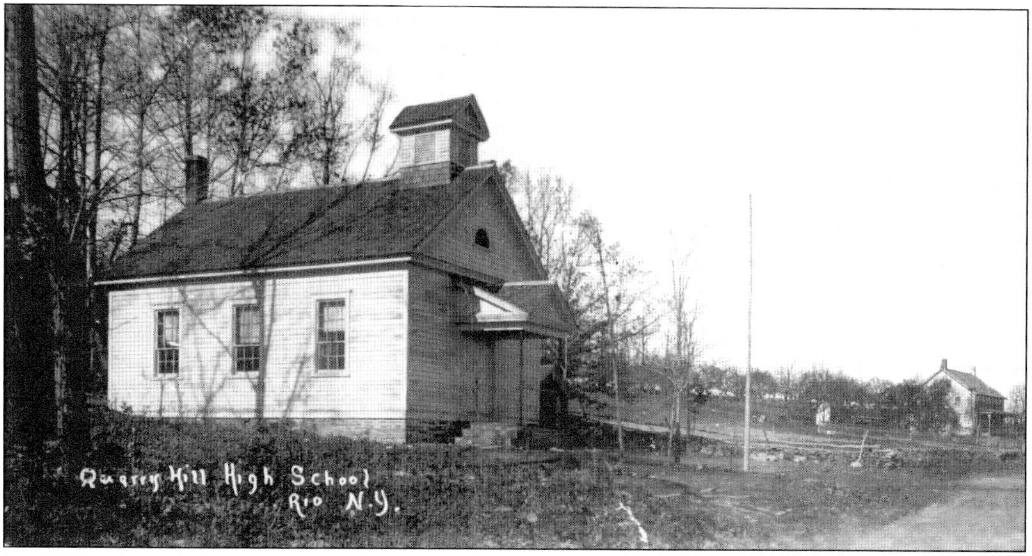

In 1900, the third and present Quarry Hill School was built to replace the old "worn-out" schoolhouse (seen in the previous photograph). The new building's windows had fifteen 9-inch by 12-inch panes, wainscoting, and blackboards across the front and back, and for the first time, a cupola for a bell. All this cost $625. The building is now a private residence. The James F. Durland homestead is in the distance. (Author's collection.)

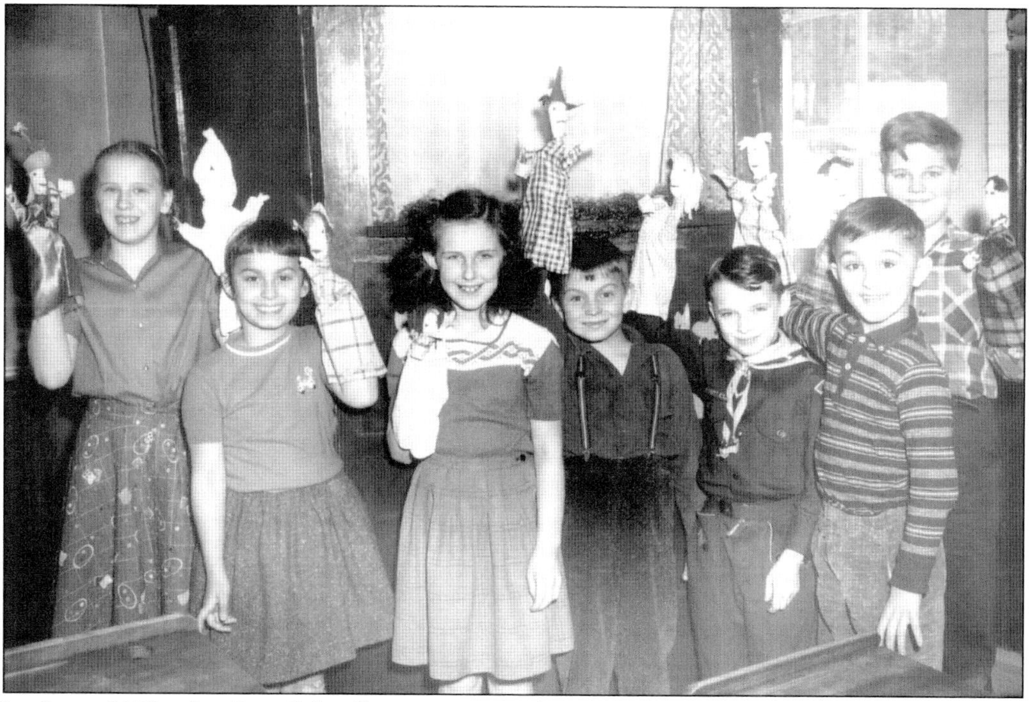

In June 1958, the Rio Schoolhouse saw its last students after Deerpark schools were centralized. Some students perform a puppet show in April 1958. They are, from left to right, Carolyn Alekna, Drusilla E. Swinton, Dawn Powers, Jerry Alekna, Glenn Poshadel, Michael R. Swinton, and Richard Stevens. Neither Keith Stevens, who was absent that day, nor the teacher, Helen Walters, are in the photograph. (Doris Swinton.)

Three

TRANSPORTATION AND INDUSTRY

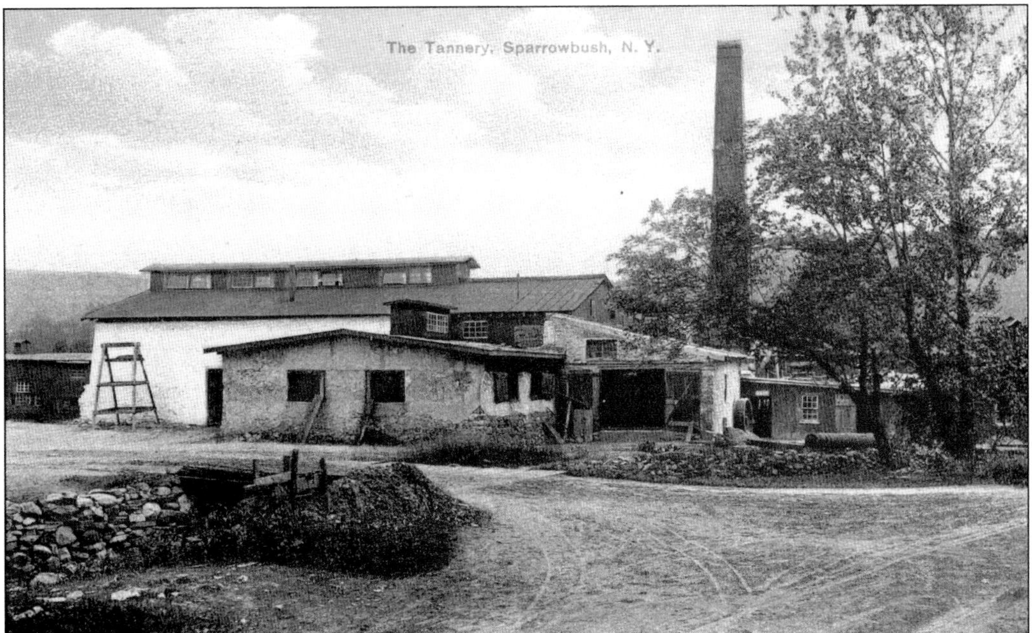

In 1850, Maurice M. Schultz built the Sparrowbush Tannery next to the Delaware and Hudson Canal, for convenient shipping. The land was donated by A.J. Raymond. In 1867, after the tannery had two fires, Charles Cooper and George W. Swasey bought, rebuilt, and enlarged the operation and continued producing all kinds of leather goods. The tannery was the town's first and only factory, producing as many as 50,000 hides in one year. In 1868, sales amounted to over $400,000. (Author's collection.)

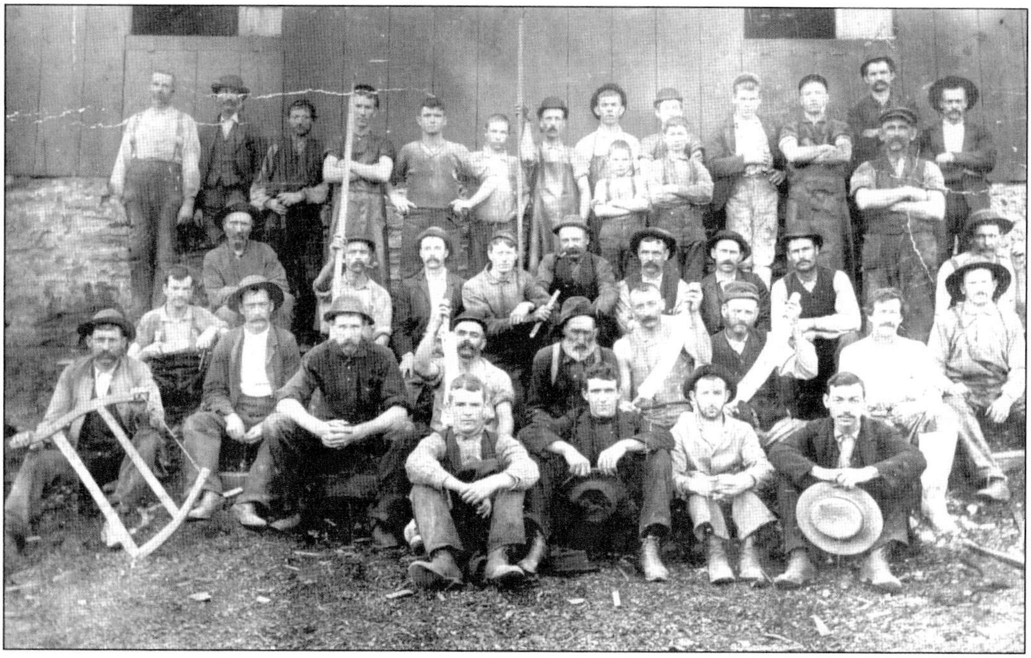

This photograph shows tannery workers holding the tools of their trade. Over the years, many new methods of tanning were developed, but the Sparrowbush Tannery used the traditional bark method. Local wooded land was stripped of oak and hemlock trees for the bark, which contained tannic acid, a key ingredient. The tannery machinery ran on a 20-horsepower steam engine built by Ray & Company of the Port Jervis Steam Engine Works. (Minisink Valley Historical Society.)

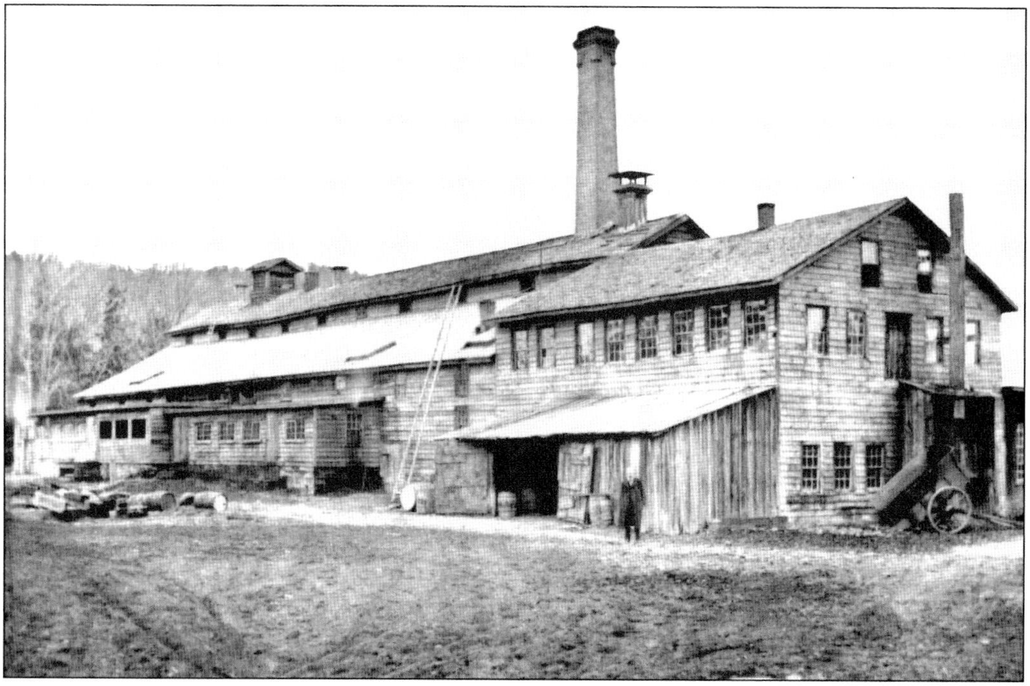

This is a late-1890s photograph of the tannery. (Nancy Dunn.)

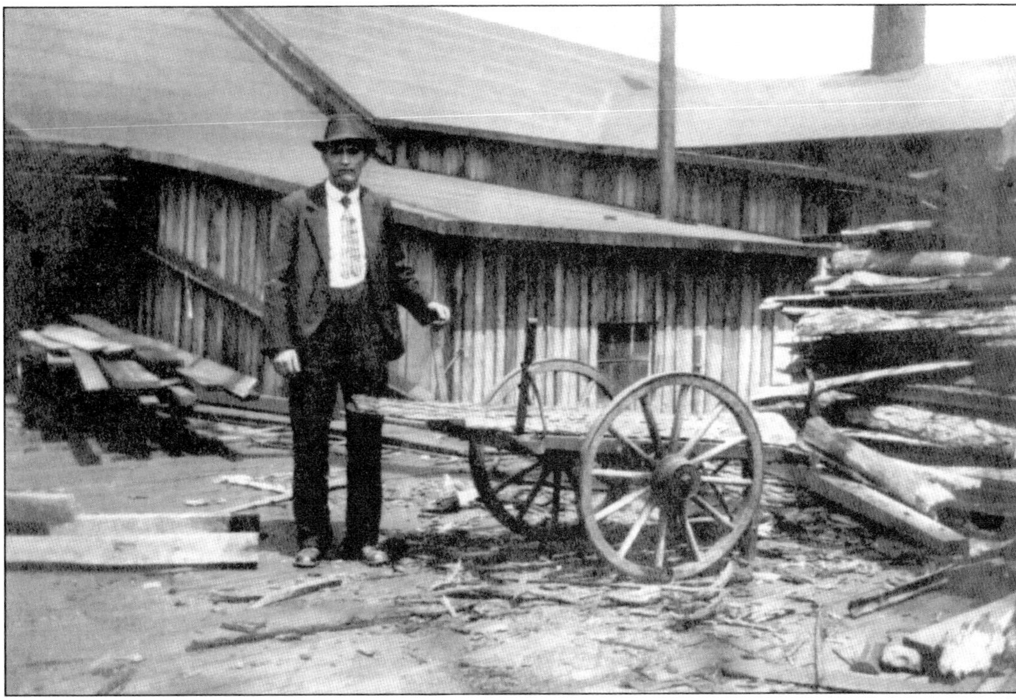

Theodore Wallace Coleman is the man in this photograph, which was probably taken at the Sparrowbush Tannery in the late 1800s. Piles of wood are being stripped of bark, the source of tannic acid used in the tanning process. In the 1860s, 4,000 cords of bark were used annually. (Nancy Coleman-Bello.)

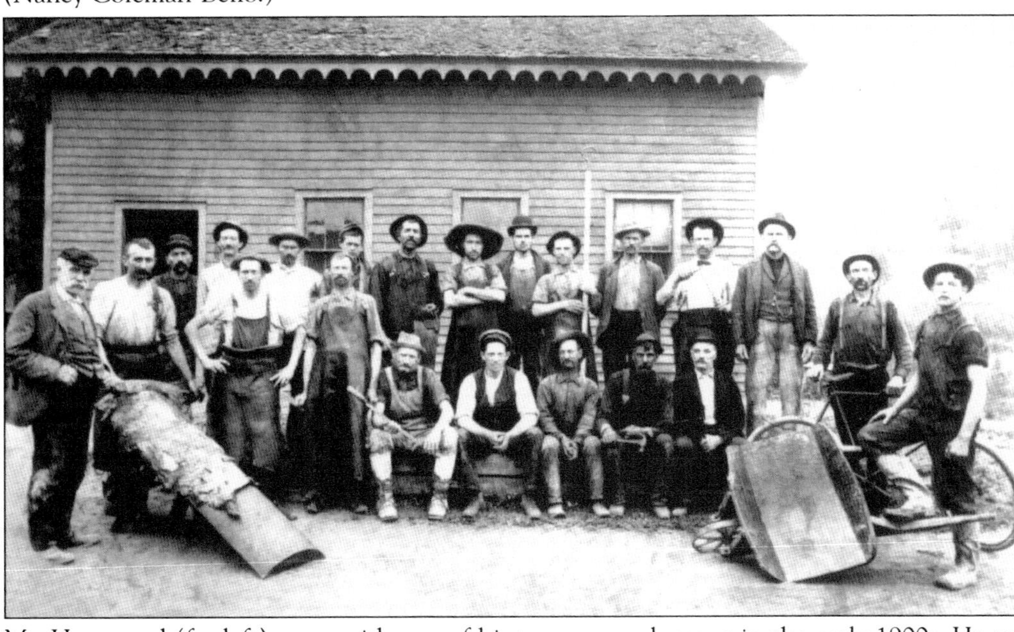

Mr. Hammond (far left) poses with one of his tannery work crews in the early 1900s. He ran a successful business until 1920. The business was sold in 1921 and became a shoe black and patent leather factory. The tannery burned to the ground in 1932. One building still stands near Routes 97 and 42. (Deerpark Historian's Office.)

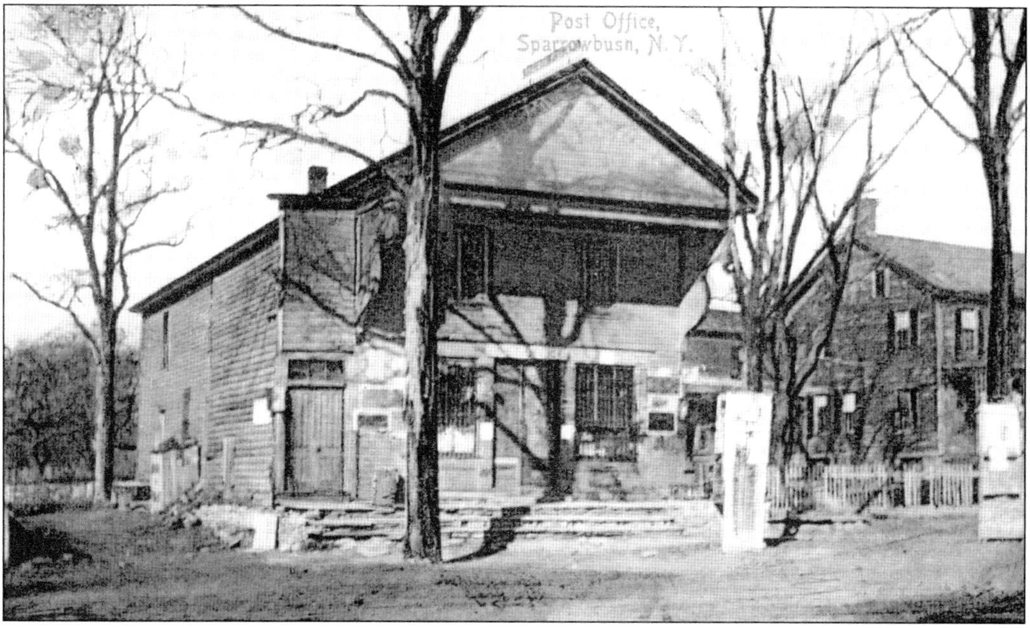

The tannery store was built by George Reymar. The store sold merchandise produced by the tannery. Starting in 1893, the building housed the post office. This view was taken in 1909. The house on the right is still standing. (Tom Patterson.)

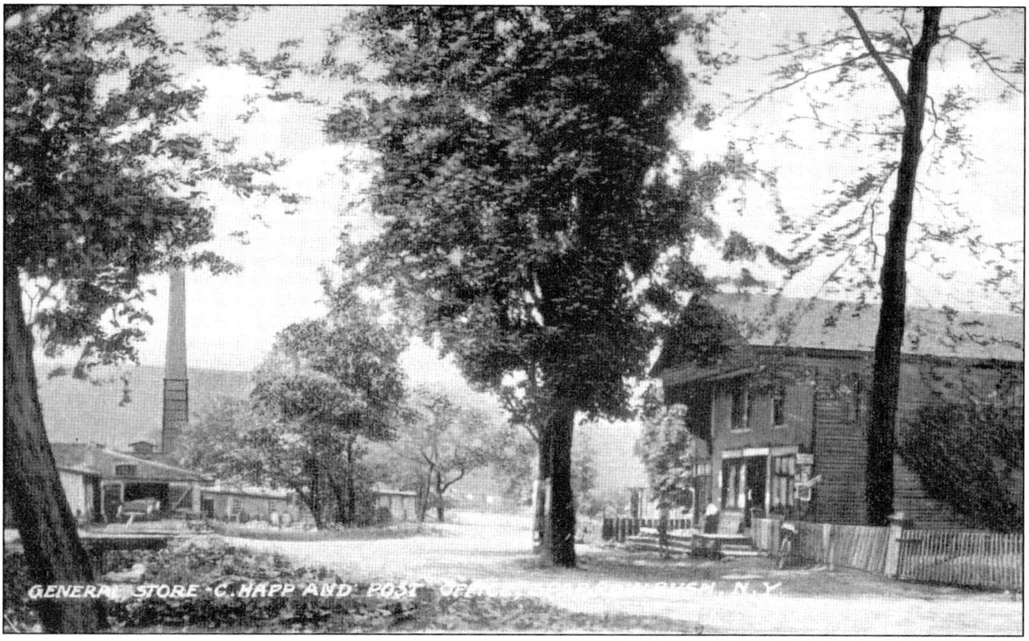

This postcard shows the proximity of the tannery and the tannery store along Lower Brook Road. When George Reymar died in 1899, Conrad Happ took over the store and acted as postmaster. When the building burned c. 1905, the post office was moved to the store owned by Henry Happ, who then served as postmaster until 1915. (Glenn R. Conklin.)

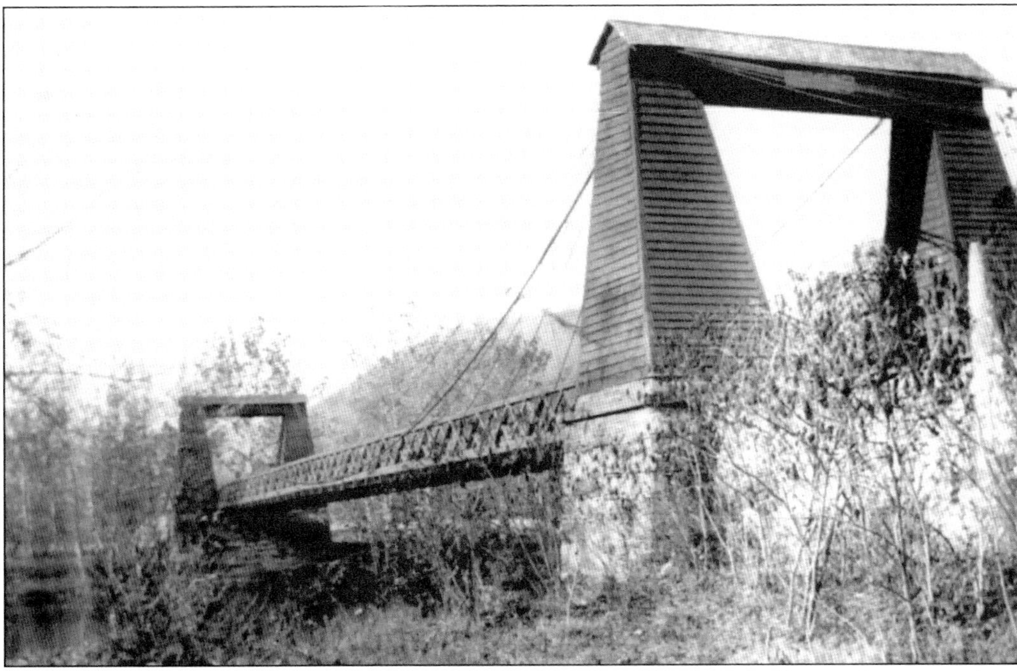

The Cuddebackville suspension bridge was built *c.* 1850 and carried traffic until it was replaced by the first one-lane iron bridge built in the early 1900s. This photograph, looking south toward Roses Point, was taken in the 1890s. (Deerpark Historian's Office.)

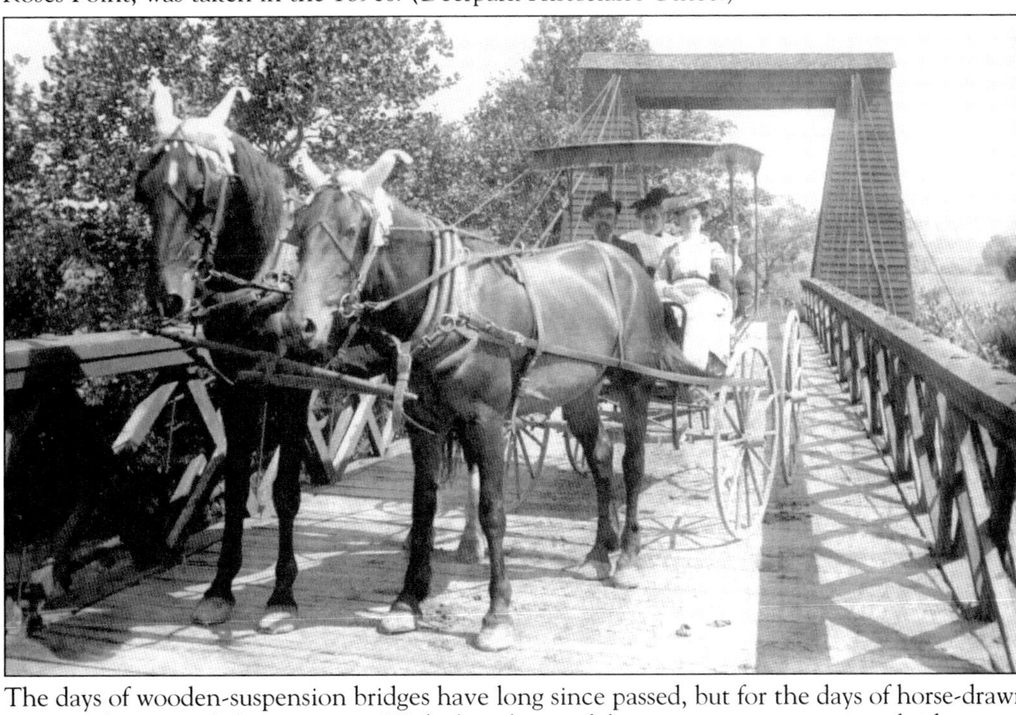

The days of wooden-suspension bridges have long since passed, but for the days of horse-drawn wagons, they served their purpose. With the advent of the motorcar, stronger iron bridges were needed. This photograph, looking south toward Godeffroy, was taken on the Cuddebackville suspension bridge in the 1880s or 1890s. (Neversink Valley Area Museum.)

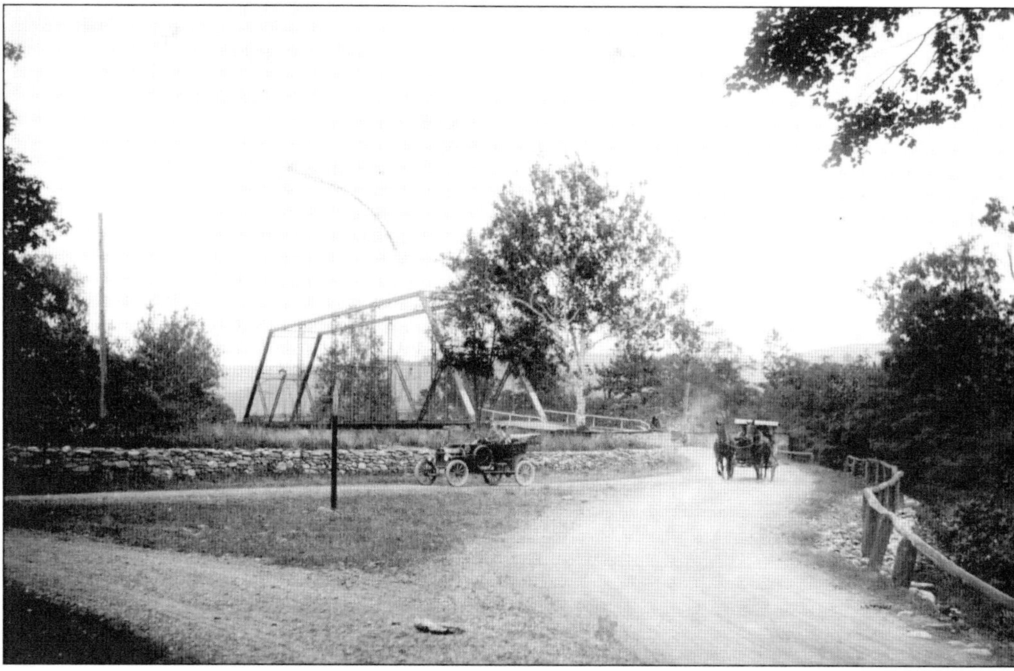

This 1910 view looking north shows the old iron bridge in Cuddebackville, a one-lane bridge that served the townsfolk and travelers until 1928. According to local information, the bridge was dismantled and moved downriver to replace the Gumaer bridge in Godeffroy. (Minisink Valley Historical Society.)

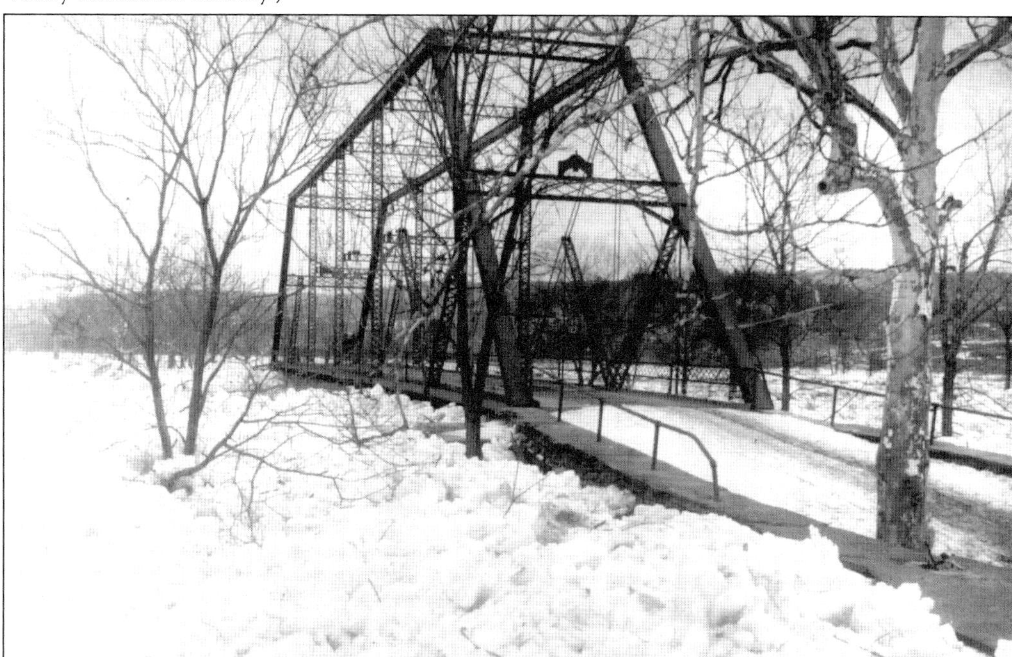

The Deerpark and Port Jervis bridges have seen their share of ice jams through the years. This view shows the 1904 ice gorge level with the Neversink River bank and touching the bottom of the old iron Cuddebackville bridge. (Deerpark Historian's Office.)

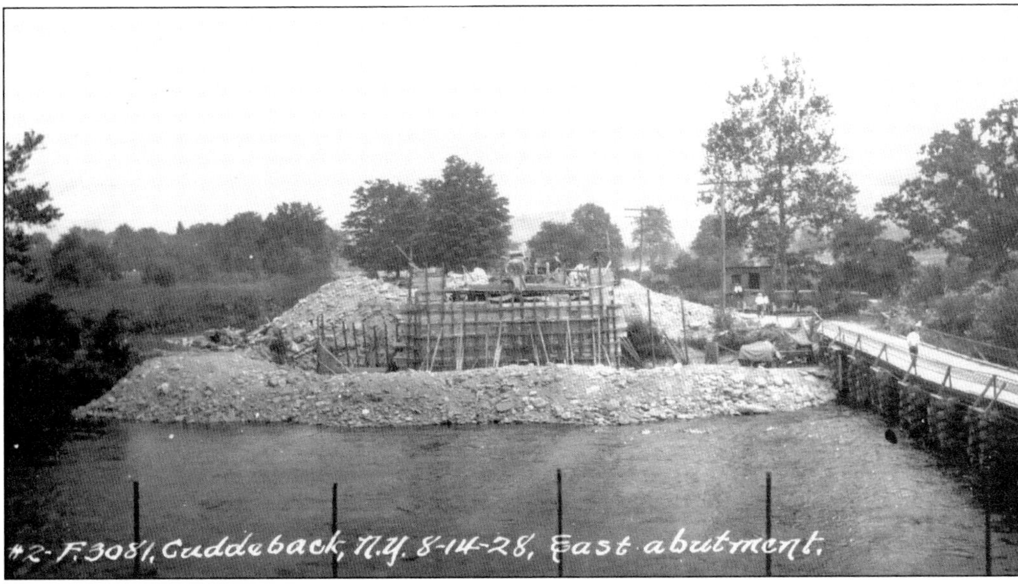

During the construction of the new Neversink River bridge in Cuddebackville, a temporary structure was built a few yards downstream to accommodate vehicles, wagons, and pedestrians. The pilings were constructed of railroad ties. A close look shows a cement mixer filling the concrete forms for the north abutment. This photograph was taken on August 14, 1928. (Author's collection.)

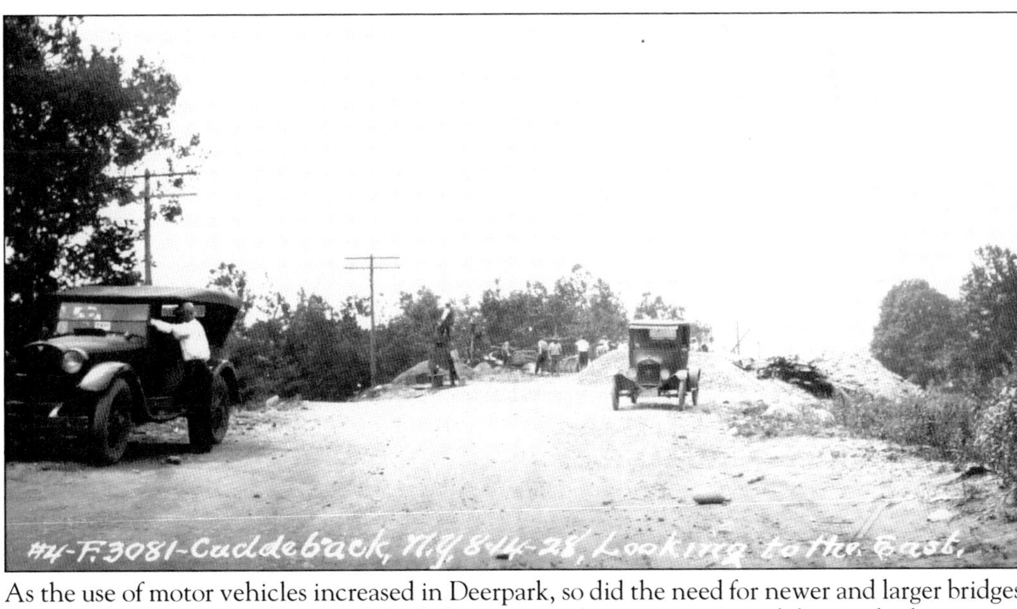

As the use of motor vehicles increased in Deerpark, so did the need for newer and larger bridges. This image, looking south toward Godeffroy, shows the construction of the north abutment of the new iron bridge. The bank height was raised to accommodate ice jams. This photograph was taken on August 14, 1928. (Author's collection.)

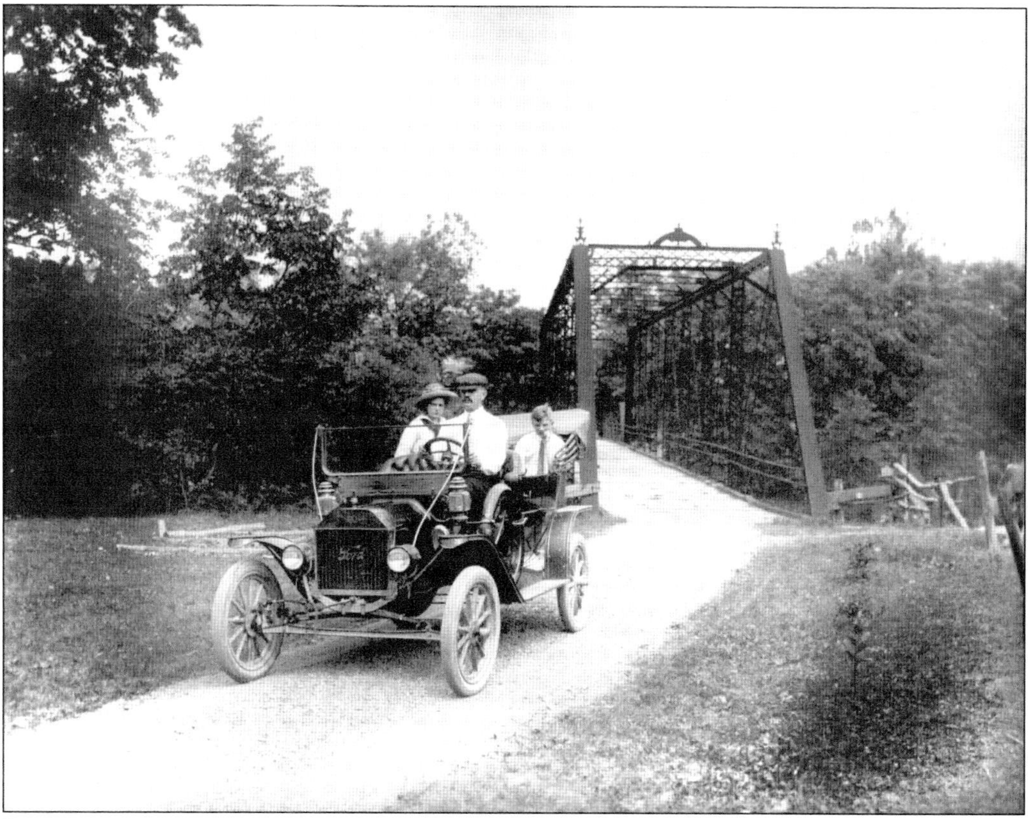

Dr. Henry B. Swartwout, the first mayor of Port Jervis, was the owner of one of the first automobiles in the area. He is seen here driving across the bridge over the Neversink River in Huguenot on the Horn Road (Neversink Drive). This photograph was taken *c.* 1909. (Minisink Valley Historical Society.)

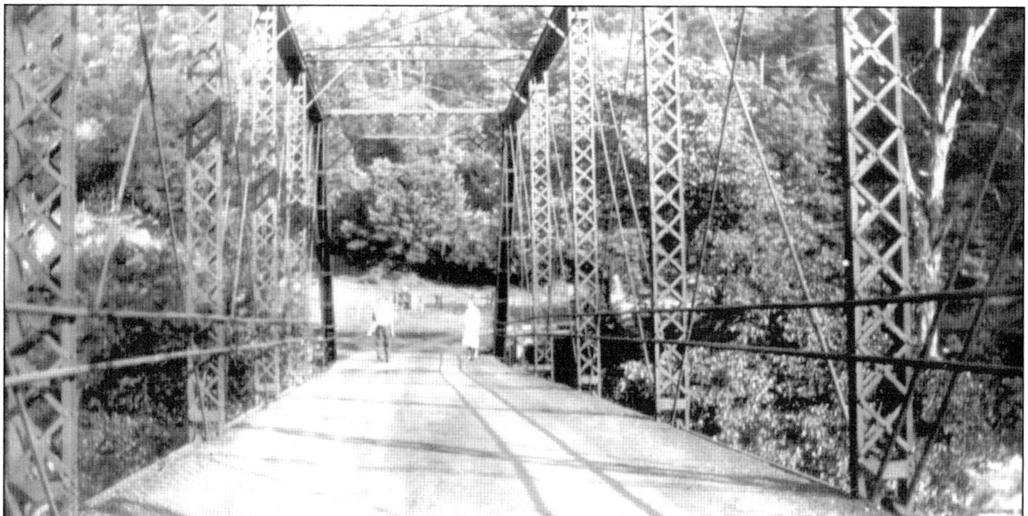

The same Huguenot bridge over the Neversink River is seen in this photograph, taken in the 1930s. (Neversink Valley Area Museum.)

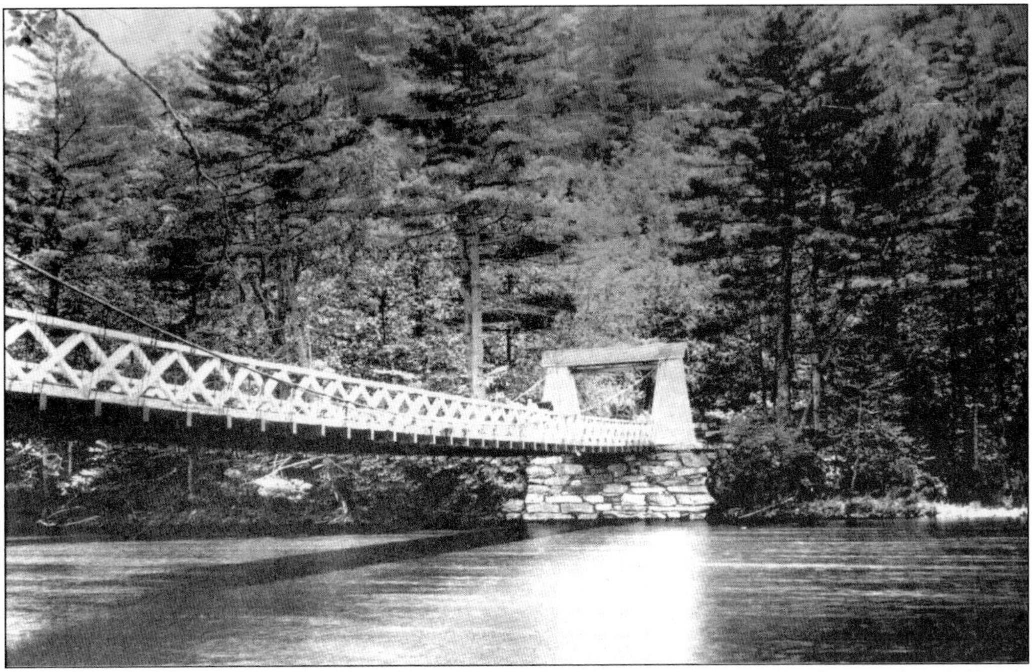

The Guymard suspension bridge, crossing the Neversink River at Port Clinton (Godeffroy), was built c. 1850 by the Gumaer family. A close look shows a horse and buggy on the bridge. Although the Cuddebackville bridge and this bridge are similar, there are differences in the site and construction details (see page 77). (Deerpark Historian's Office.)

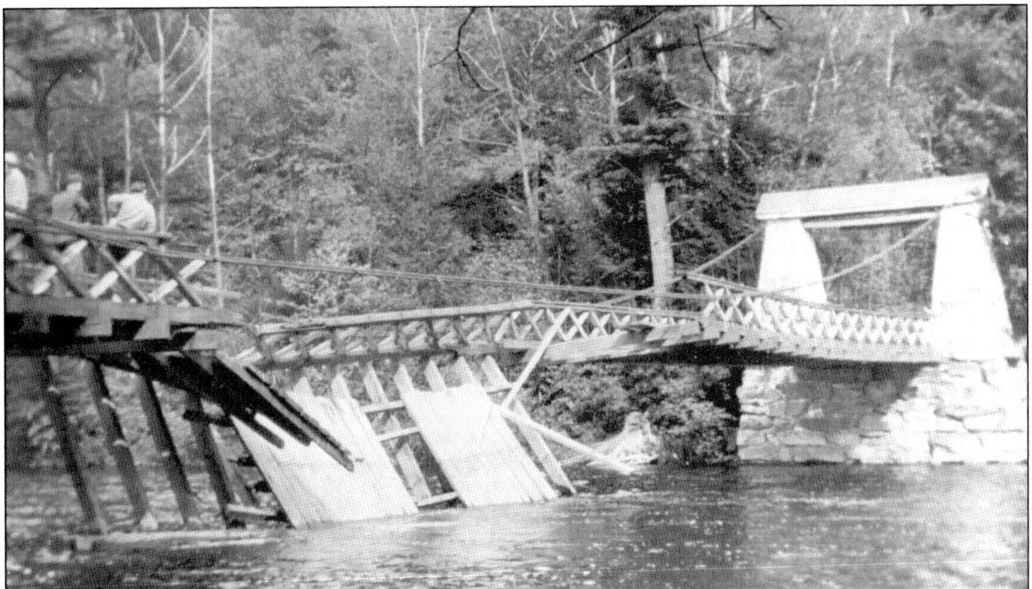

Wooden suspension bridges were built to handle the weight of horse-drawn wagons. In this May or June 1927 photograph of the Neversink River Guymard bridge, the bridge suspension has not collapsed and people are standing nonchalantly at the edge of the remaining roadway. An overloaded truck caused the collapse with $1,000 reported in damages. (Deerpark Historian's Office.)

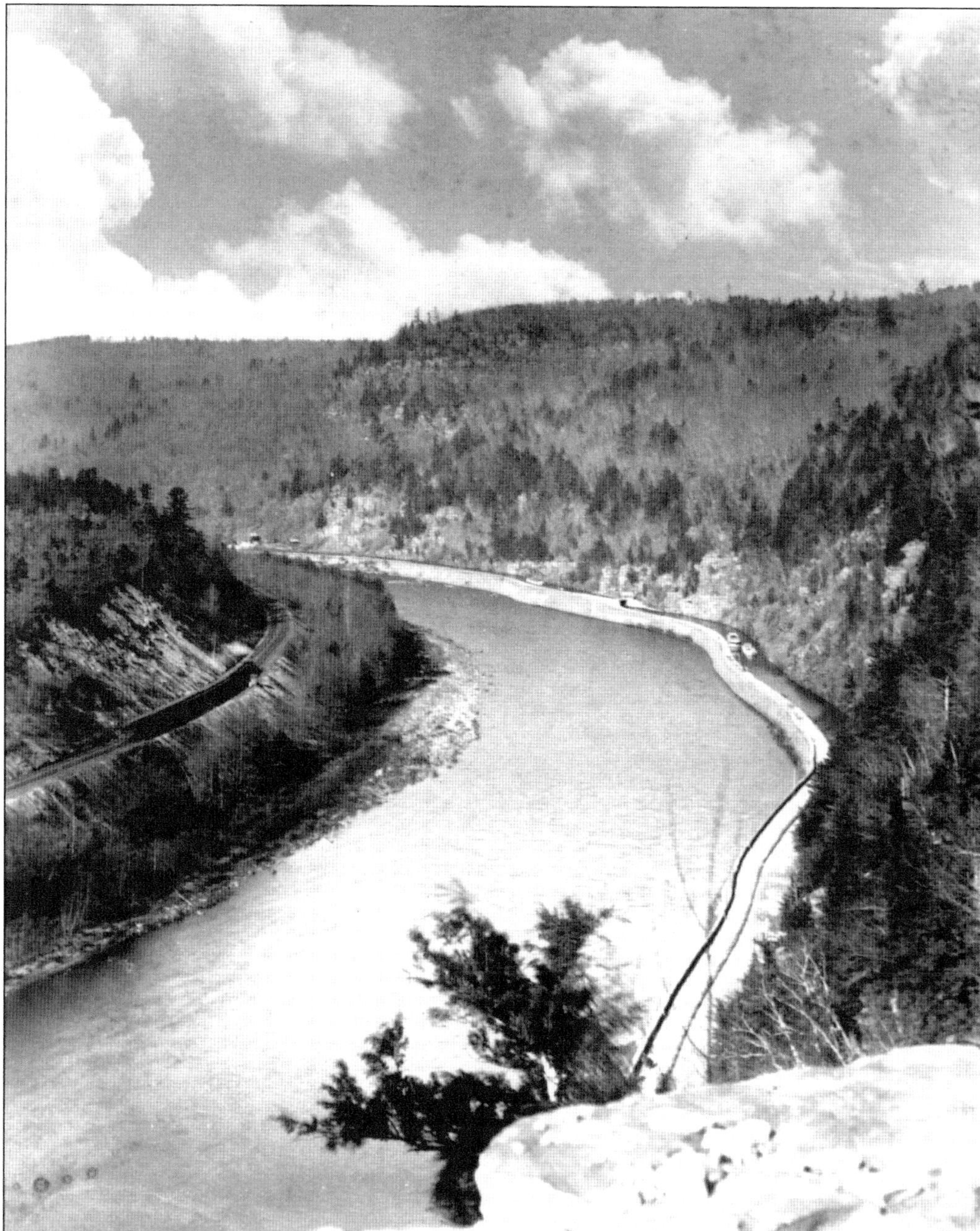

In this 1880s view from the Hawk's Nest on Route 97 in Sparrowbush, we can see how the Delaware and Hudson Canal hugged the bank of the Delaware River. The lock tender's house can be seen much further upstream. On the opposite side of the river, an Erie Railroad train can be seen. Time and ice flowing downriver in the winter have slowly eroded away any signs of the Delaware and Hudson Canal in this section. (Minisink Valley Historical Society.)

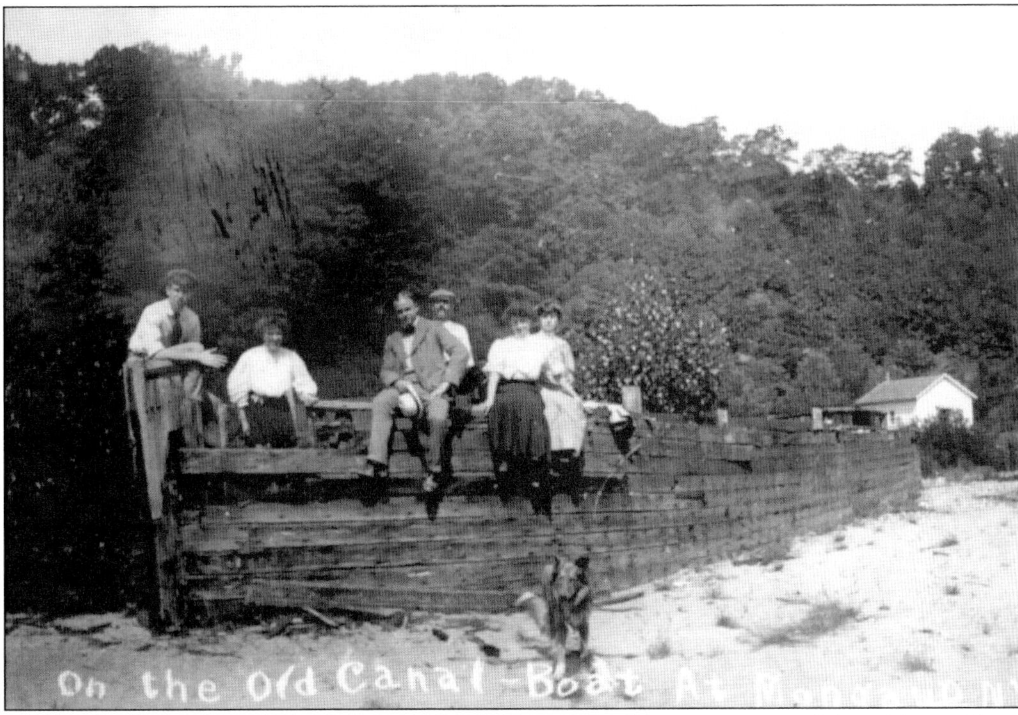

At this site in Mongaup, many searches have been done for any remains of this old canal boat. No searches have been successful. The photograph dates from c. 1907. (Author's collection.)

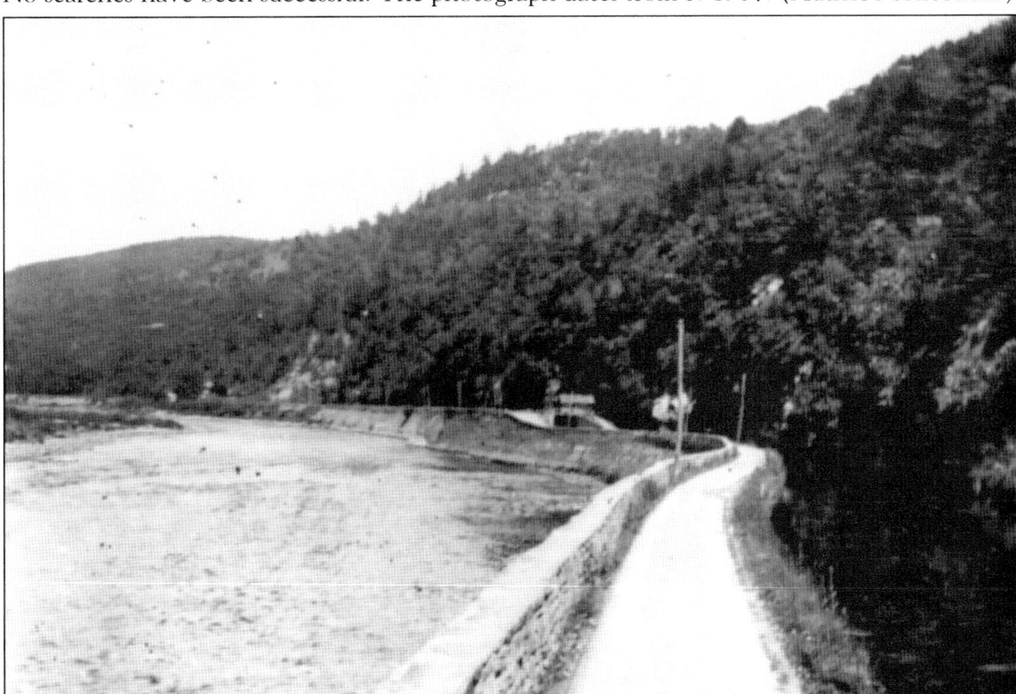

Butler's Lock, No. 57, was located below the Hawk's Nest along the banks of the Delaware River. The lock tender's house was located about a half a mile upstream. (Deerpark Historian's Office.)

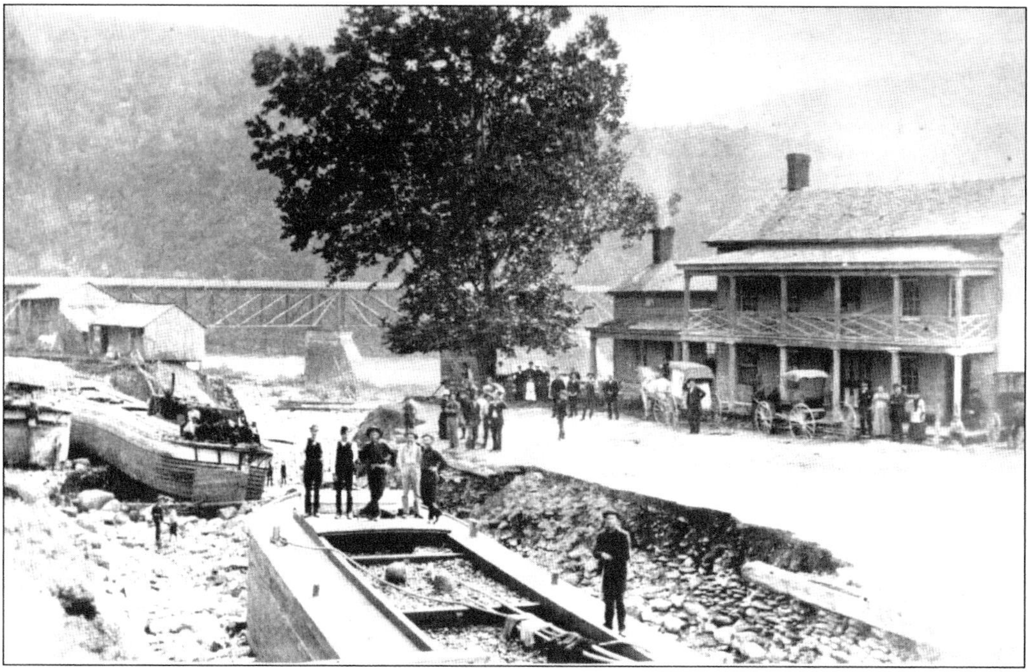

A severe storm on August 5, 1885, caused a breach in the Delaware and Hudson Canal at Bolton Basin in Sparrowbush. The water from the canal emptied into the Delaware River. Extensive damage was done. Mrs. Simpson (third from the right) stands in front of the Simpson Hotel. The bridge in the background is the Erie Bridge No. 2 over the Delaware River. (Deerpark Historian's Office.)

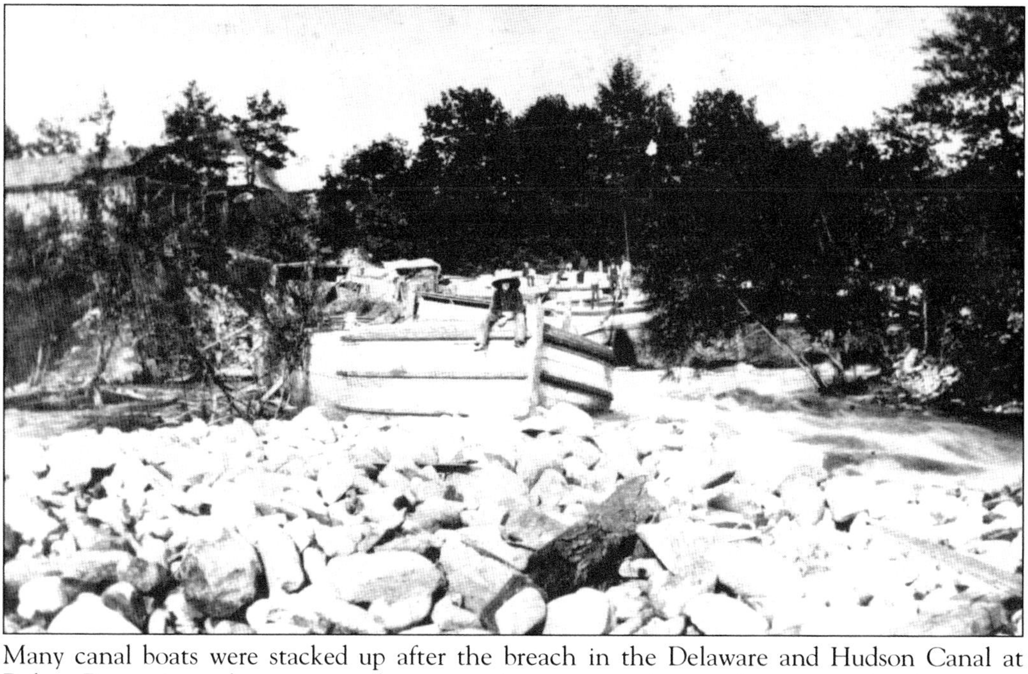

Many canal boats were stacked up after the breach in the Delaware and Hudson Canal at Bolton Basin. According to research sources, the repair on the breach was completed in a very short time. (Deerpark Historian's Office.)

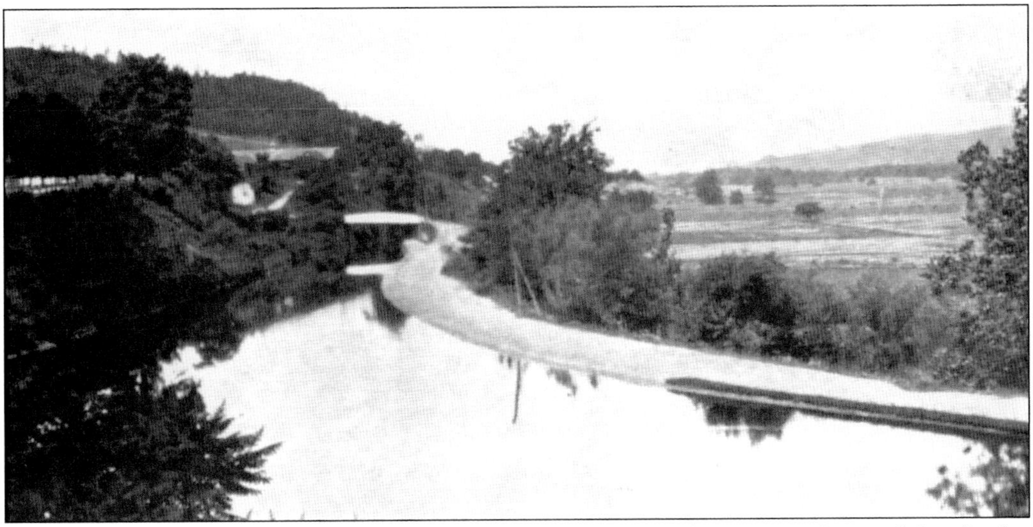

This image of the Delaware and Hudson Canal in Huguenot shows an early canal foot bridge (center) that was just below the Hotel Huguenot. The bridge was known to boatmen as the Spring House Bridge, named after one of the original names of the hotel. In this section of the canal, four stop locks were needed because the current flowed against the loaded boats, making travel to Kingston slow and difficult. (Author's collection.)

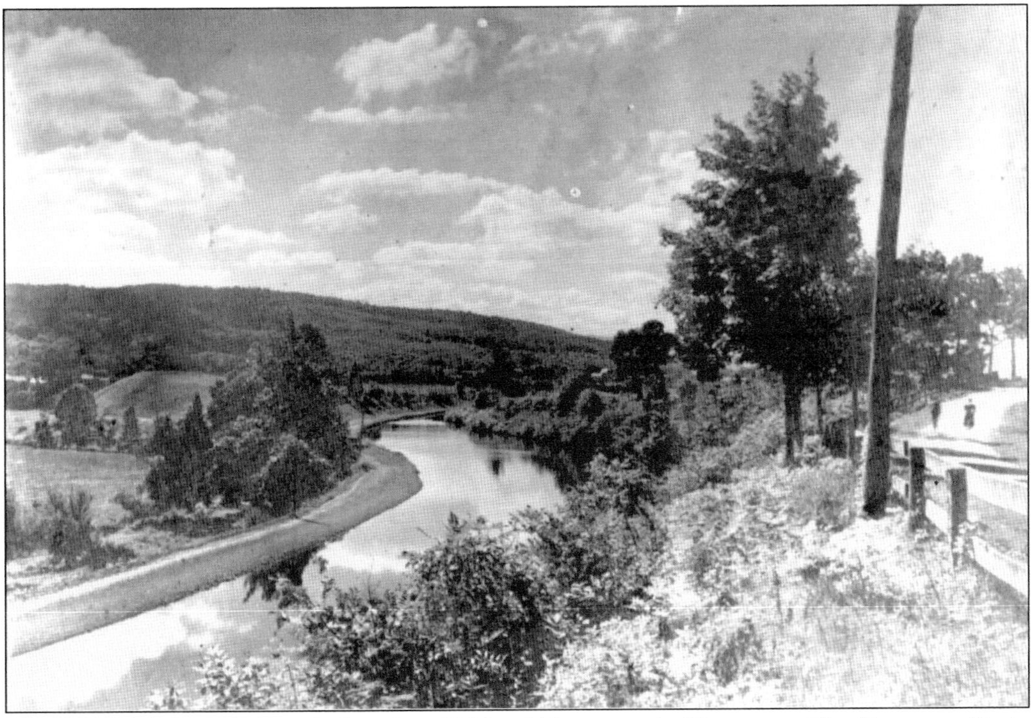

This part of the canal is just below the old Hotel Huguenot in Huguenot. The Huguenot Basin and Birdsall's Boatyard, with two dry docks, were located in this section of the canal. This view was taken looking south in the late 1800s. (Deerpark Historian's Office.)

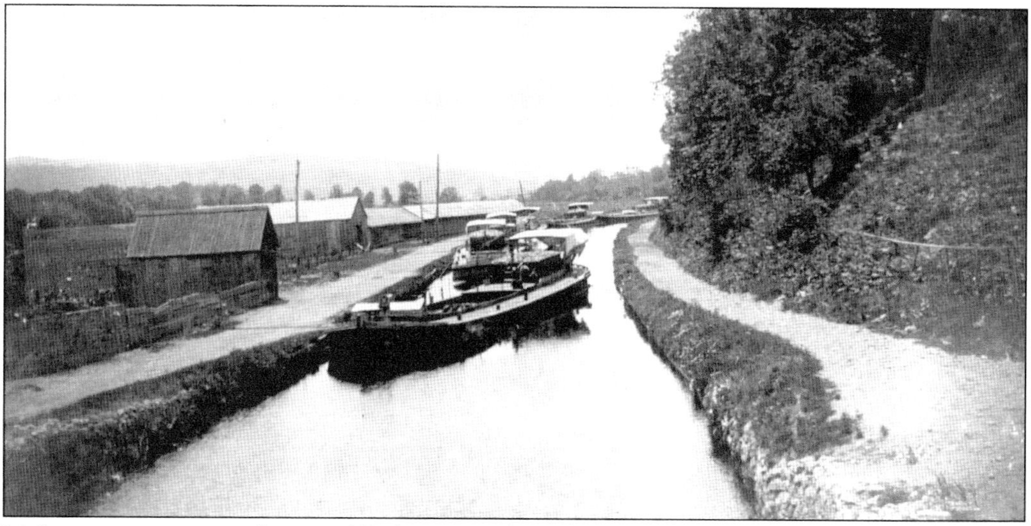

Mules were an essential part of Delaware and Hudson Canal operations. In this late-1800s view, several mule barns and buildings can be seen on the south side of Guymard Turnpike in Godeffroy, and six canal boats are tied up. It is unusual to see multiple boats in one photograph. (Minisink Valley Historical Society.)

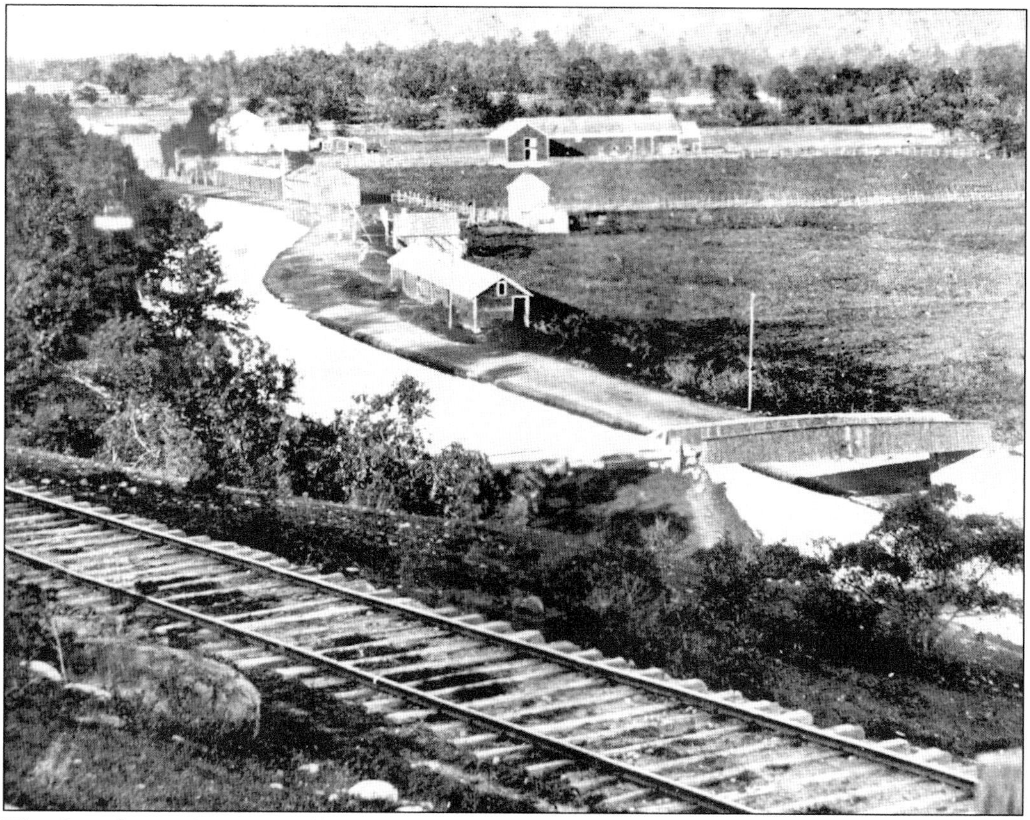

The Port Jervis & Monticello Railroad and the Delaware and Hudson Canal both passed through Godeffroy. The Peter E. Gumaer farm is in the background. In the center are canal mule barns. (Minisink Valley Historical Society.)

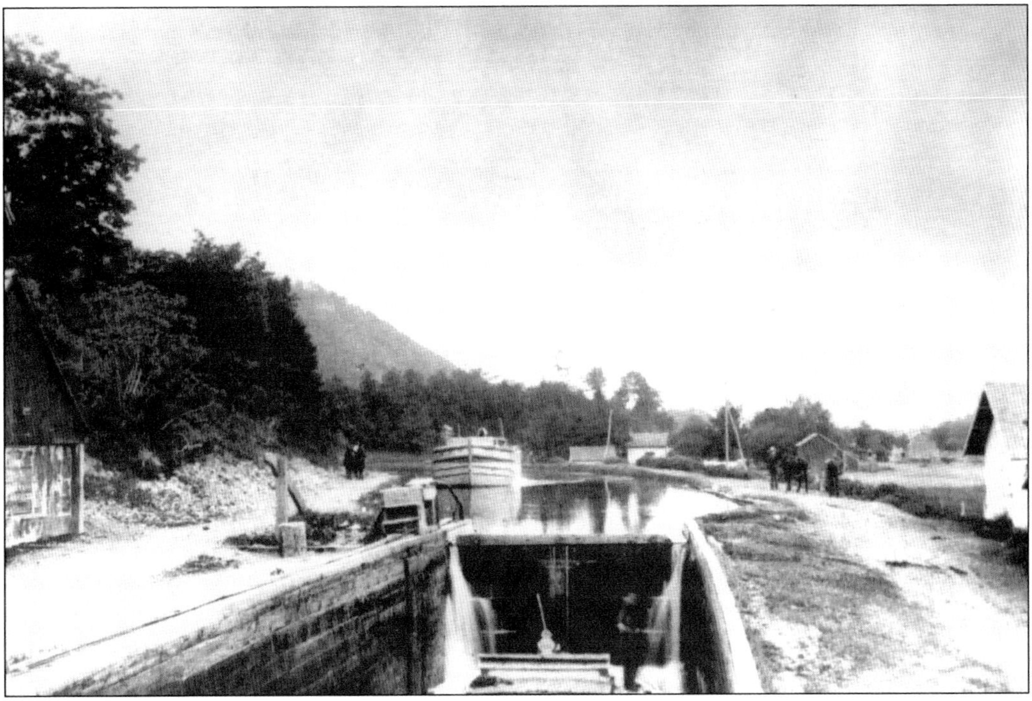

This is the Mineral Springs Lock, No. 56, in Port Clinton (now Godeffroy). Mules wait on the towpaths while lock tenders lock through a boat. Another boat awaits its turn. Roses Point is in the background. (Deerpark Historian's Office.)

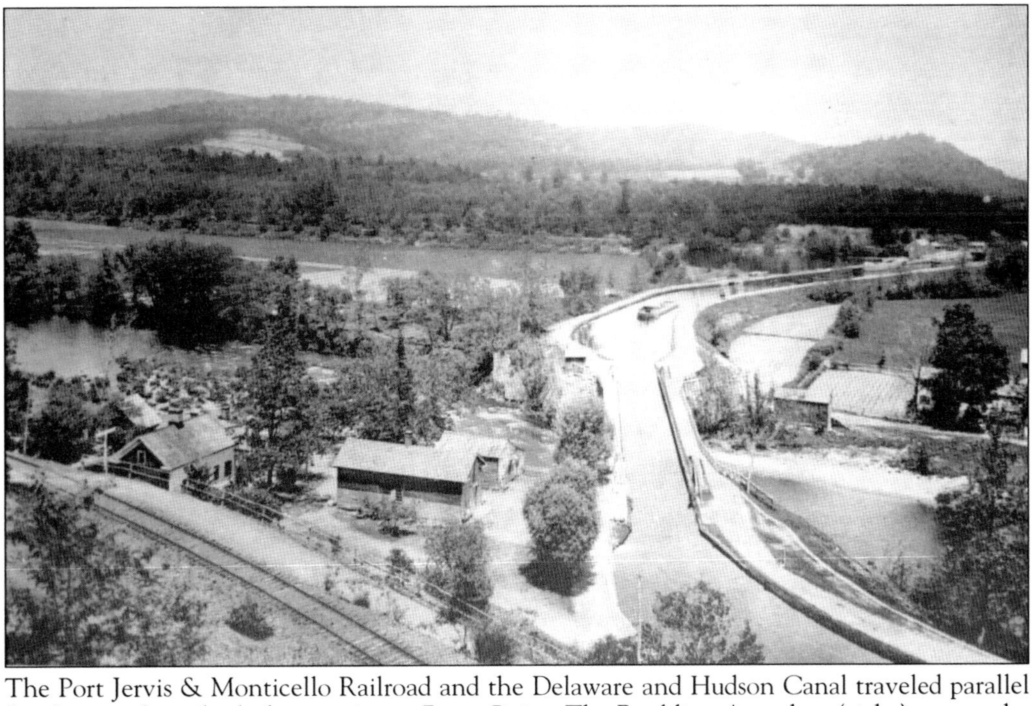

The Port Jervis & Monticello Railroad and the Delaware and Hudson Canal traveled parallel for about eight miles before parting at Roses Point. The Roebling Aqueduct (right) crosses the Neversink River. (Robbie Smith.)

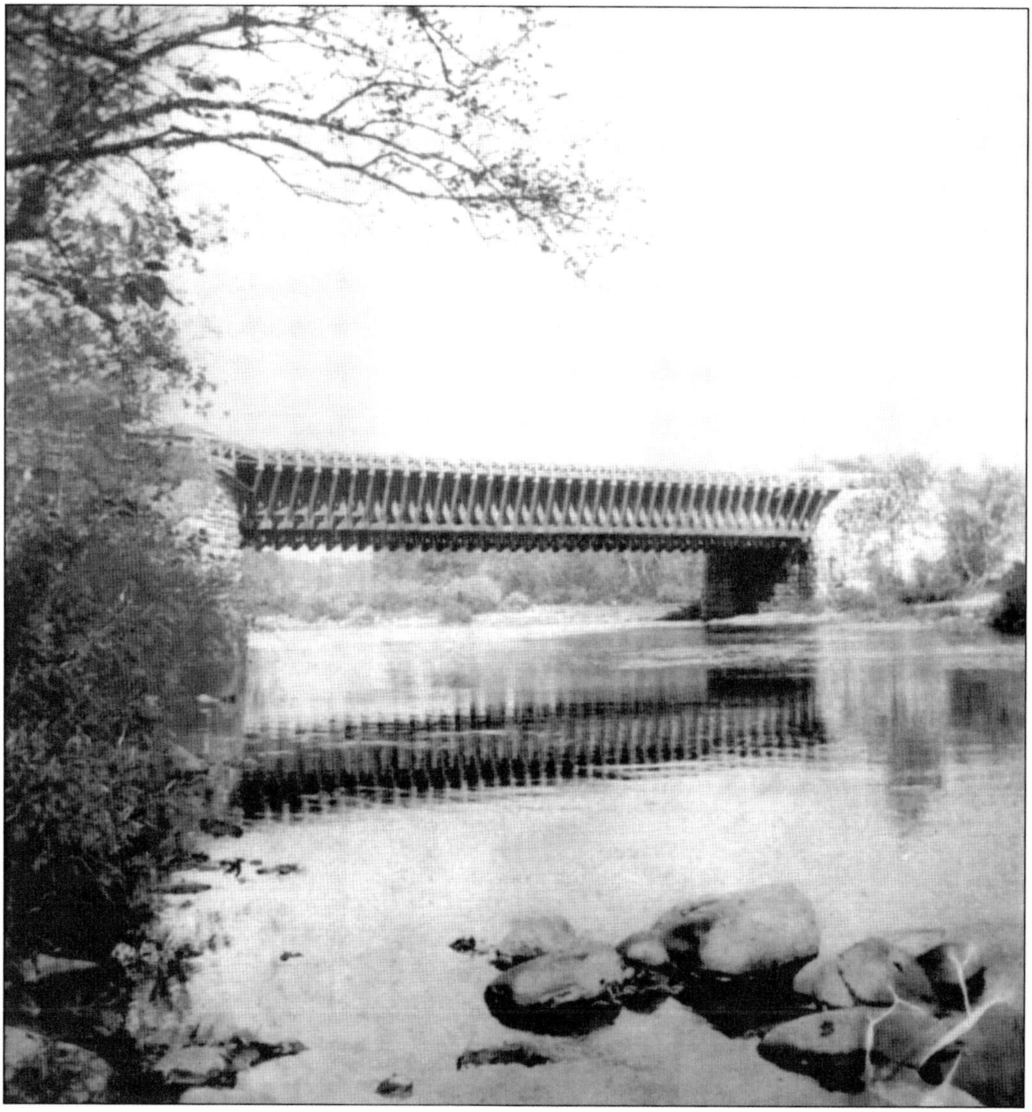

Work on the Roebling Aqueduct started in 1849 and was completed in time for the 1851 season. The structure was about 100 feet downstream from the first aqueduct. Designed by John B. Jervis, the double arch stone-and-wood truss aqueduct was built between 1827 and 1829. The Roebling construction was completed while the old aqueduct was still in use. (Deerpark Historian's Office.)

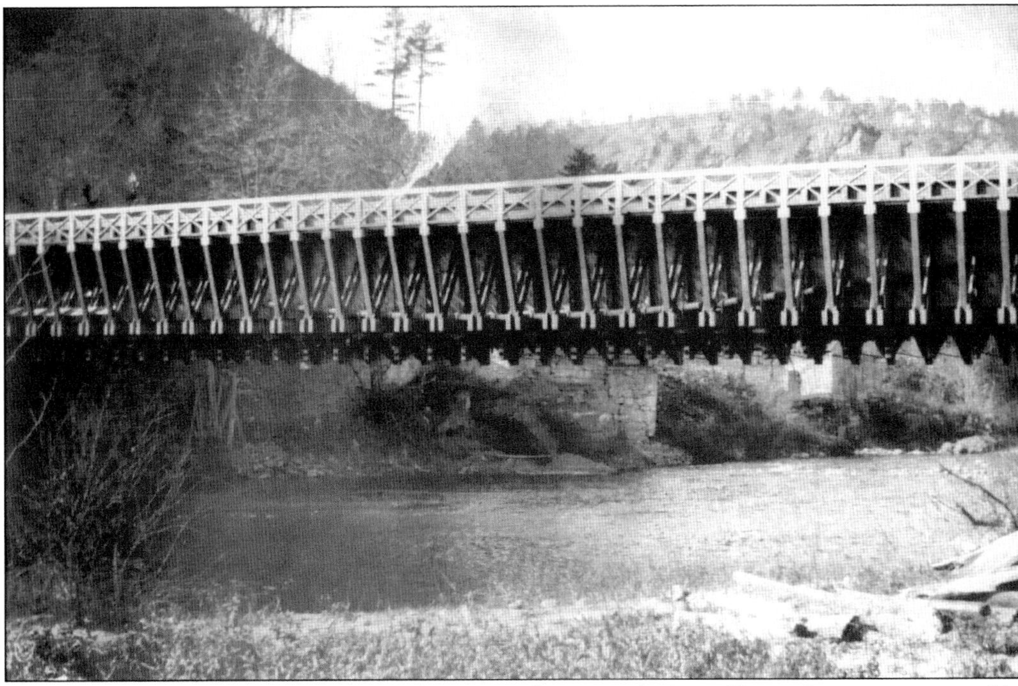

This closeup of the Neversink Aqueduct provides a good idea of how the suspension cables and hangers were attached. The Neversink Aqueduct cost $25,130 to build. Like the Delaware Aqueduct, the trunk measured 17 feet, 6 inches wide at the bottom, 20 feet at the top, and 9 feet deep. The surface of the river was about 21 feet below the aqueduct. (Neversink Valley Area Museum.)

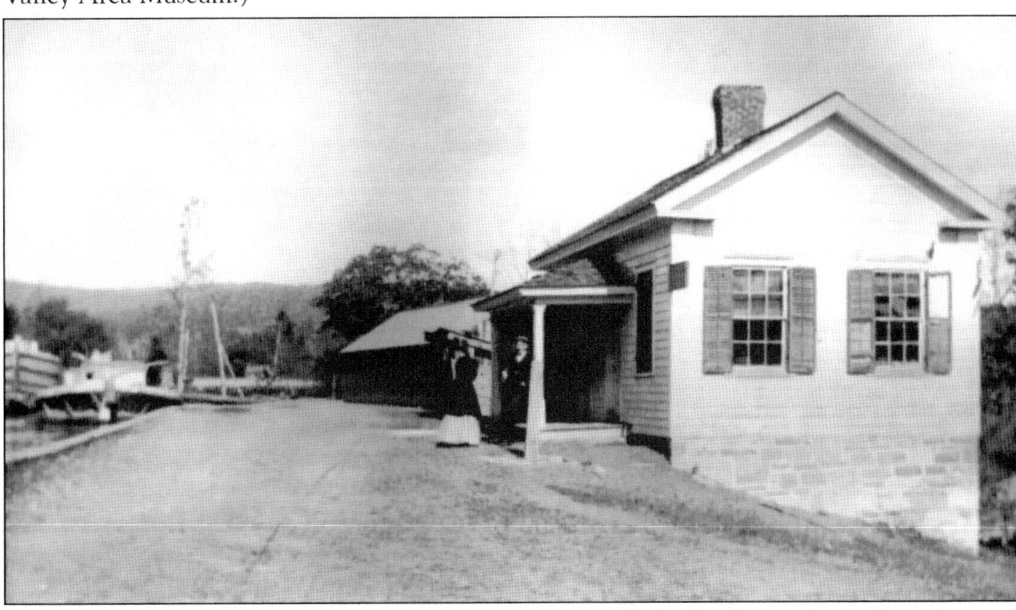

The Delaware and Hudson Canal telegraph office in Cuddebackville was located on the south side of the aqueduct at Lock 52. Still standing on Prospect Hill Road, this building is now part of a private residence. In this photograph, the aqueduct is in the distance and two canal boats are on the left. (Deerpark Historian's Office.)

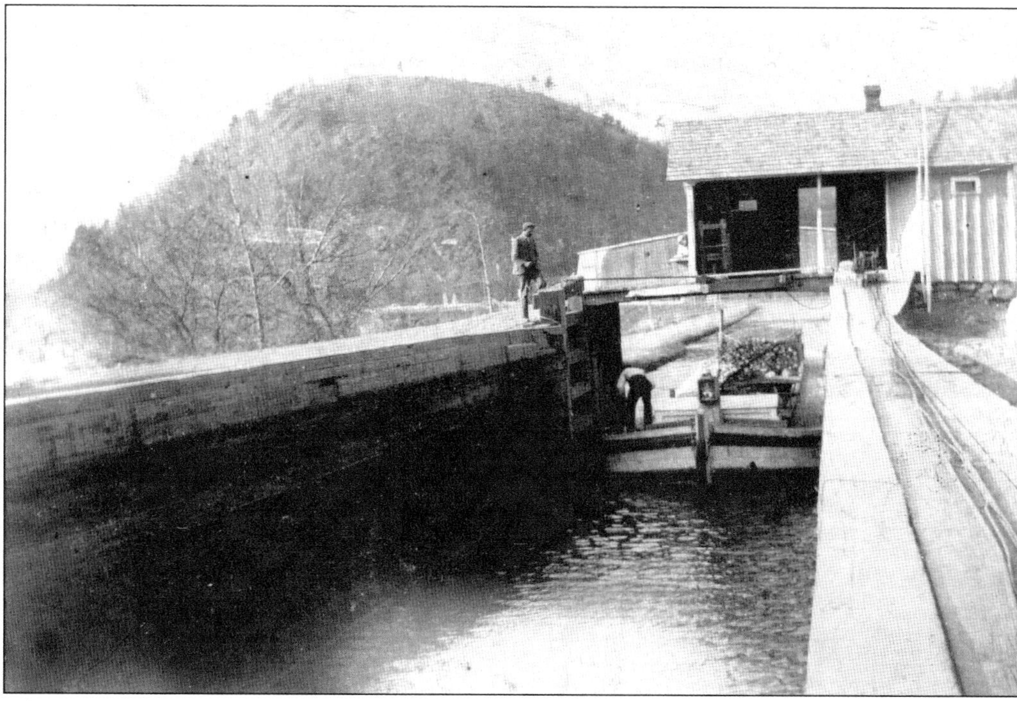

Abe Hoag looks down as a boat enters the lower end of the Pie Lock, No. 51. Roses Point can be seen in the distance. Shortly after crossing the Neversink Aqueduct, canal boats approached the Pie Lock, which got its name from Mary Casey and her famous rice custard pies. Canawlers would wait in line for her 15¢ pies. (Deerpark Historian's Office.)

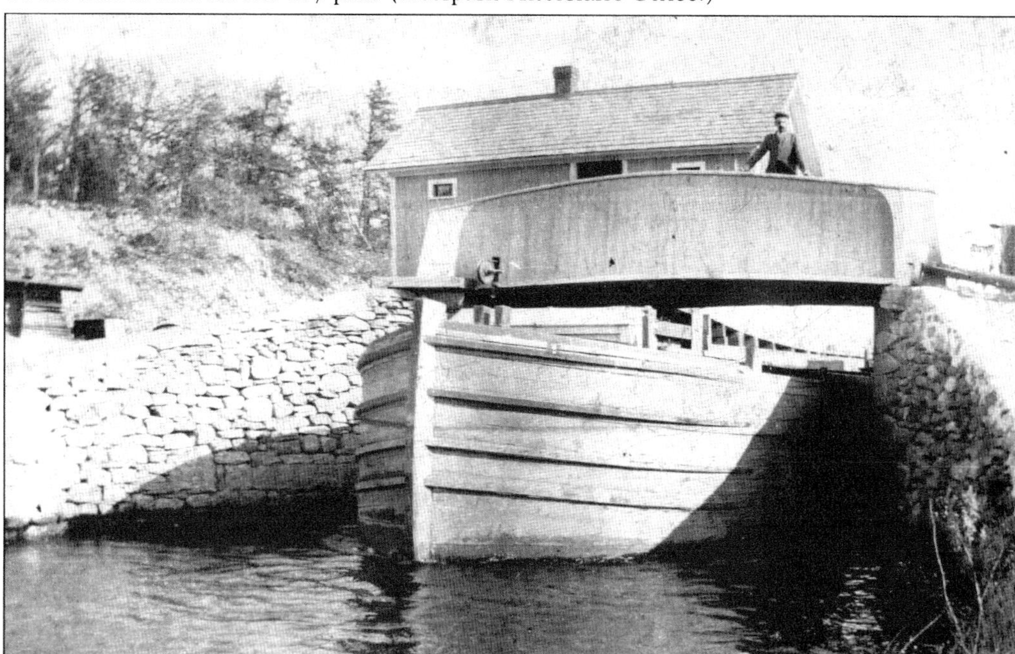

At the Pie Lock, Abe Hoag looks down from the bridge as a light boat emerges after being locked through. (Deerpark Historian's Office.)

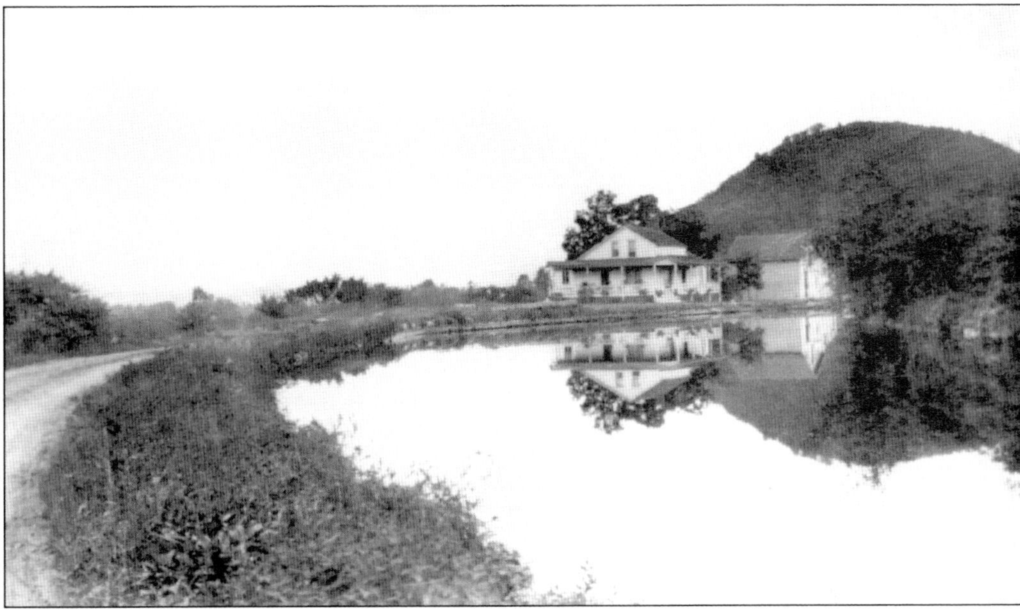

The Hoag family lived in the lock tender's house next to the towpath, near Lock No. 51. This early-1900s view of the canal was taken looking south toward the aqueduct. (Neversink Valley Area Museum.)

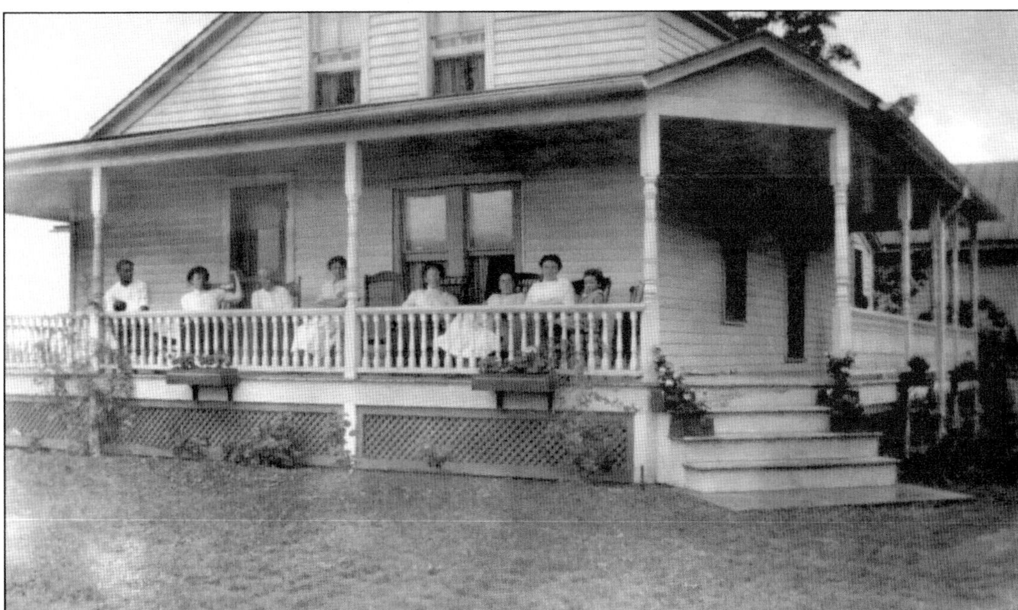

The Hoags spend some time on their front porch. This home is located within the Orange County Delaware and Hudson Canal Park on Hoag Road in Cuddebackville. (Neversink Valley Area Museum.)

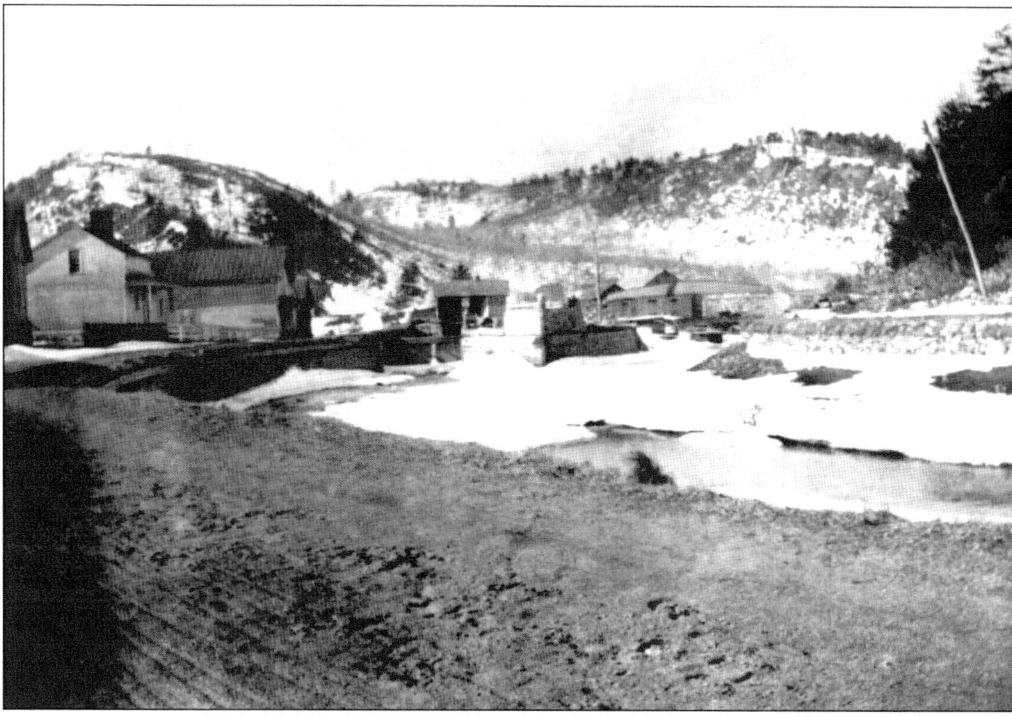

This canal basin was located near Lock No. 51. Mule barns and other canal buildings can be seen surrounding the basin. (Deerpark Historian's Office.)

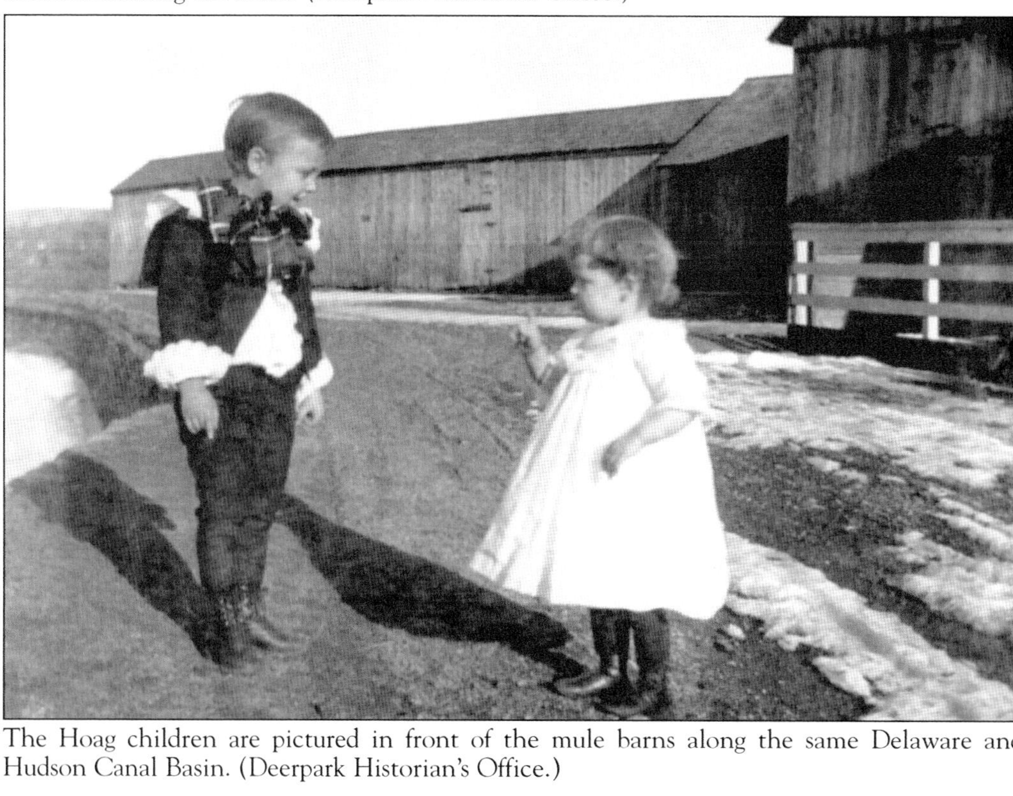

The Hoag children are pictured in front of the mule barns along the same Delaware and Hudson Canal Basin. (Deerpark Historian's Office.)

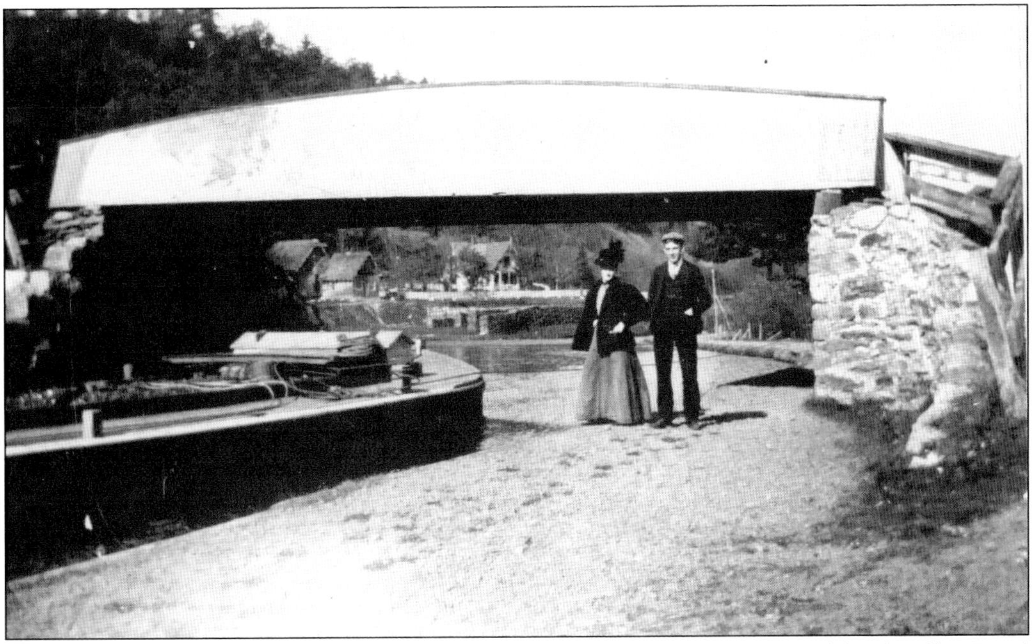

In Cuddebackville, a loaded canal boat makes its way north under the Oakland Valley Road Bridge, on its way into a freight basin. The Gordons' house is in the distance. (Minisink Valley Historical Society.)

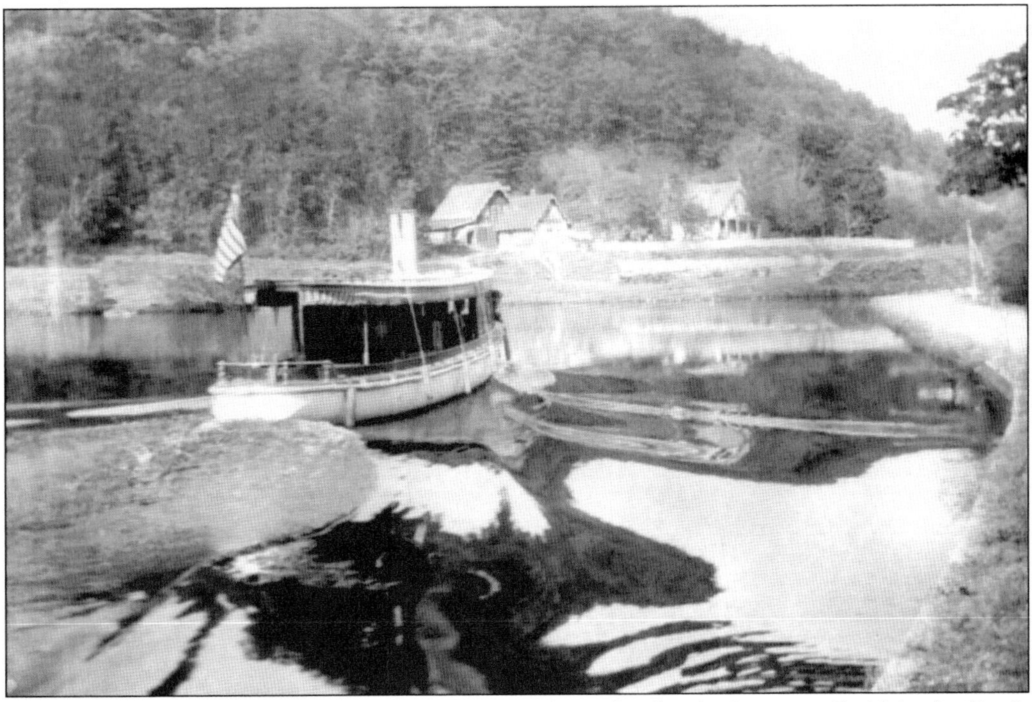

The *D & H*, a steam launch, chugs its way north in the freight basin at Cuddebackville. It was also known as the paymaster's boat. In all likelihood, this was a chartered trip during the canal's last years of operation. The Gordons' home can be seen in the background. (Deerpark Historian's Office.)

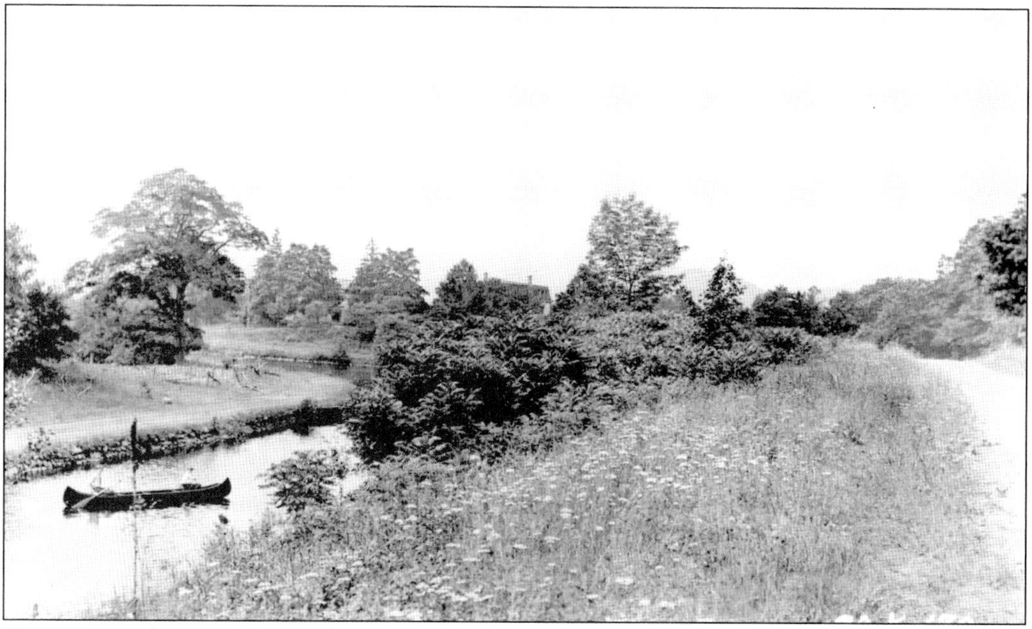

Canoeing and swimming in the canal were popular pastimes after the abandonment of the Delaware and Hudson Canal. A one-mile stretch in the Orange County Delaware and Hudson Canal Park in Cuddebackville has remained full of water. (Neversink Valley Area Museum.)

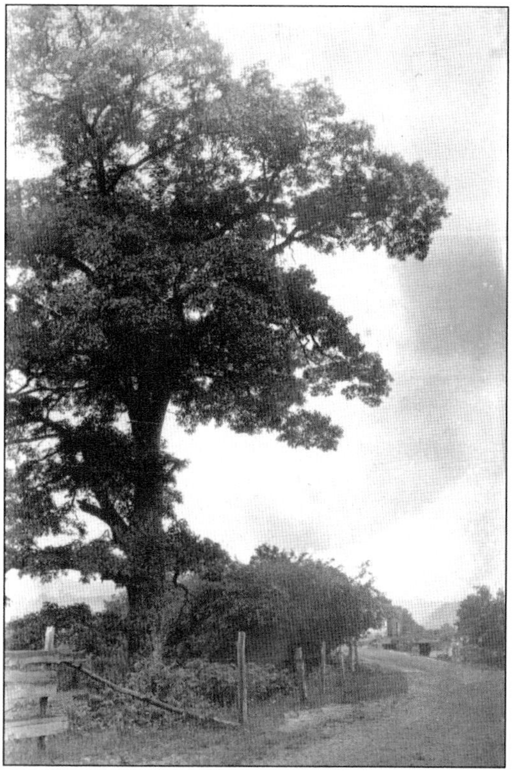

This old oak tree captured the photographer's eye near the freight basin in Cuddebackville. The old Delaware and Hudson Canal Store and the Oakland Valley Road Bridge over the canal are visible in the distance. The same tree can be seen on the left side of the previous photograph. (Author's collection.)

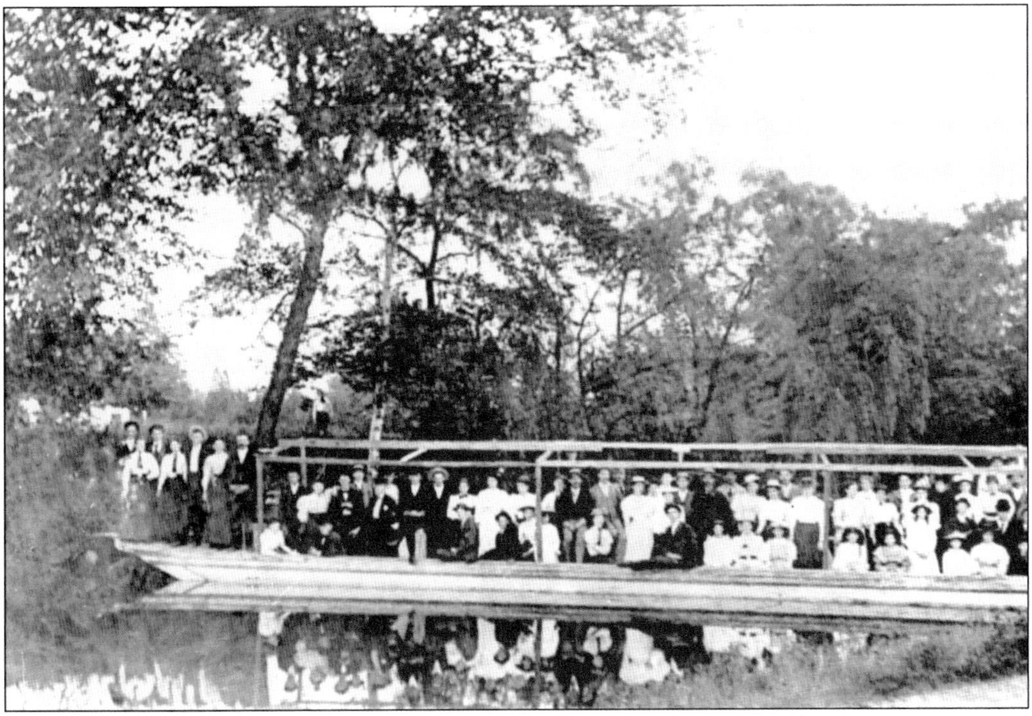

In the late 1800s, the Sparrowbush Methodist Church and Sunday school went on picnic excursions on the Delaware and Hudson Canal up to Cuddebackville. The exciting part of the trip was passing through the locks. This photograph was taken in 1895 in Cuddebackville. (Minisink Valley Historical Society.)

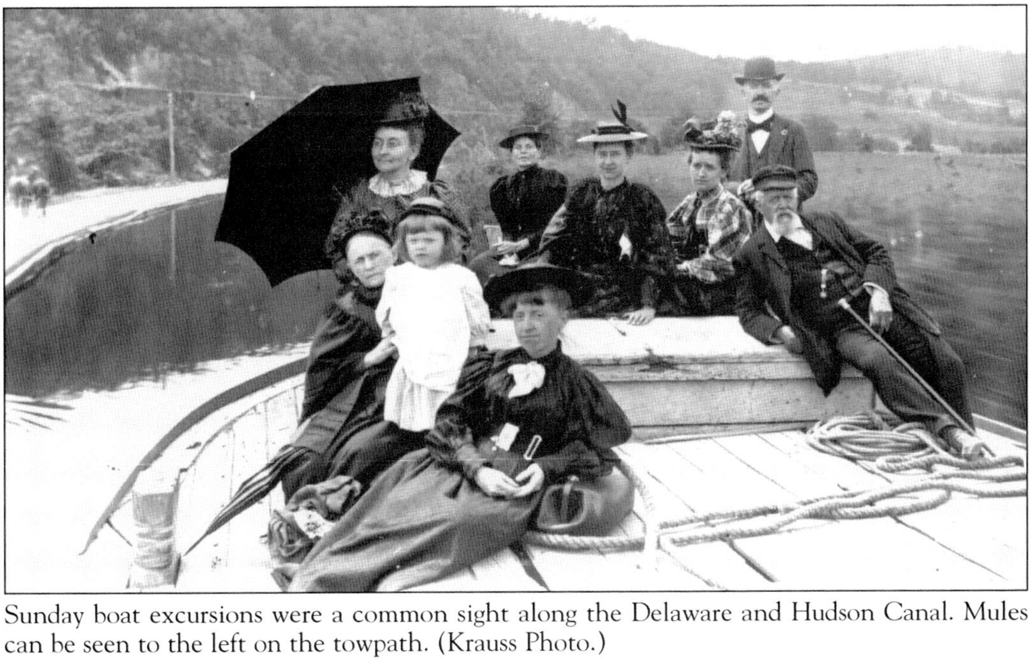

Sunday boat excursions were a common sight along the Delaware and Hudson Canal. Mules can be seen to the left on the towpath. (Krauss Photo.)

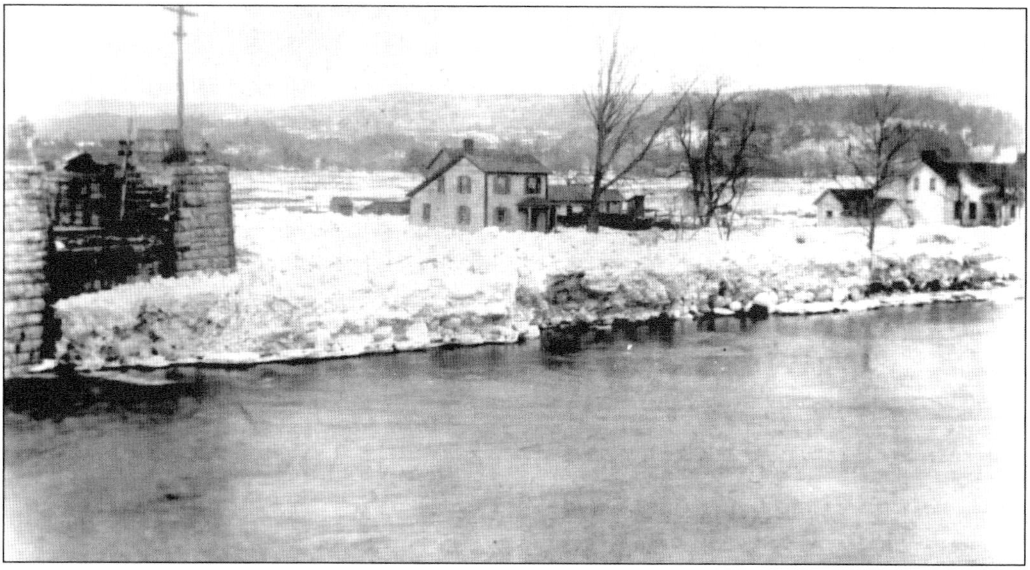

The ice gorges of 1902, 1903, and 1904 caused a lot of damage on both the Neversink and Delaware Rivers. This view, taken in March 1904, shows the north abutment of the Neversink Aqueduct two years after the aqueduct was dismantled. The building in the center was the blacksmith's house. This building and the one to the right are now home to the Neversink Valley Area Museum. (Deerpark Historian's Office.)

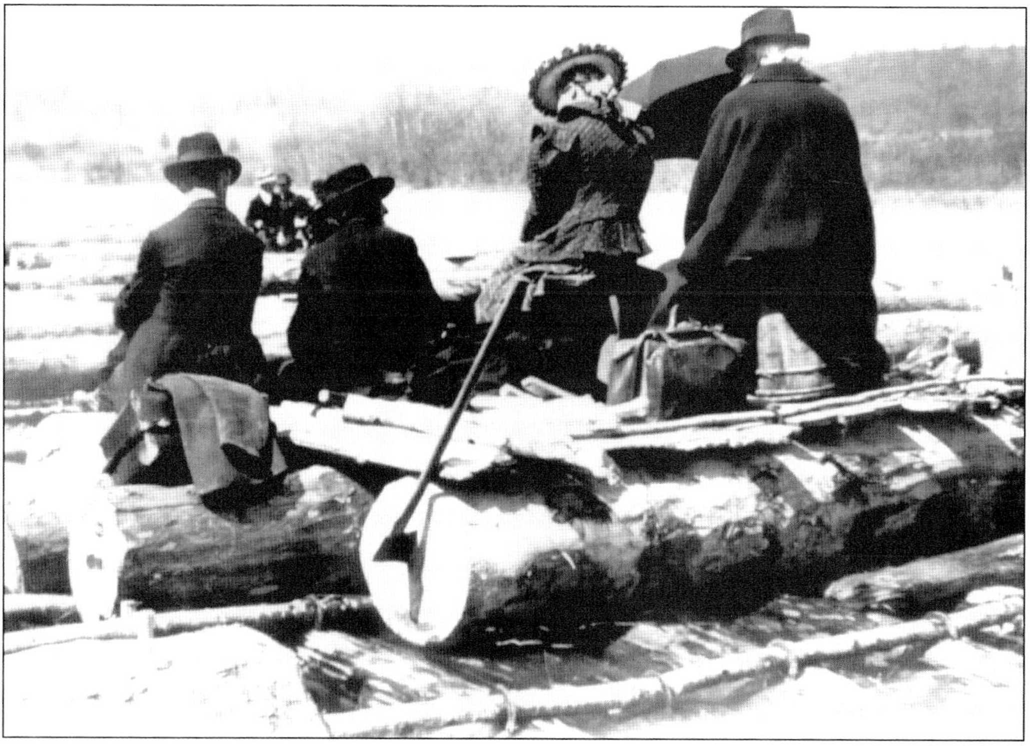

From the 1760s to 1908, timber was rafted down area rivers. It appears as if passengers traveled along with the timber. A favorite stop was Eddy Farm. This photograph was taken on the Delaware River. (Minisink Valley Historical Society.)

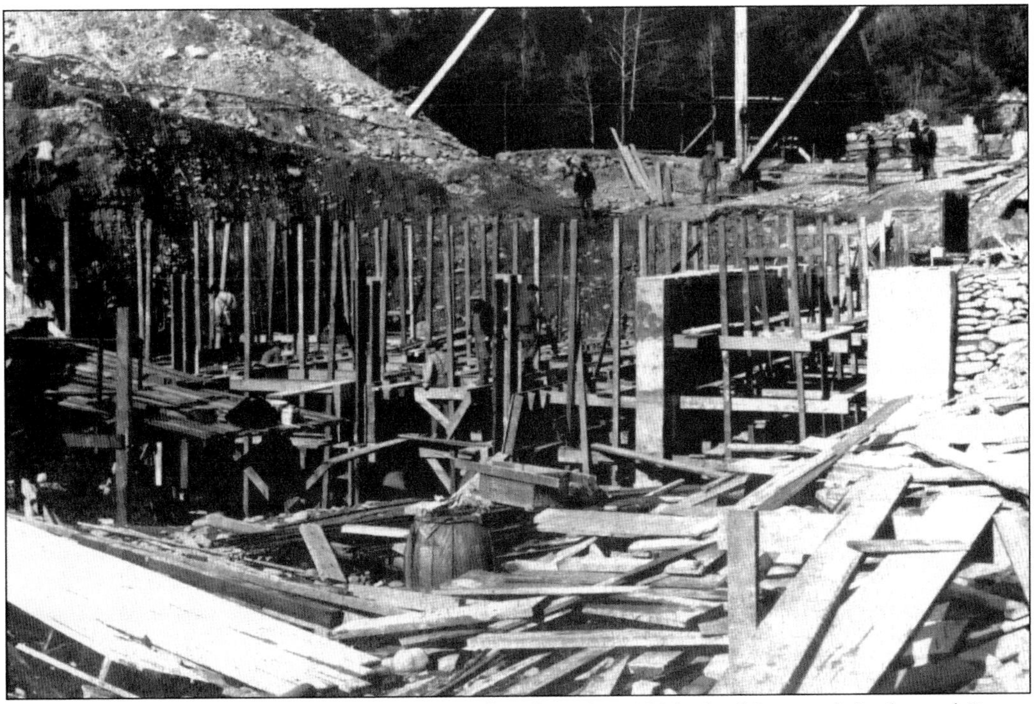

After the Delaware and Hudson Canal was abandoned in 1900, the Neversink Light and Power Company purchased the works for the canal in Cuddebackville. It was a perfect location for a hydroelectric power plant. These works included a steady water supply diverted from the Neversink River by means of a dam and feeder. Construction began at the Pie Lock, No. 51, in 1902. This photograph shows construction of the power plant in its early stages. Wood forms were built and concrete was delivered by large wooden cranes. (Neversink Valley Area Museum.)

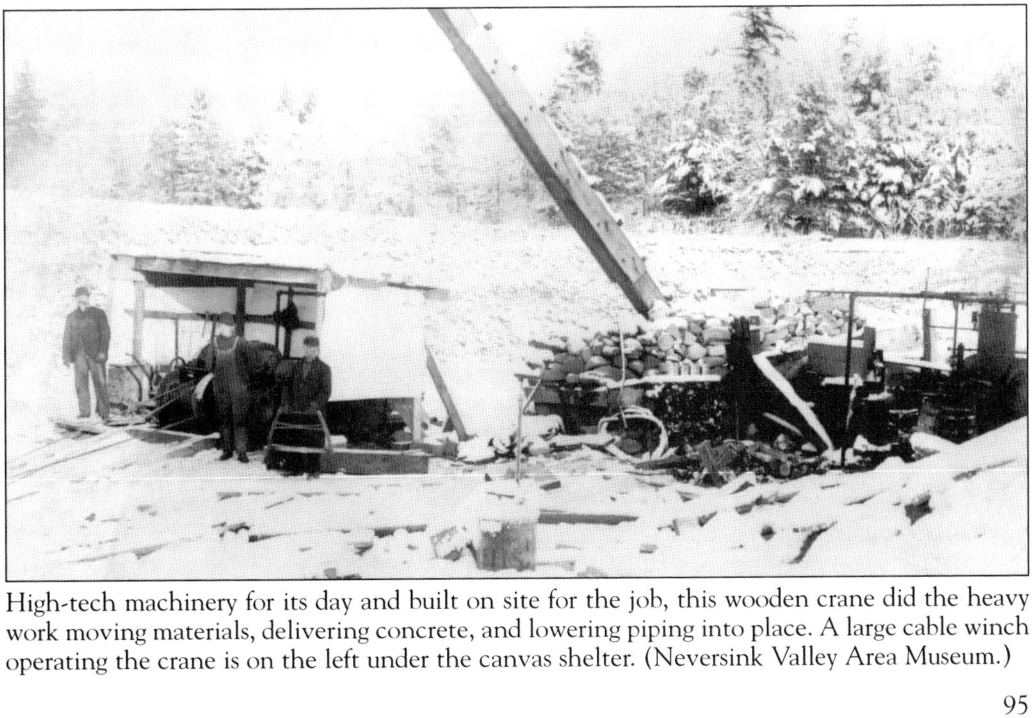

High-tech machinery for its day and built on site for the job, this wooden crane did the heavy work moving materials, delivering concrete, and lowering piping into place. A large cable winch operating the crane is on the left under the canvas shelter. (Neversink Valley Area Museum.)

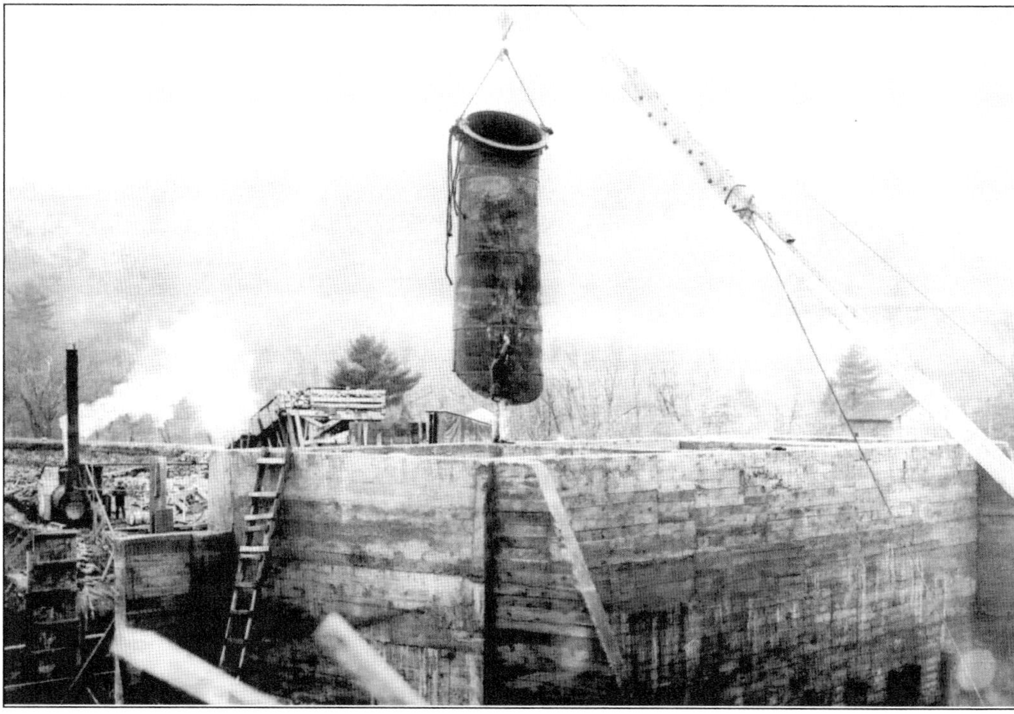

The crane is lowering a large flume into place inside the power plant. A small steam engine is on the far left. (Neversink Valley Area Museum.)

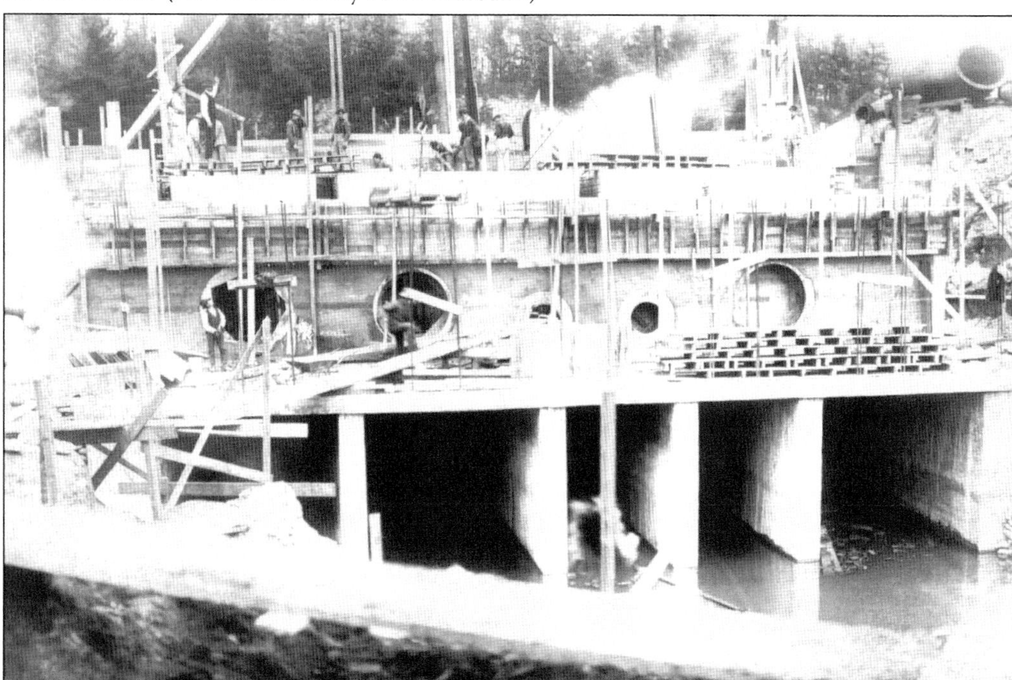

Farther along in its construction, the power plant is now recognizable. One story and the gallery are yet to be built. (Neversink Valley Area Museum.)

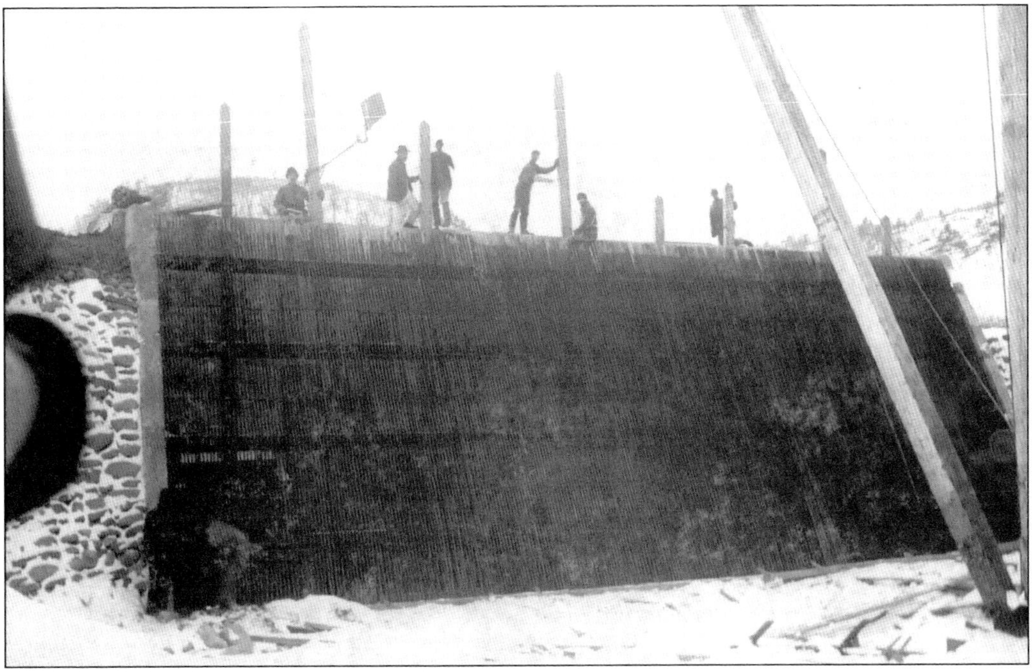

From the forebay, or storage reservoir, water flowed through an inclined iron rack that prevented ice and debris from entering the large chamber in front of the penstocks. The rack covered an area of 1,200 square feet. (Neversink Valley Area Museum.)

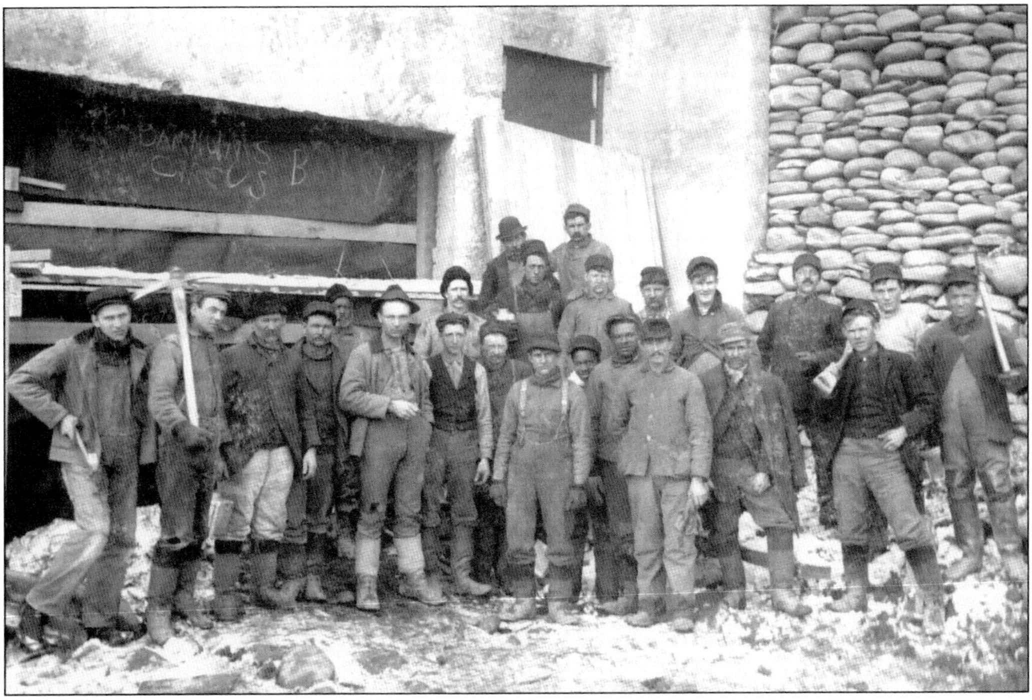

Workers pause for a photograph *c.* 1902. The stone wall is holding up the embankment, behind which is the forebay. A joker has written on the canvas covering the door to the powerhouse "Barnums Bailey Circus." (Neversink Valley Area Museum.)

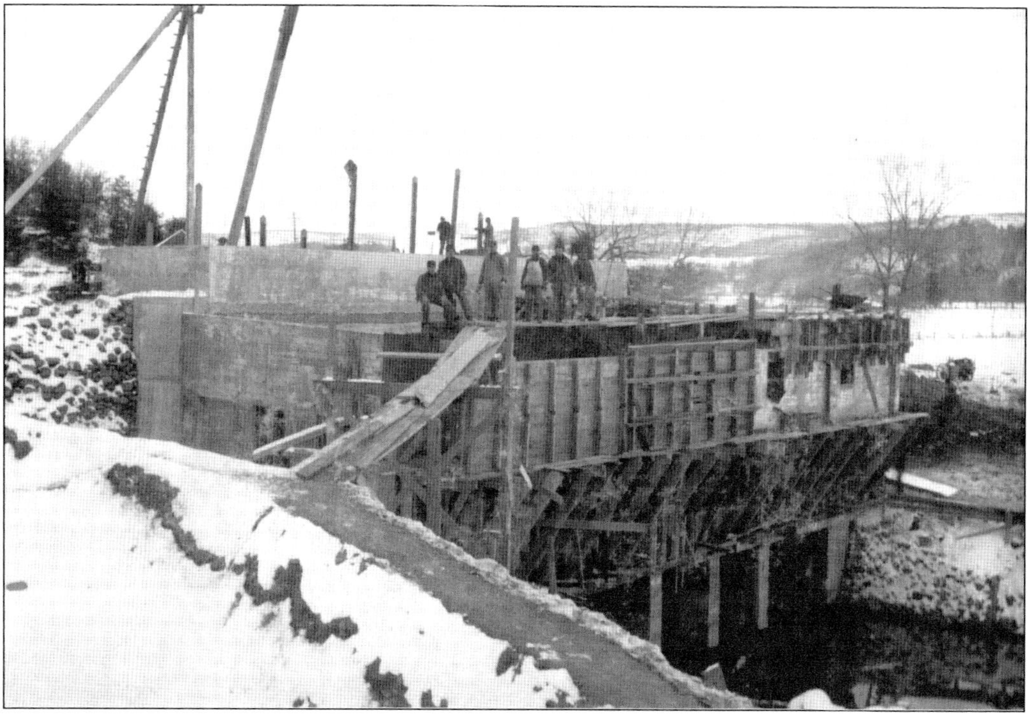

Work continues on the gallery and final floor. (Neversink Valley Area Museum.)

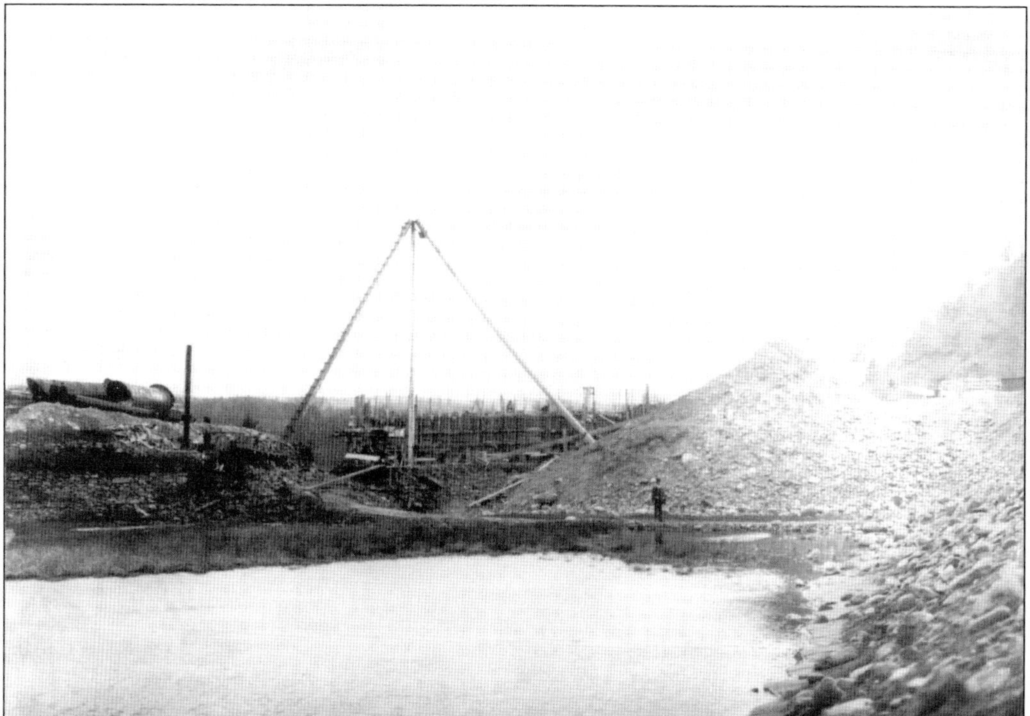

A reservoir had to be constructed behind the power plant to supply the plant with water. In addition, the embankments were raised about 40 feet. (Neversink Valley Area Museum.)

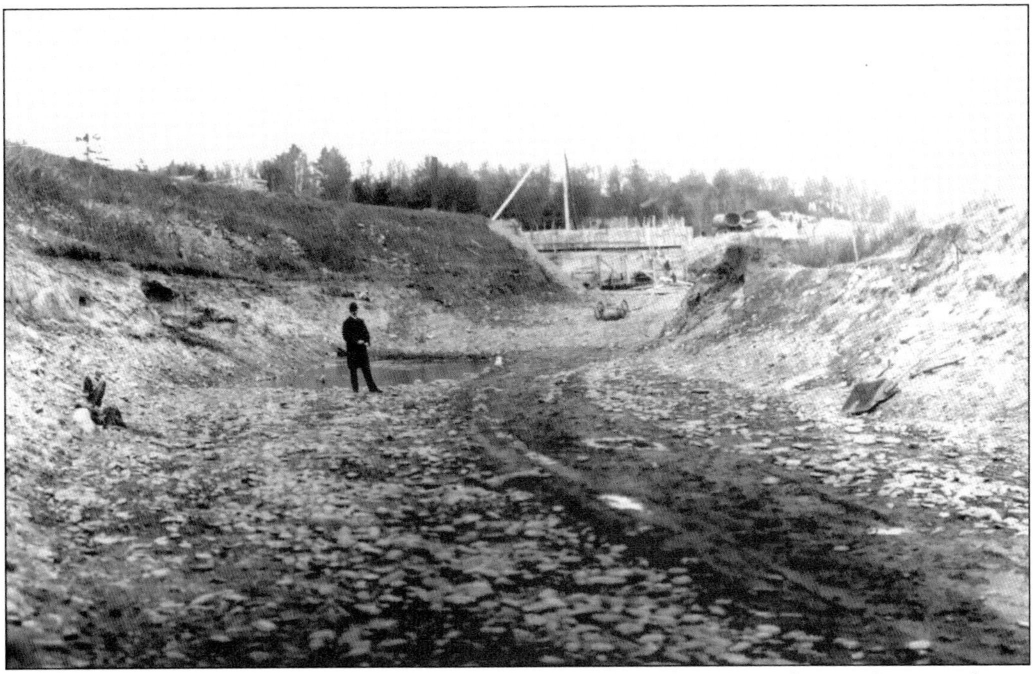

The tail race was the waste weir. It carried water away from the power plant and returned it to the Neversink. Its size has been greatly reduced by the 100 years of vegetation and debris that have filled it in. (Neversink Valley Area Museum.)

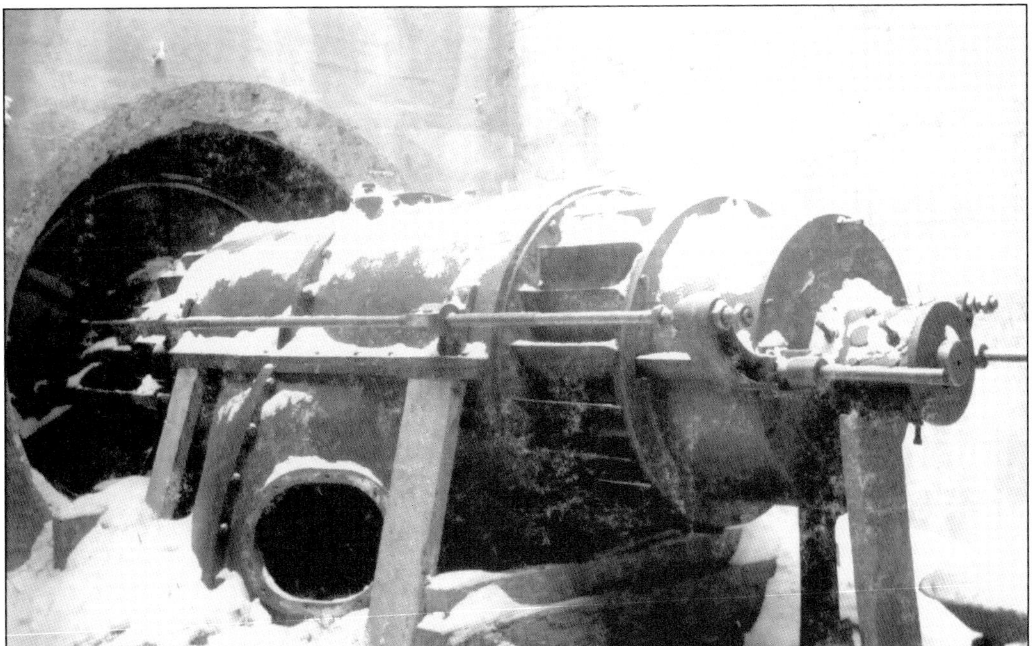

Construction was often slowed down or stopped during the winter months. Pictured is one of the four turbines ready for installation. The generators were furnished by General Electric. They were each of 300-kilowatt capacity, three phase, 60 cycle, 600 volts, revolving field type, and running at 300 revolutions per minute. (Neversink Valley Area Museum.)

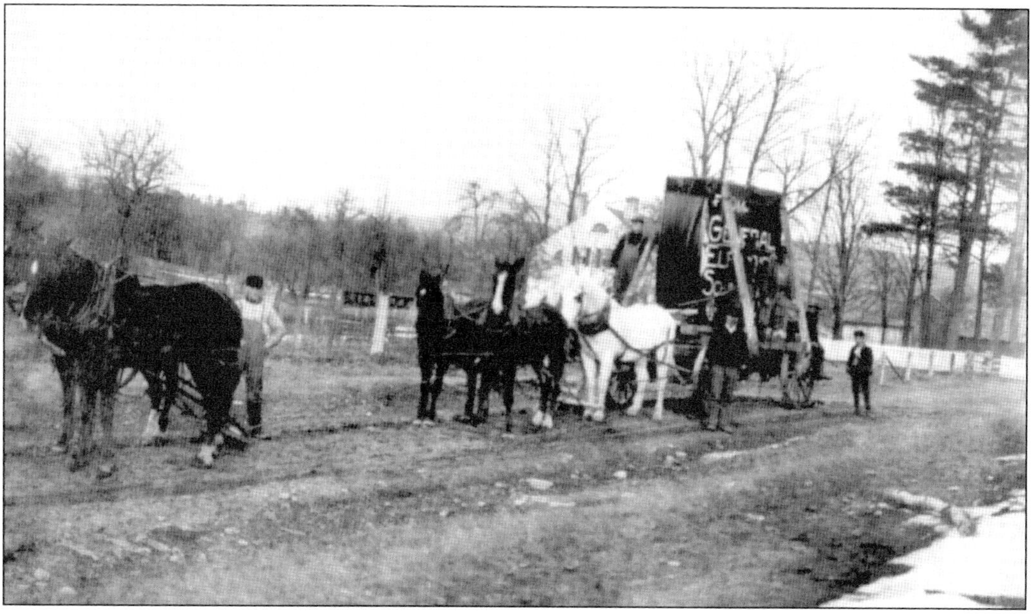

General Electric supplied many of the components. Shown are parts for the Neversink Light and Power Plant, a tough heavy load, being delivered by a team of six horses over the mountain via Route 211. In the background is the William Cuddeback homestead and farm. (Neversink Valley Area Museum.)

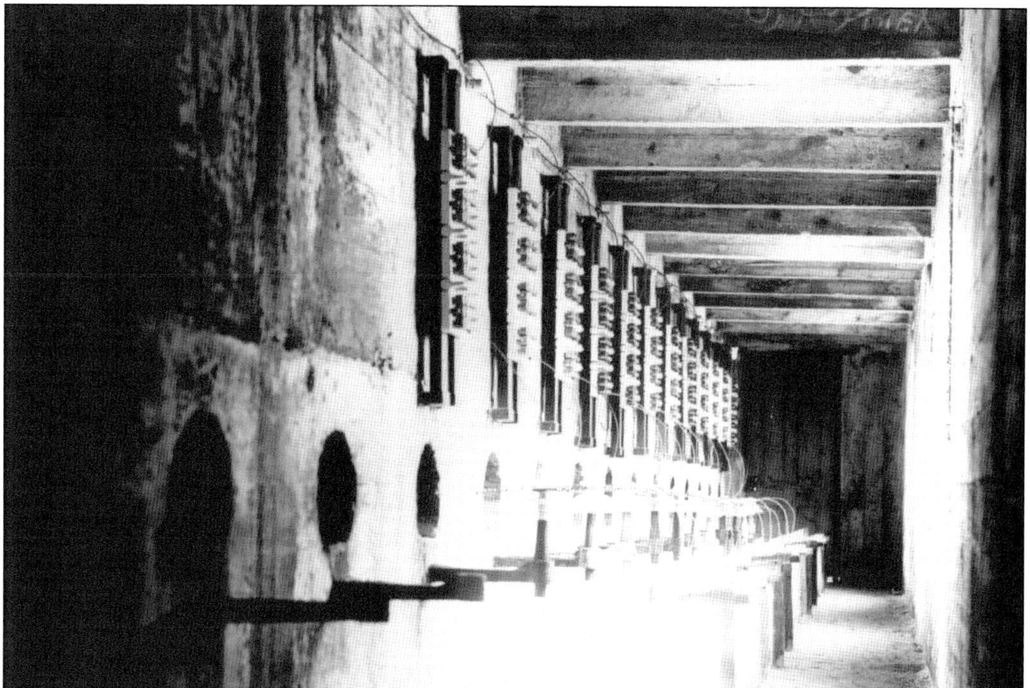

The gallery overhangs the tail race, creating a separate room known as the lightning arrester room. The room extends across the entire south side of the building. (Neversink Valley Area Museum.)

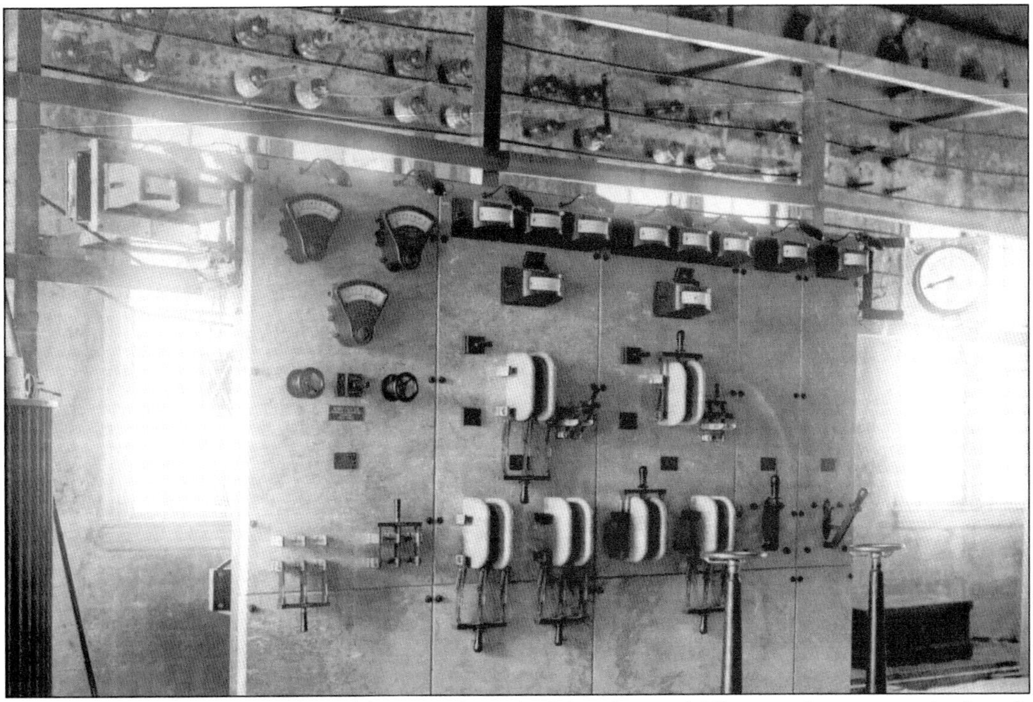

The switchboard, made of marble, was furnished by General Electric. It was supplied with all the latest and most modern instruments, such as voltmeters, wattmeters, and switches. (Neversink Valley Area Museum.)

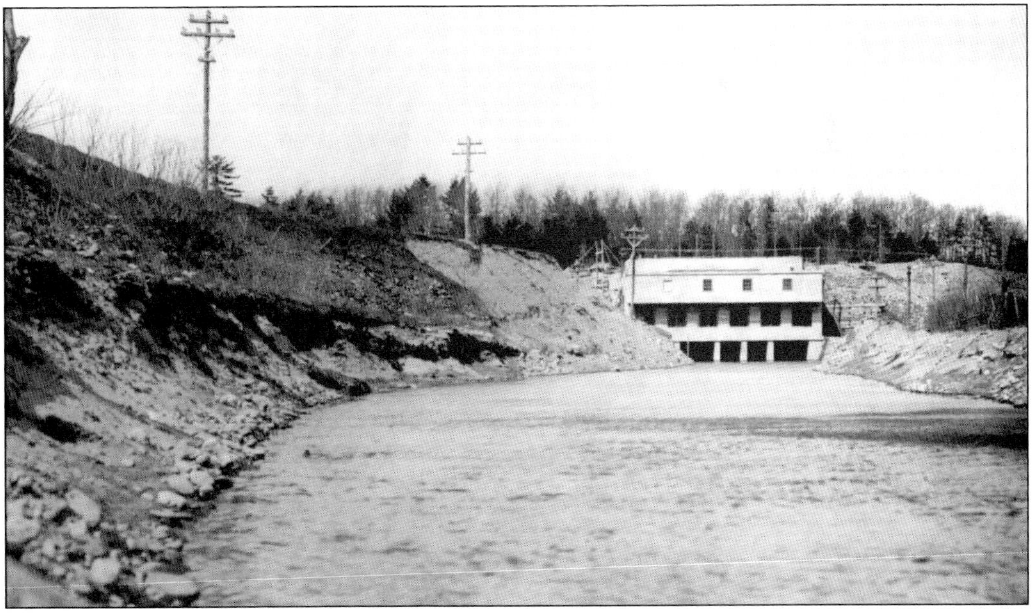

The power plant was operational in 1903. Interesting statistics about the structure include the following: the powerhouse was made of steel and concrete throughout, including the roof, floors, girders, walls, and foundations; it was built under the Ransome patents; and it measured 40 feet by 60 feet, with a 45-foot height. The building still exists in the Orange County Delaware and Hudson Canal Park on Hoag Road in Cuddebackville. (Neversink Valley Area Museum.)

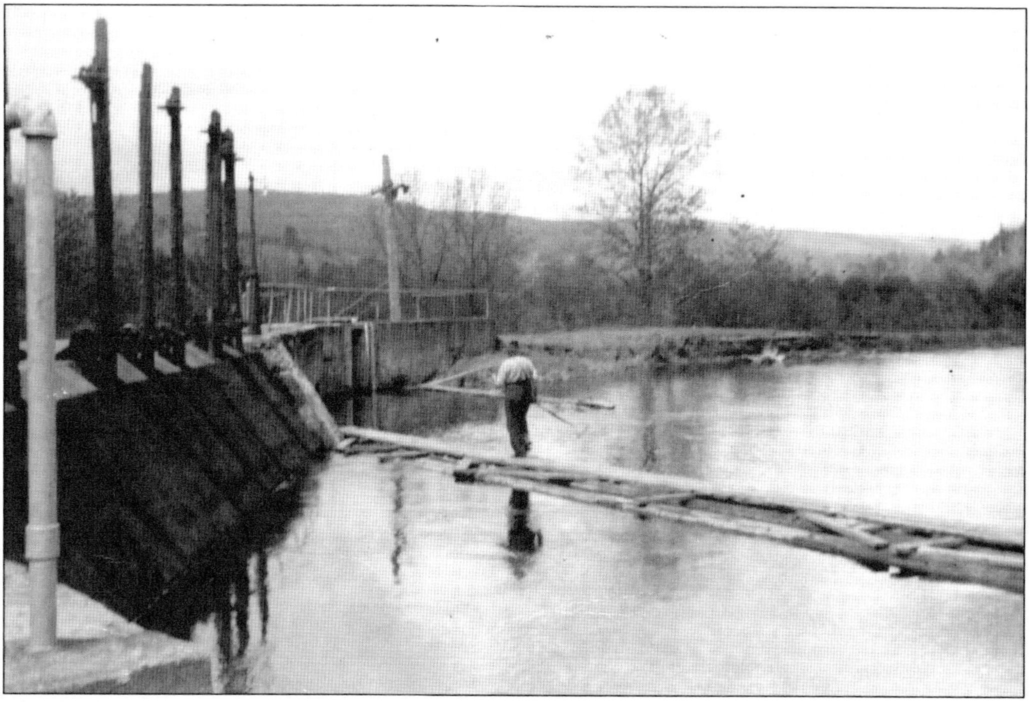

The forebay, located behind the power plant, served as the storage reservoir filled by the feeder. Joseph Lewis, walking on the floating plank, performs routine maintenance. (Author's collection.)

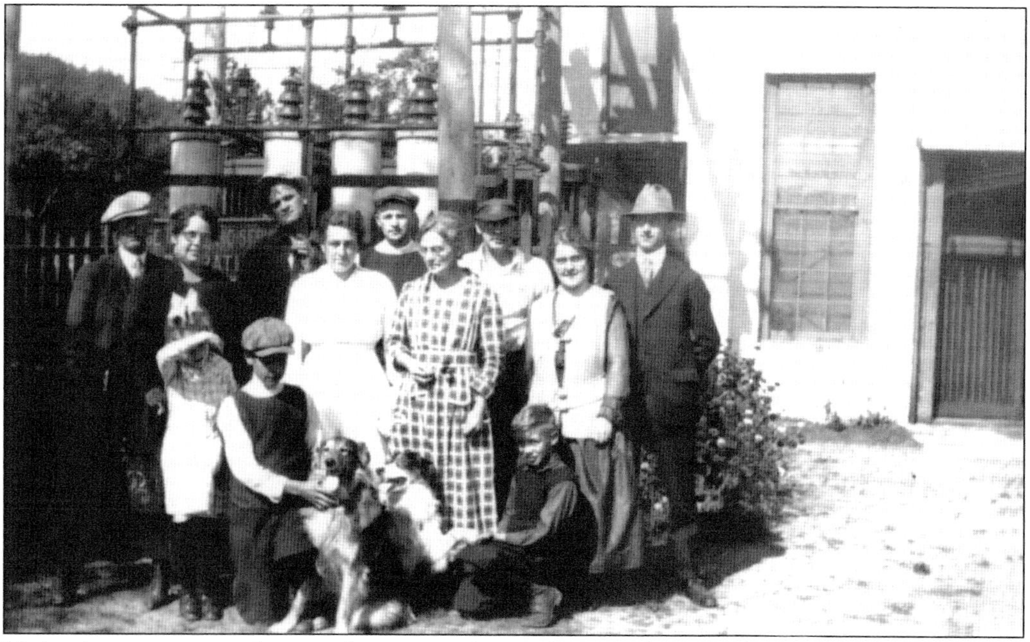

Hydroelectric power plant workers pose for a photograph with their wives and children. Joseph B. Lewis stands second from the right in the back row, and his wife, Emmaline Case Lewis, stands second from the right in the center row. Joseph Lewis worked from the time the plant opened *c.* 1903, until he was laid off in 1948. The plant closed in 1950. The photograph was taken in the 1920s next to the entrance of the plant. (Author's collection.)

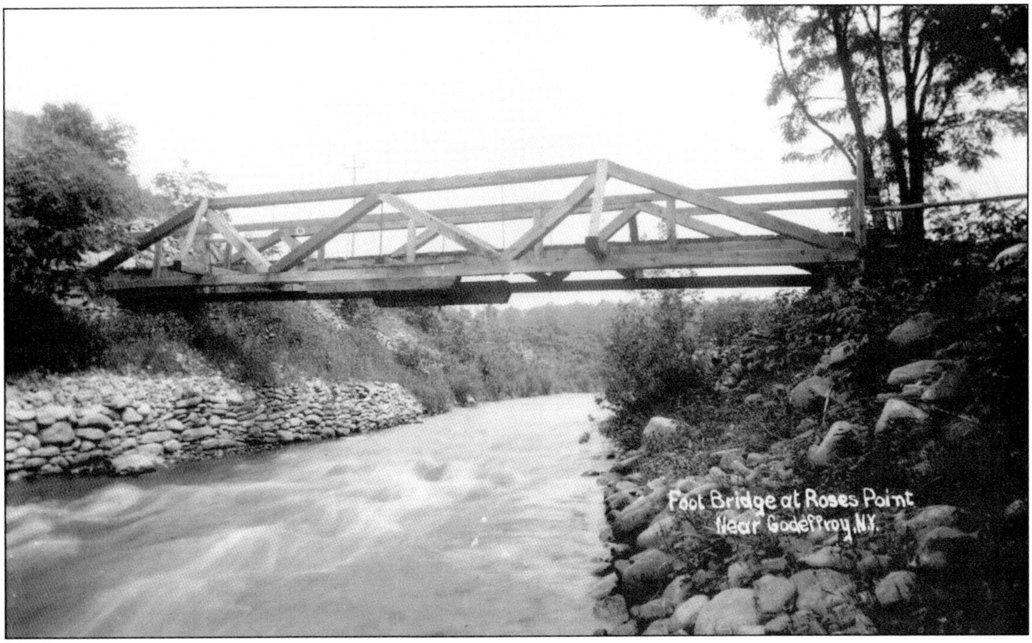

This footbridge once crossed the tail race, or waste weir, from the hydropower plant. At this junction, the tail race emptied into the Neversink River. A few rocks of the stone wall can still be seen near the north abutment of the aqueduct. (Minisink Valley Historical Society.)

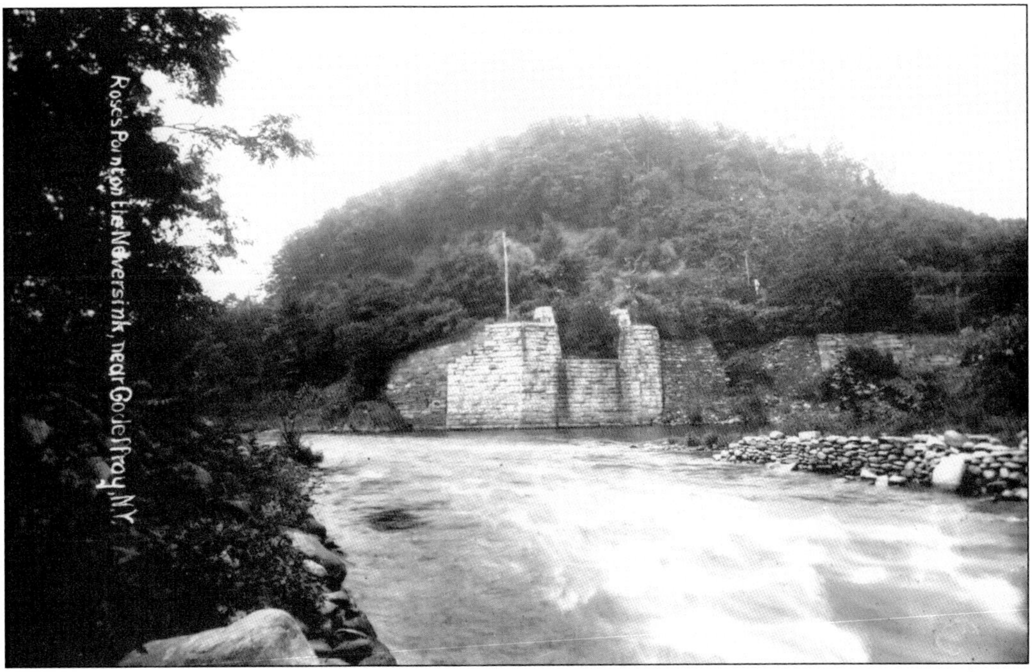

This early-1900s photograph is very important in that it clearly shows the ruins of both the Jervis and Roebling Aqueducts. The remains of the Jervis Aqueduct can be seen on the right. The Roebling Aqueduct was built to the left of the Jervis structure This photograph was taken from the footbridge, pictured above, over the power plant tail race. (Minisink Valley Historical Society.)

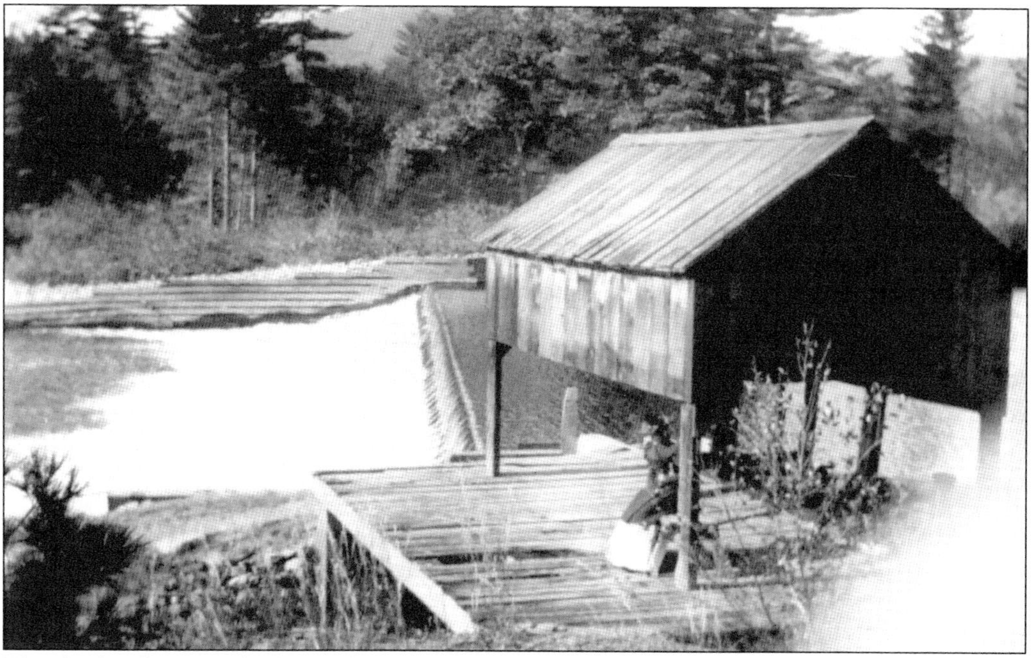

The feeder dam was built on the Neversink River to divert water to supply the Delaware and Hudson Canal. This photograph shows what it looked like during canal use. (Deerpark Historian's Office.)

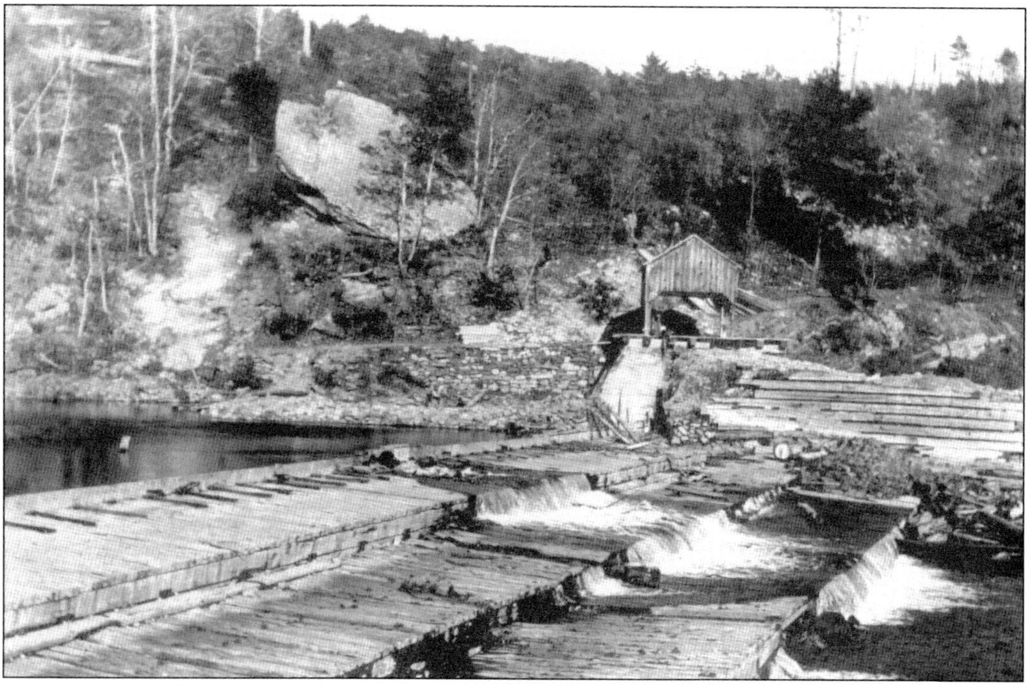

Ice gorges in 1902, 1903, and 1904 caused major damage to the feeder dam. Many structural changes occurred during this period, including changes in building materials from stonework and timbers to concrete. Changing the dam to this step-down dam was probably the first change. (Neversink Valley Area Museum.)

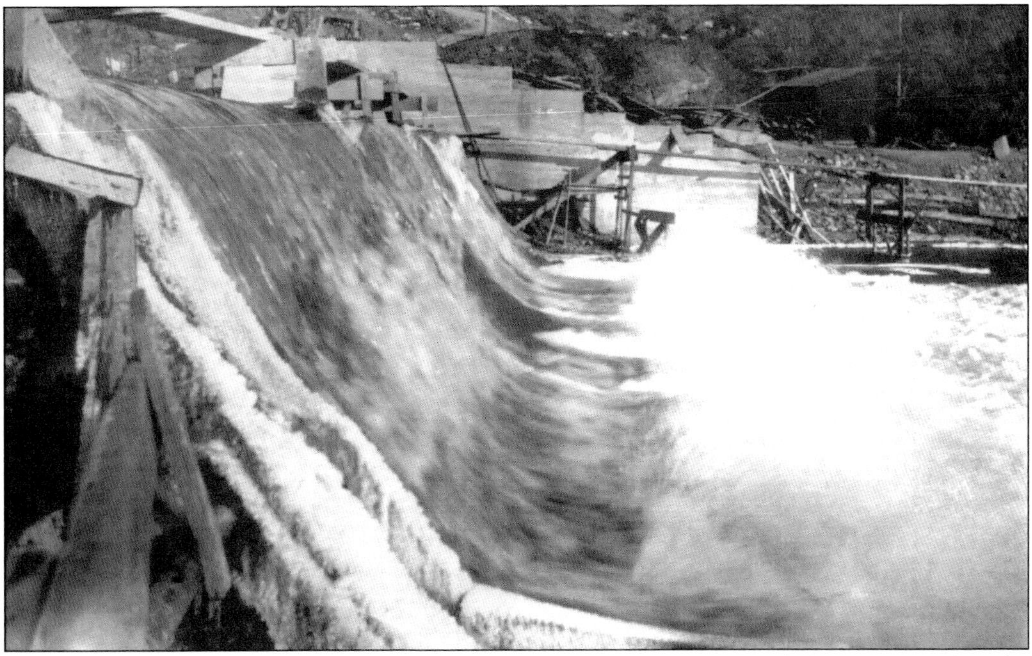

The reconstruction work on the dam shown in this photograph is likely being done after the 1904 ice damage. At this time, the most extensive changes were made: the timber sides were replaced with concrete; the dam was again raised, replacing the step-down style; and the intake gate was reconstructed with concrete replacing the laid stone and wood. (Neversink Valley Area Museum.)

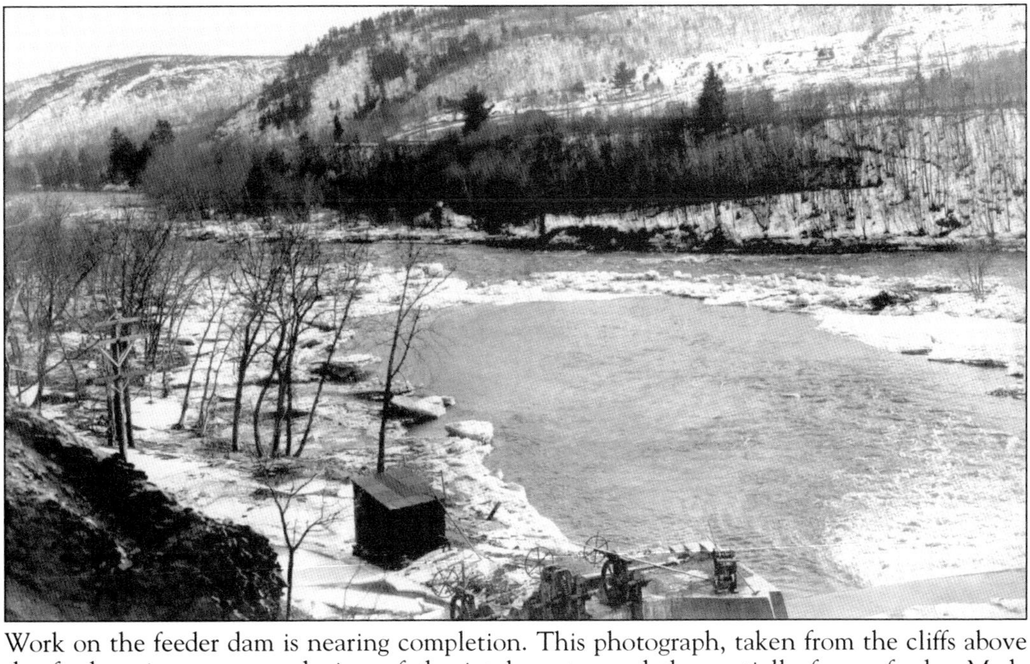

Work on the feeder dam is nearing completion. This photograph, taken from the cliffs above the feeder, gives us a good view of the intake gates and the partially frozen feeder. Made of heavy oak beams, the gates were operated by a system of three large wheels and gears. (Neversink Valley Area Museum.)

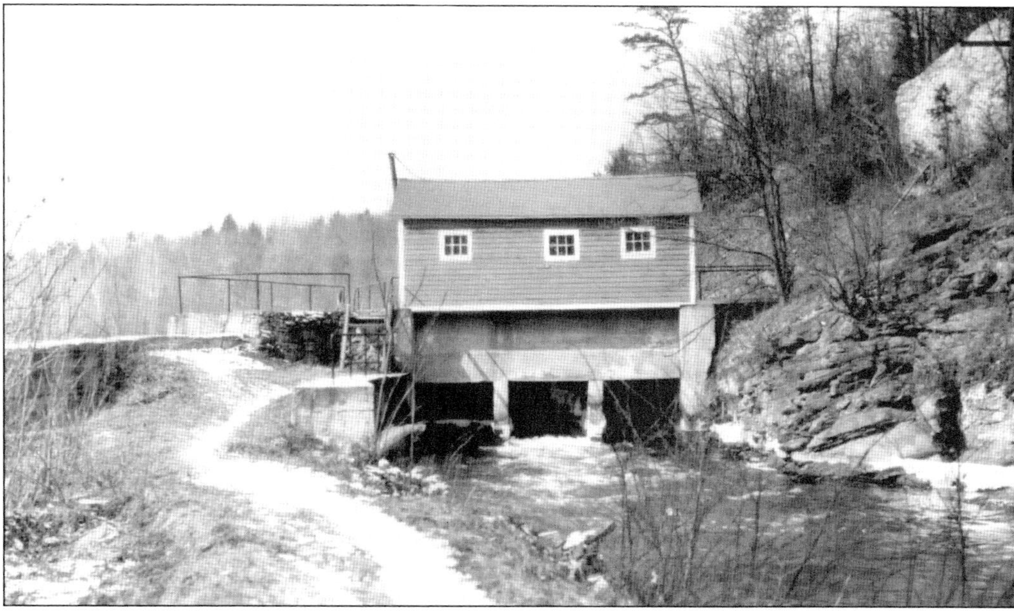

The feeder dam is completed, and the gates are in working order. The function of the gatehouse was to protect the gears from the weather. Some 50 years after the closing of the power plant, little is left of the dam. Over time, ice and the flow of the river have washed away large portions of it. (Neversink Valley Area Museum.)

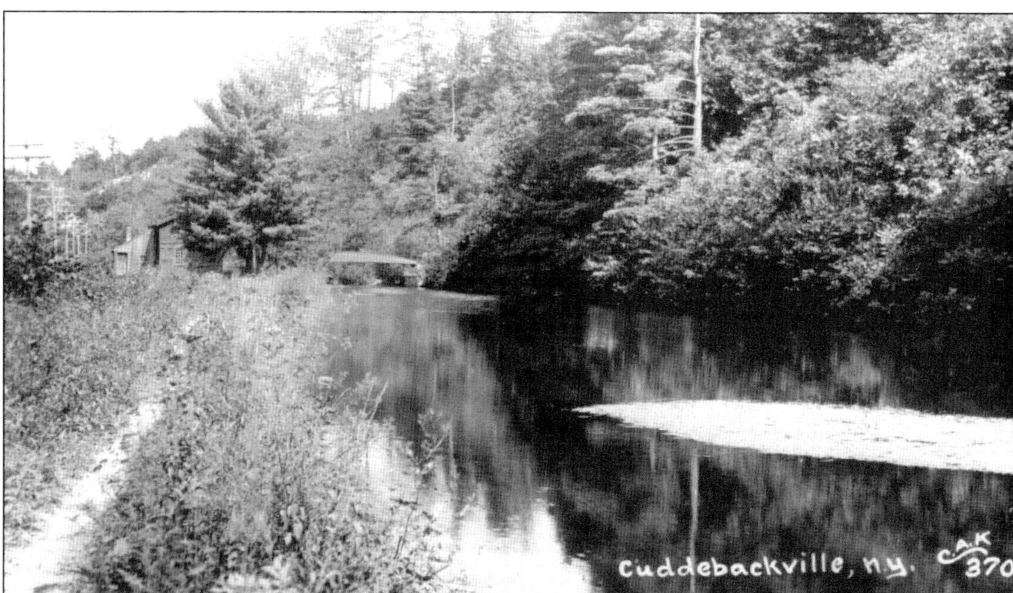

Shown are the feeder canal, tender's house, and footbridge. The feeder delivered water diverted from the Neversink River dam one mile to where it filled the Delaware and Hudson Canal. This feeder later supplied the power plant. (Neversink Valley Area Museum.)

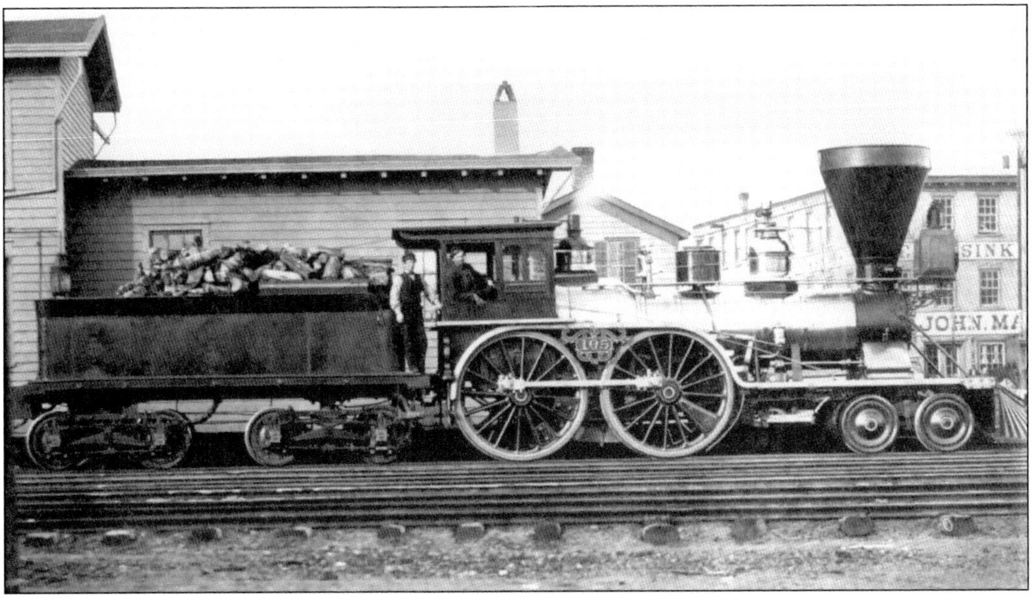

Erie No. 105 was one of the first wood-burning steam engines to chug into Port Jervis. It was built by Rogers, Ketcham, and Grasninor in 1851. As were most early 6-foot gauge trains, Erie No. 105 was an inside connector, with 17- by 20-inch cylinders and 72-inch drivers. This type of train was used on the Port Jervis & Monticello Railroad. This flat-out side view was taken at the end of Sussex Street in 1855. The Neversink Foundry can be seen in the background to the right. (Deerpark Historian's Office.)

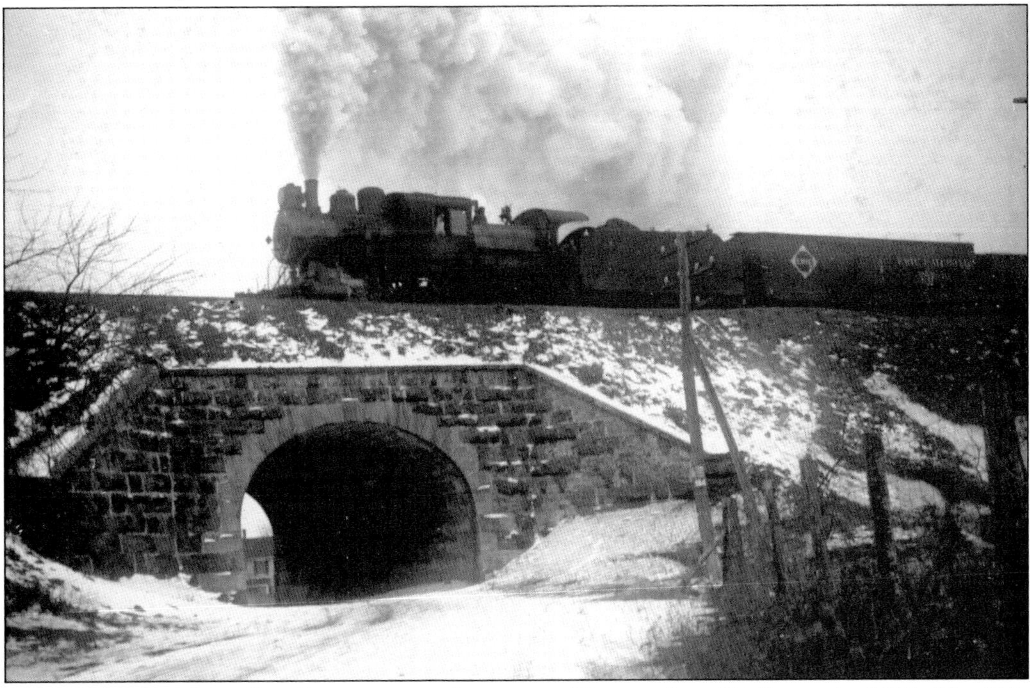

A steam engine from Port Jervis enters the town of Deerpark at Tri-States in 1904. The Erie Railroad tracks follow the Deerpark-Mount Hope boundary line. This tunnel, located at the end of Neversink Drive, is still in use. (Minisink Valley Historical Society.)

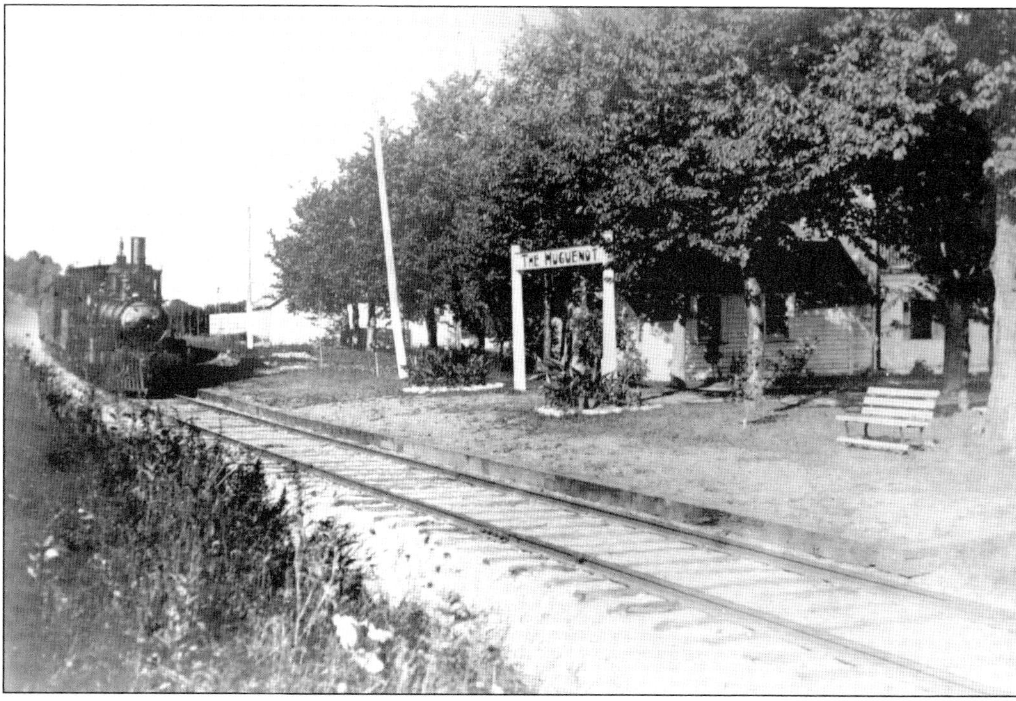

Believe it or not, Huguenot had its own railroad depot. With brakes smoking from the long downgrade from Monticello, the Port Jervis & Monticello Railroad (later the New York, Ontario & Western) train arrives at the Huguenot station, with passengers and goods. The station was at the rear of the hotel. The photograph dates from c. 1900. (Minisink Valley Historical Society.)

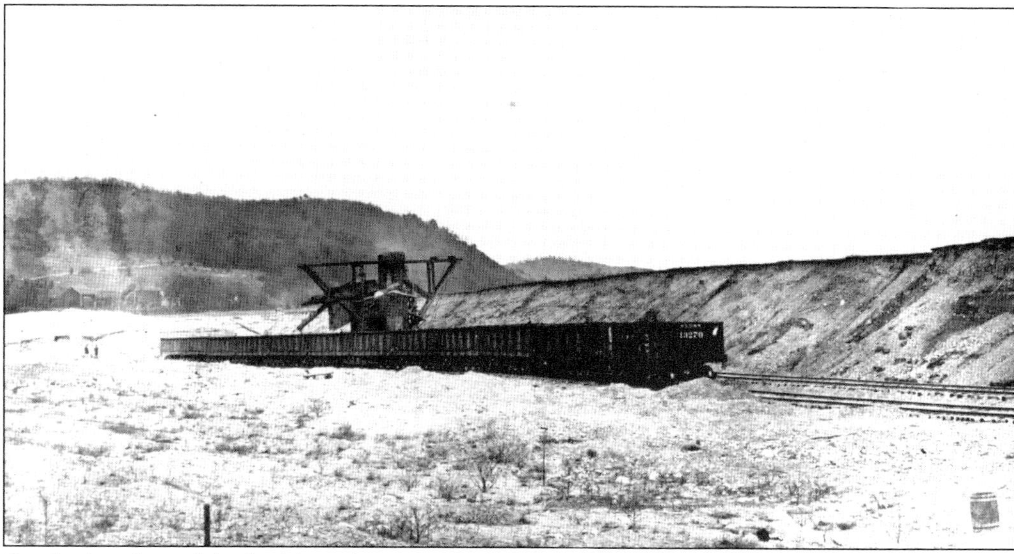

Crushed rock used for building the New York, Ontario & Western Railroad bed (early 1900s) through the valley came from a large hill known as the sandbank, located on the Swartwout farm in Huguenot. This photograph shows removal of the ballast. Later, Empire Tube built a factory on this leveled land. Now, the Deerpark Town Hall and C & D Technologies are located on this land. (Deerpark Historian's Office.)

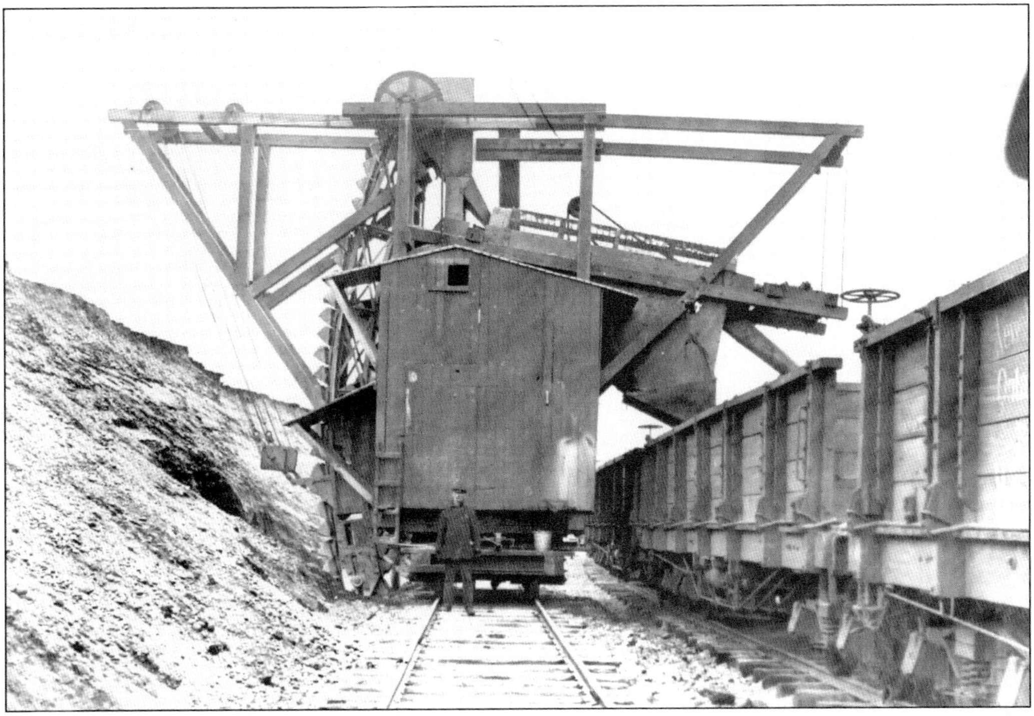

This view shows the gravel loader in action as it scoops away at the sandbank and dumps the ballast into the cars. (Deerpark Historian's Office.)

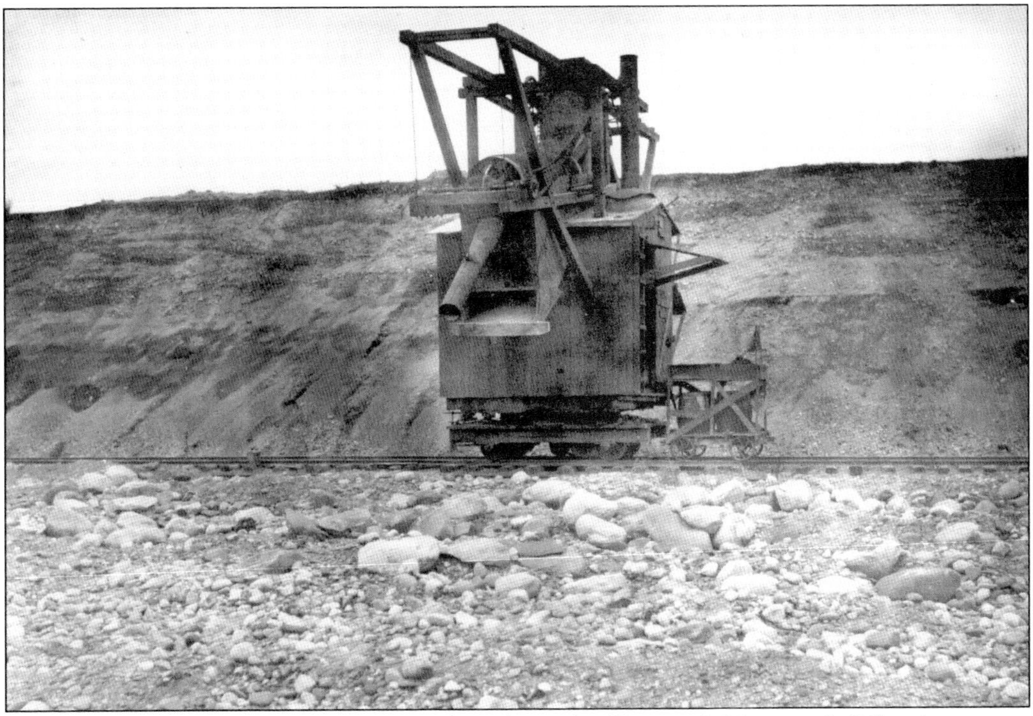

This is a view of the gravel loader from the other side. (Deerpark Historian's Office.)

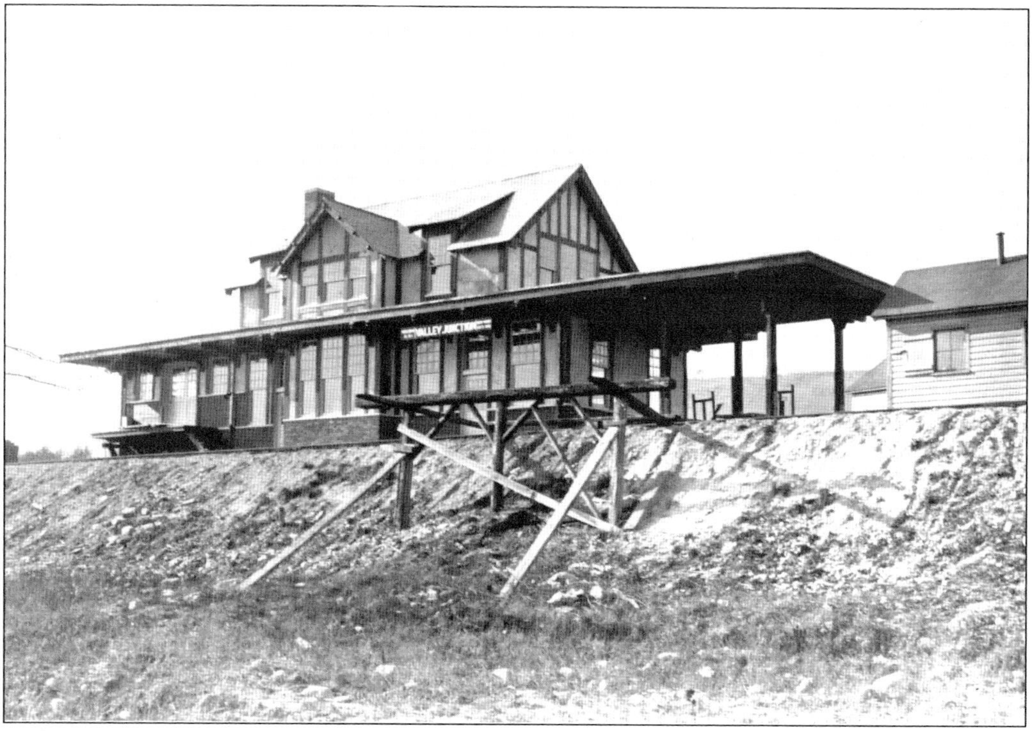

Both the old and new Valley Junction Railroad Stations are shown in this 1913 photograph. The second Valley Junction Station (left) was grander than the first one. (Deerpark Historian's Office.)

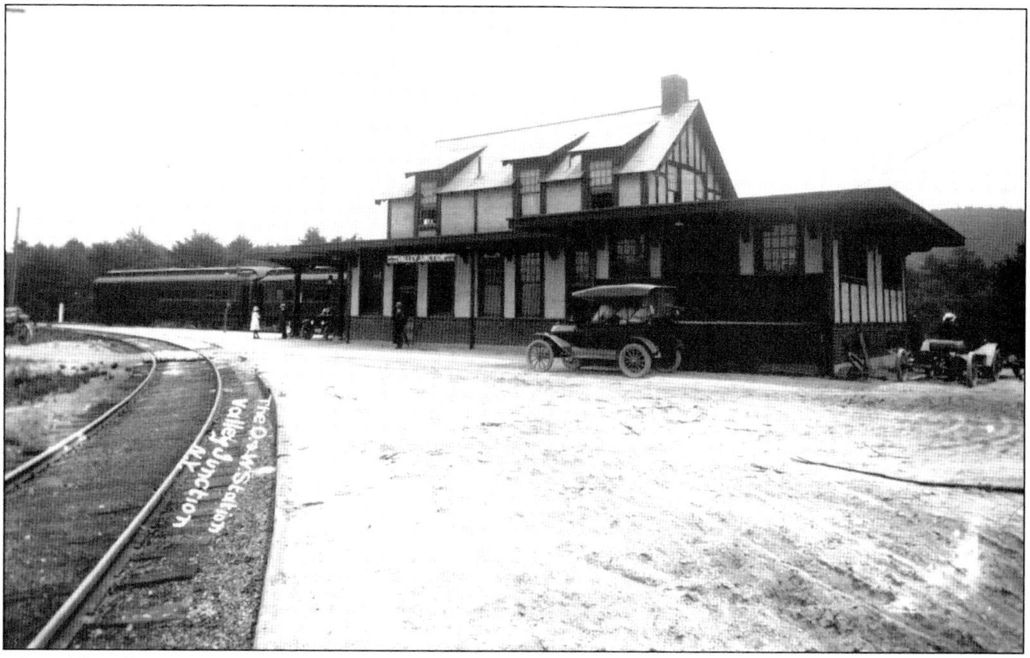

The old Valley Junction Station was removed when the new station opened. Here, a New York, Ontario & Western passenger train arrives. (Minisink Valley Historical Society.)

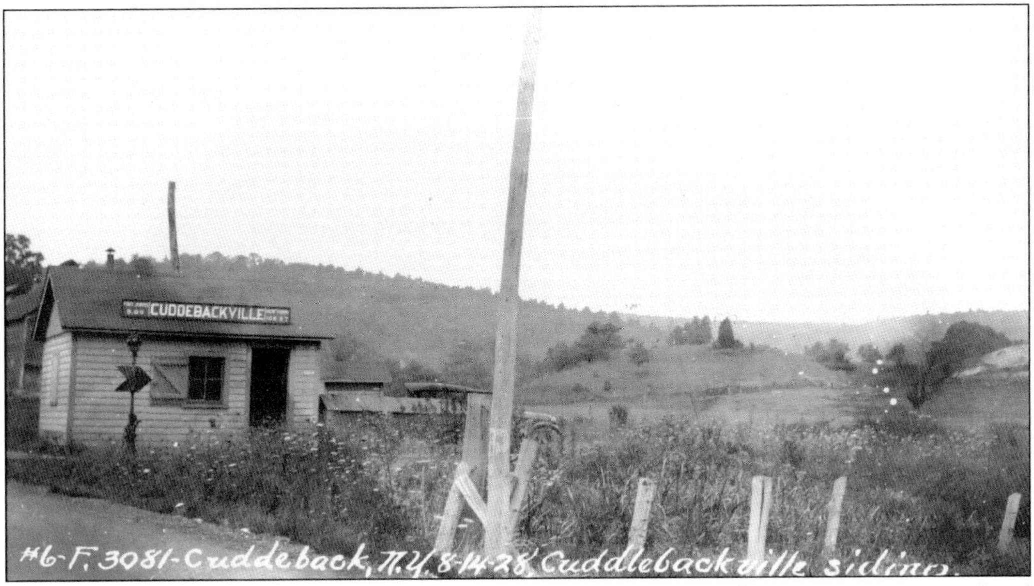

In the late 1800s, the Port Jervis , Monticello, & New York Railroad Company reorganized and purchased the Port Jervis & Monticello Railroad Company for $127,000. Later, a branch was built from Roses Point to Summitville. This photograph shows the station in Cuddebackville on August 14, 1928. The William Cuddeback farm can just be seen behind the station. (Author's collection.)

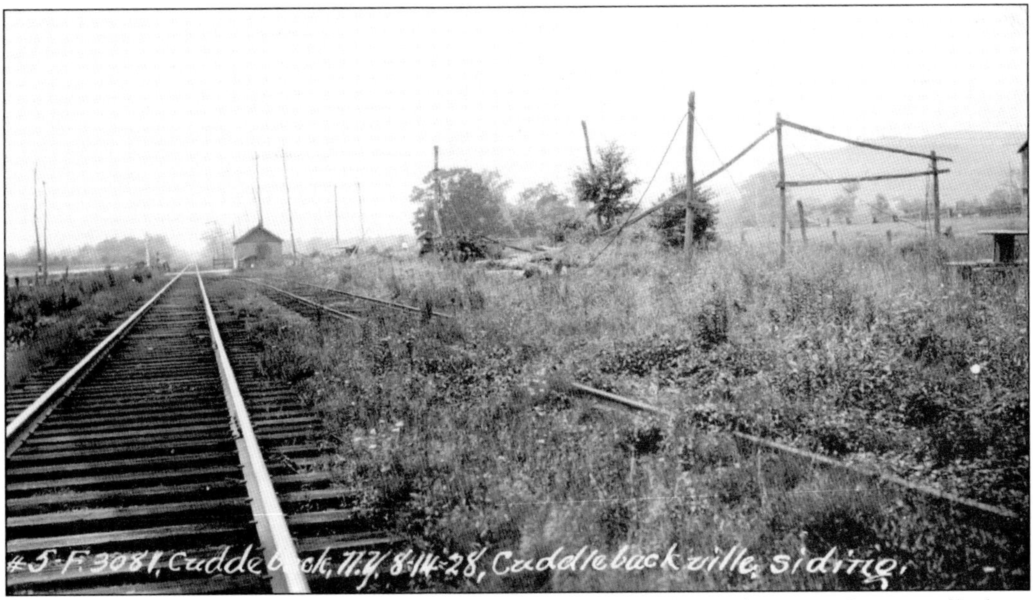

Looking toward Port Jervis on August 14, 1928, this view shows the same Summitville line. D.W. Griffith and silent film stars arrived at this little station. The William Cuddeback farm is to the extreme right. The barns are now home of the Old Red Barn Auction. (Author's collection.)

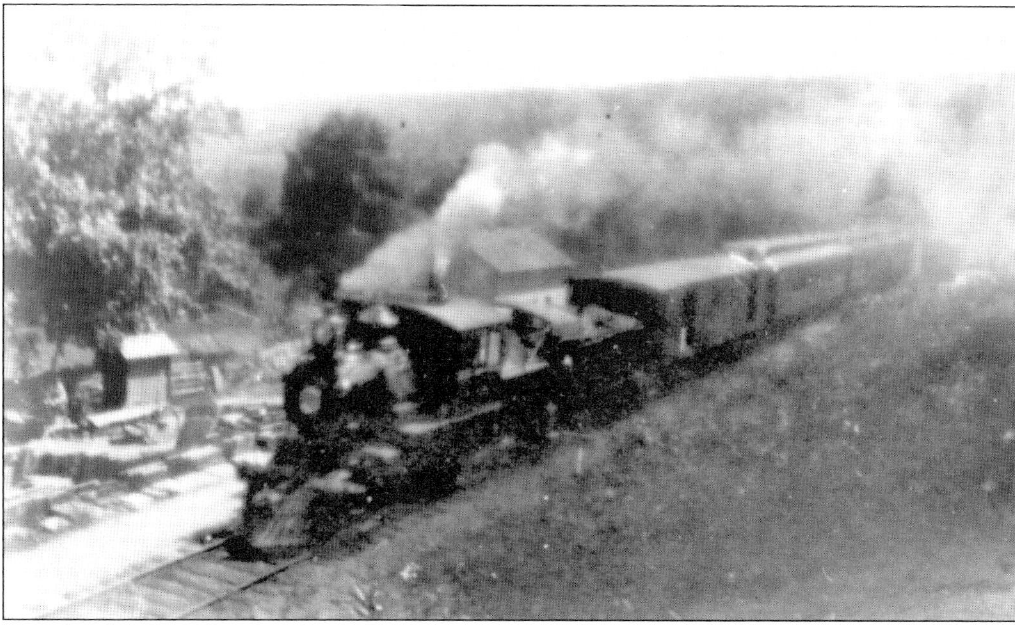

A Port Jervis & Monticello engine makes its way between Cuddebackville and Oakland Valley-Paradise on its way to Monticello in the 1890s. The train may be waiting to be loaded with cut stones produced by the North River & Oakland Bluestone Company. The railroad was taken over by the New York, Ontario & Western in 1903. (Author's collection.)

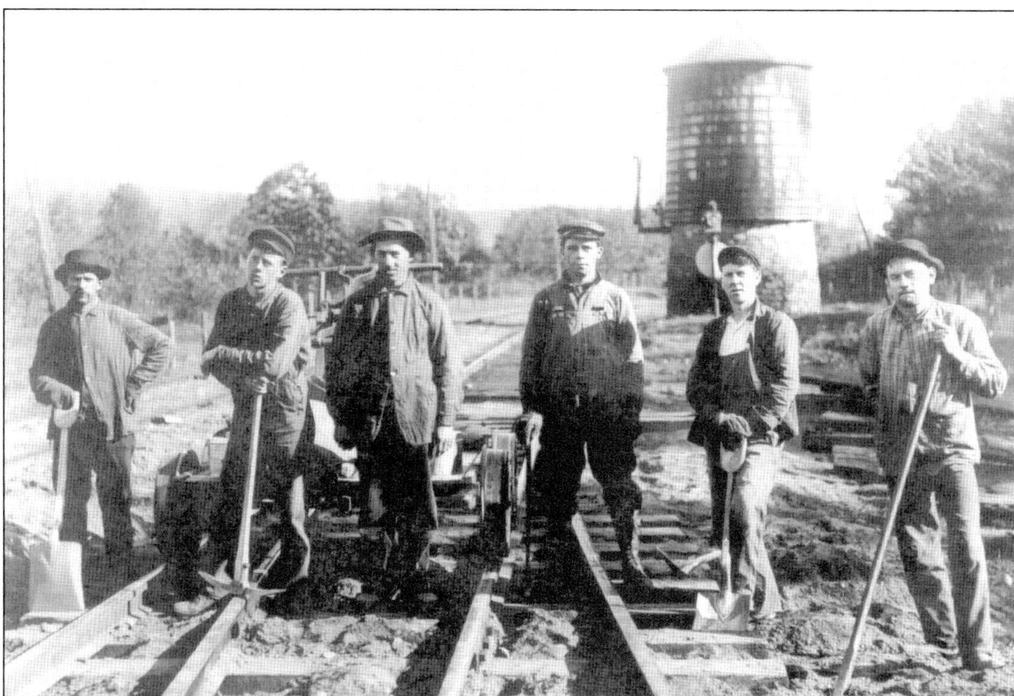

New York, Ontario & Western workers rest after replacing the rotting ties near a siding in Paradise in 1910. They are, from left to right, William Runnalls, Ray Decker, Tracy Turner, Clarence Ogden, Edward Decker, and Donald Gordon. (Bill Flieger.)

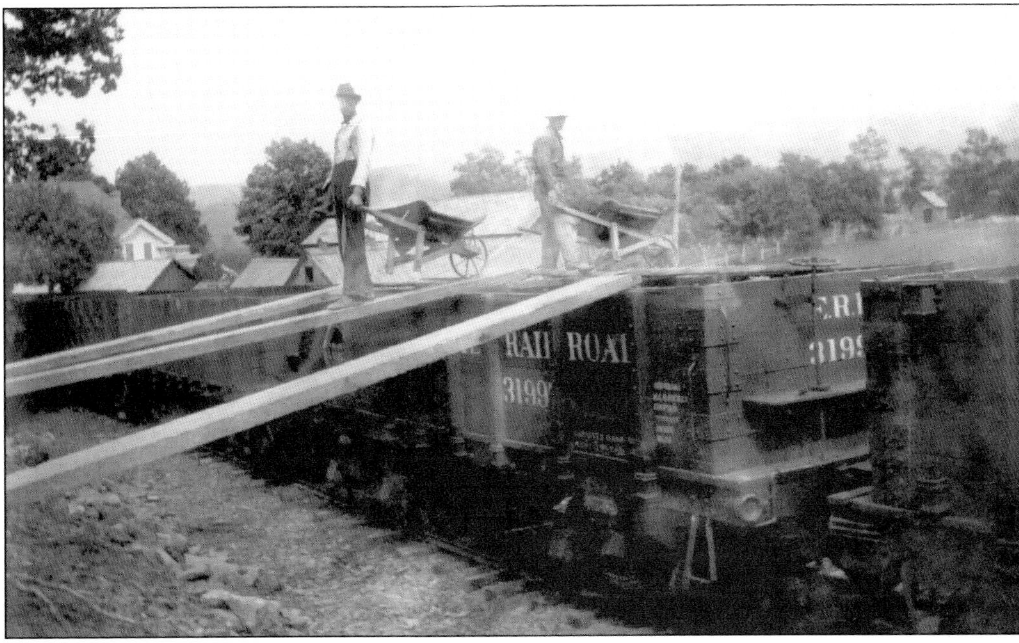

The New York, Ontario & Western Railroad often rented cars from the Erie Railroad. Here, in 1901, men are dumping calcareous shale into drop-bottom gondola cars in Godeffroy. The Peter E. Gumaer farm is in the background. Route 209 and other local roads were made of this shale, which was said to produce "a billiard-table-like surface." Average gondola cars held 25 yards, each yard weighing 2,650 pounds. (Neversink Valley Area Museum.)

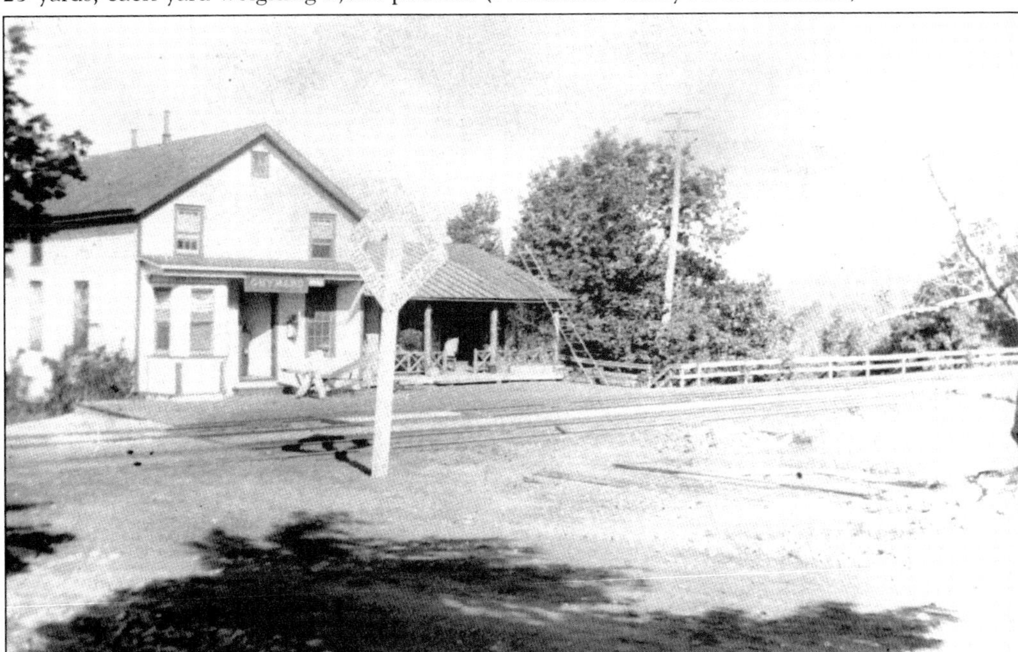

The Guymard Erie Railroad Depot was a stop on the way to Middletown and served as a grocery store and post office. This photograph was taken on October 6, 1890. (Minisink Valley Historical Society.)

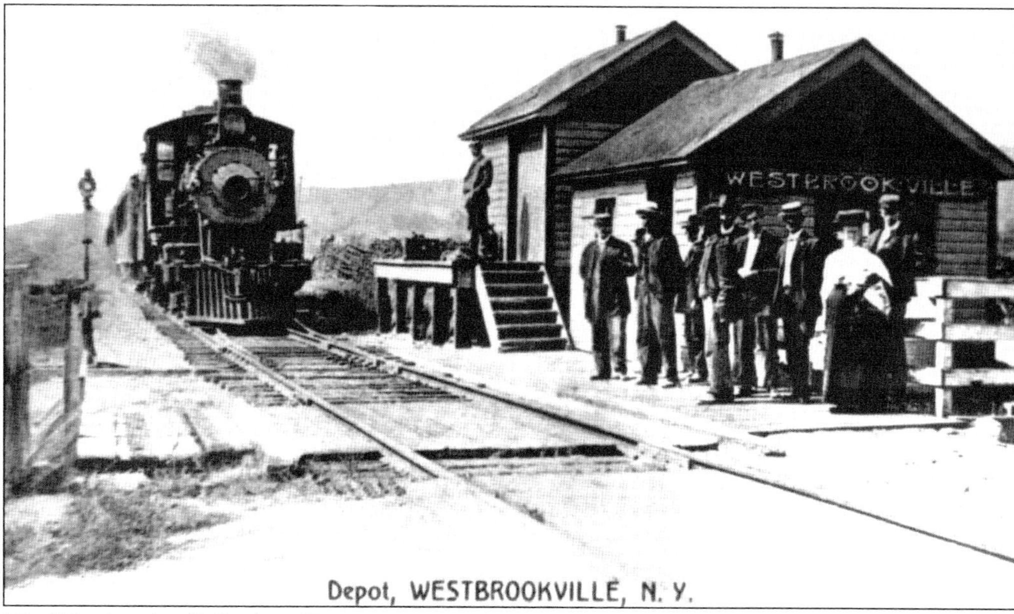

The Westbrookville Railroad Depot was one of several stops for the New York, Ontario & Western on the Cuddebackville-to-Summitville branch. (Minisink Valley Historical Society.)

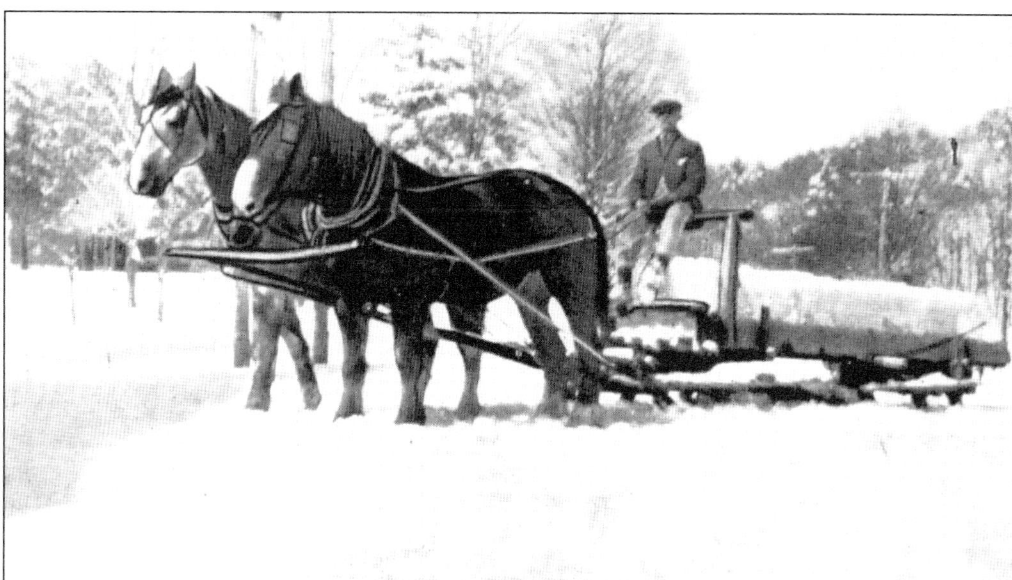

Every winter, the townsmen had the task of harvesting ice. This man has a full load of ice on his sleigh, ready for a trip to his icehouse. In Cuddebackville, the Delaware and Hudson Canal offered a large supply of ice. Harvesting ice on the canal was safe in comparison to cutting ice on lakes and rivers. This early-1900s photograph was likely taken near the canal freight basin. (Deerpark Historian's Office.)

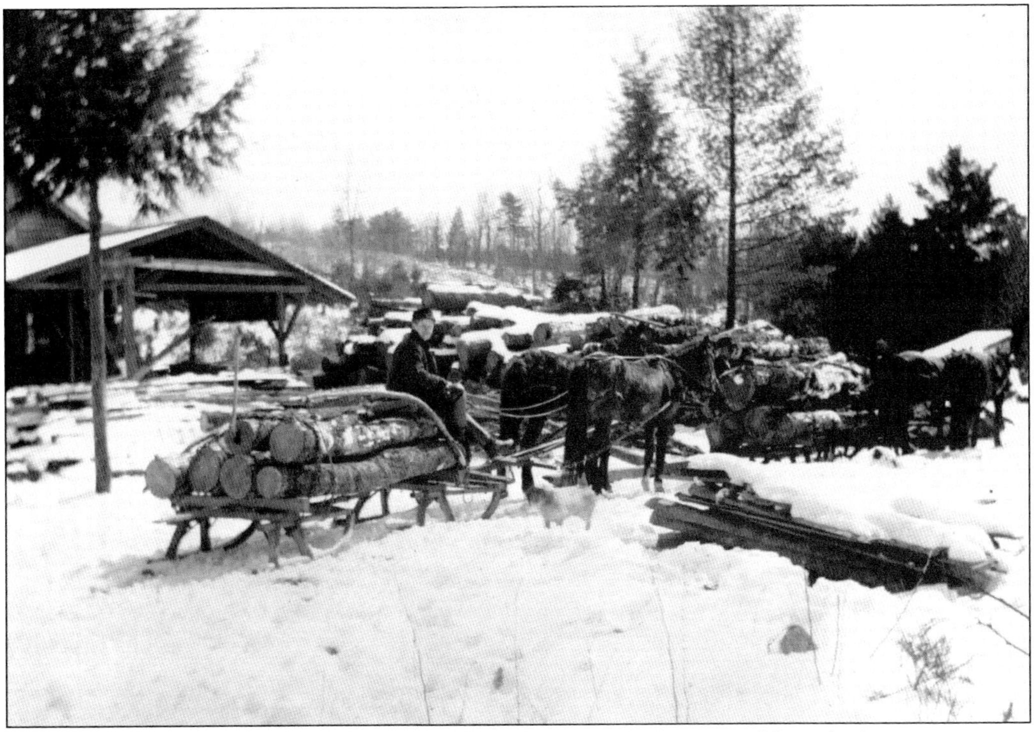

The location of this logging camp and sawmill remains a mystery. Although there were many camps like this one throughout Deerpark, this camp was likely located in Woodland Park in Huguenot. (Deerpark Historian's Office.)

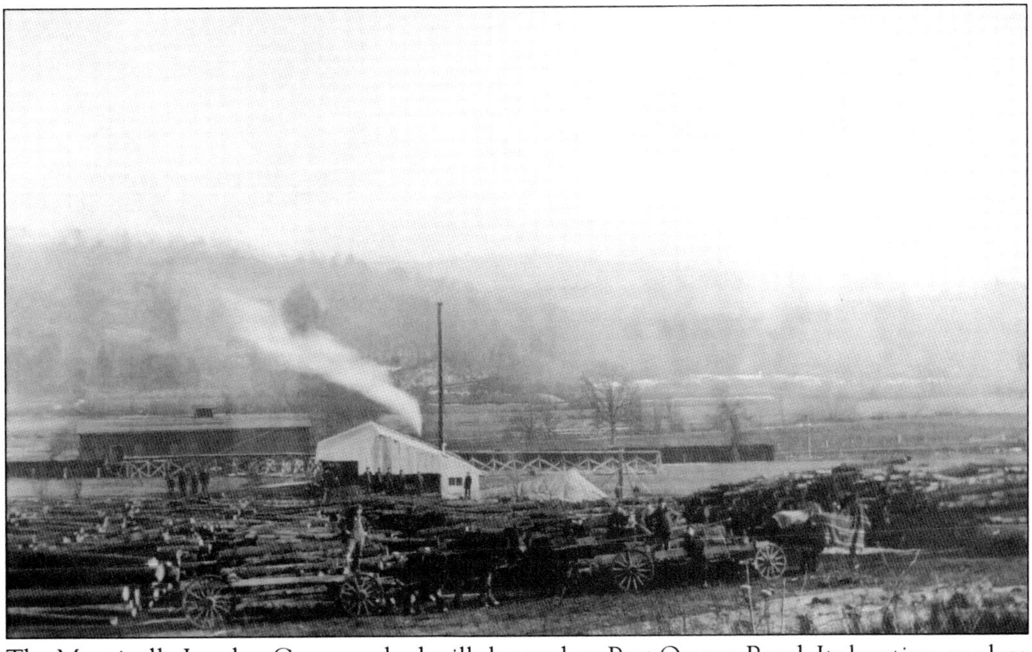

The Monticello Lumber Company had mills located on Port Orange Road. Its location, so close to the Delaware and Hudson Canal, was perfect for shipping lumber. The Basha Kill is in the background of this c. 1907 photograph. (Author's collection.)

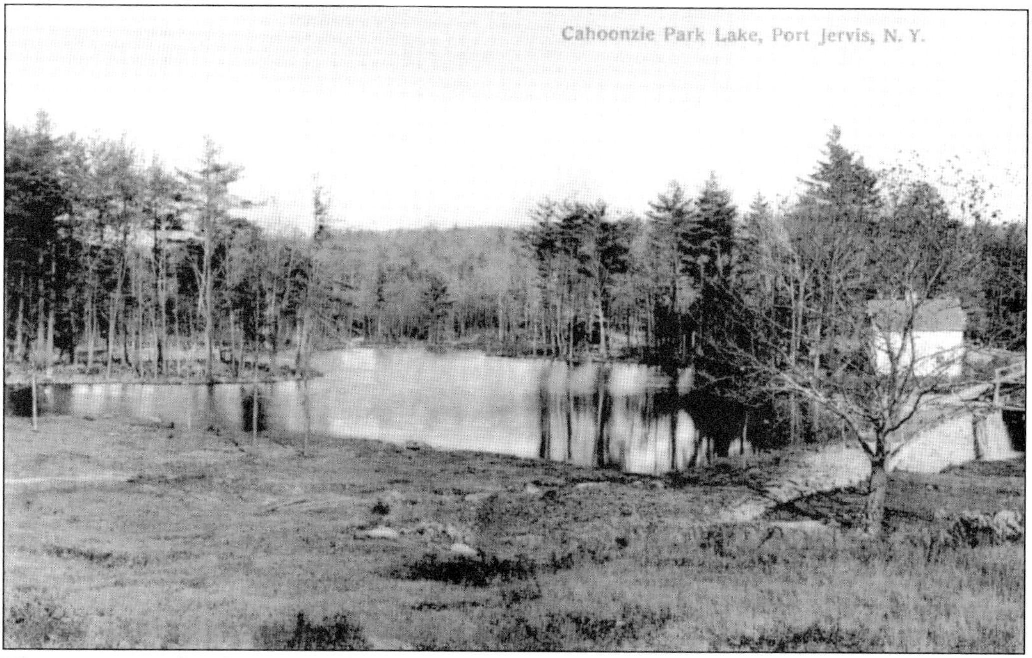

This is a view of Cahoonzie Park Lake in Cahoonzie on Route 42. At one time, there was an ice-manufacturing plant near this site. (Nancy Dunn.)

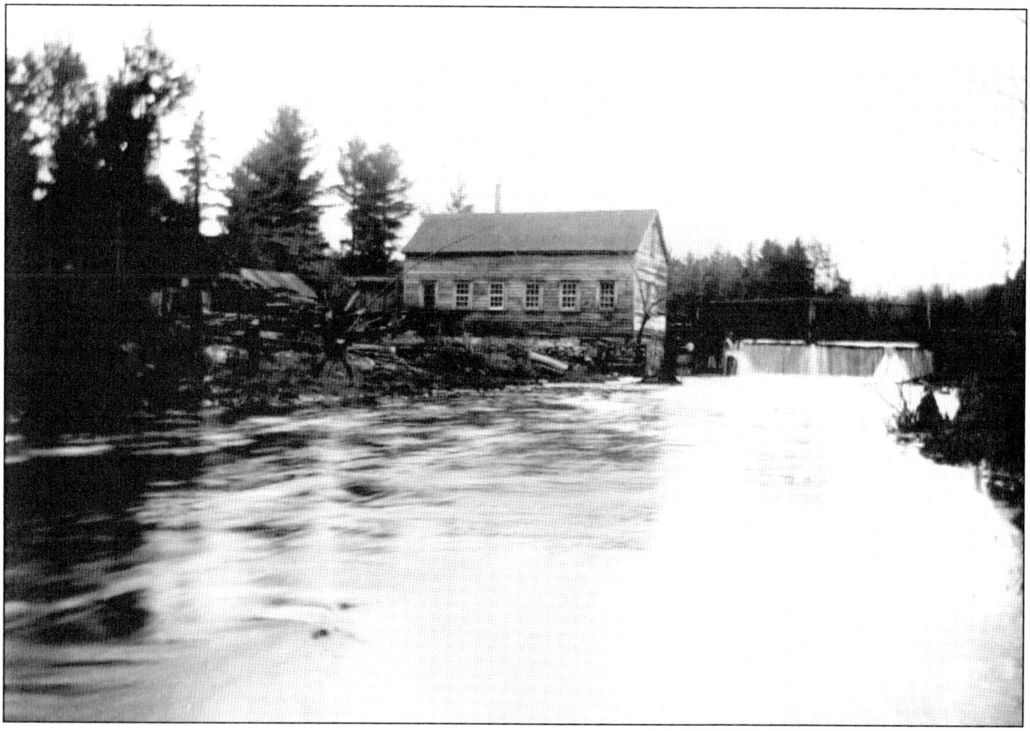

The dam at Cahoonzie Park Lake later became a fish hatchery. In this early photograph, it looks as though the mill may still be in operation. Note the man fishing on the left with the long bamboo pole. (Deerpark Historian's Office.)

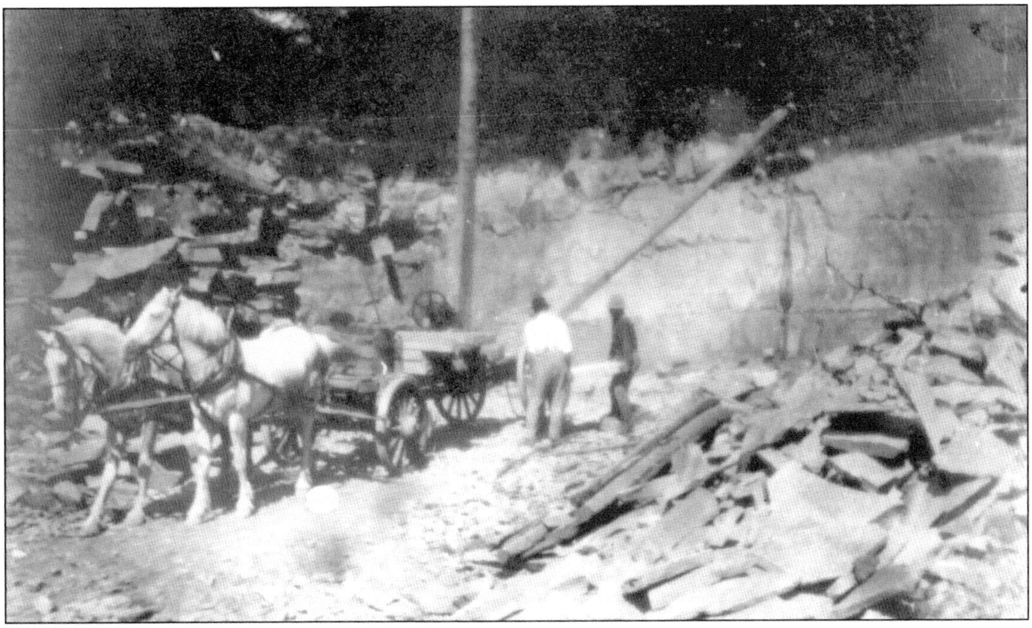

In Deerpark, there were many bluestone quarries. This quarry was most likely located on the James Lewis homestead in Oakland Valley near Buttermilk Falls. This photograph was taken in the 1890s. (Author's collection.)

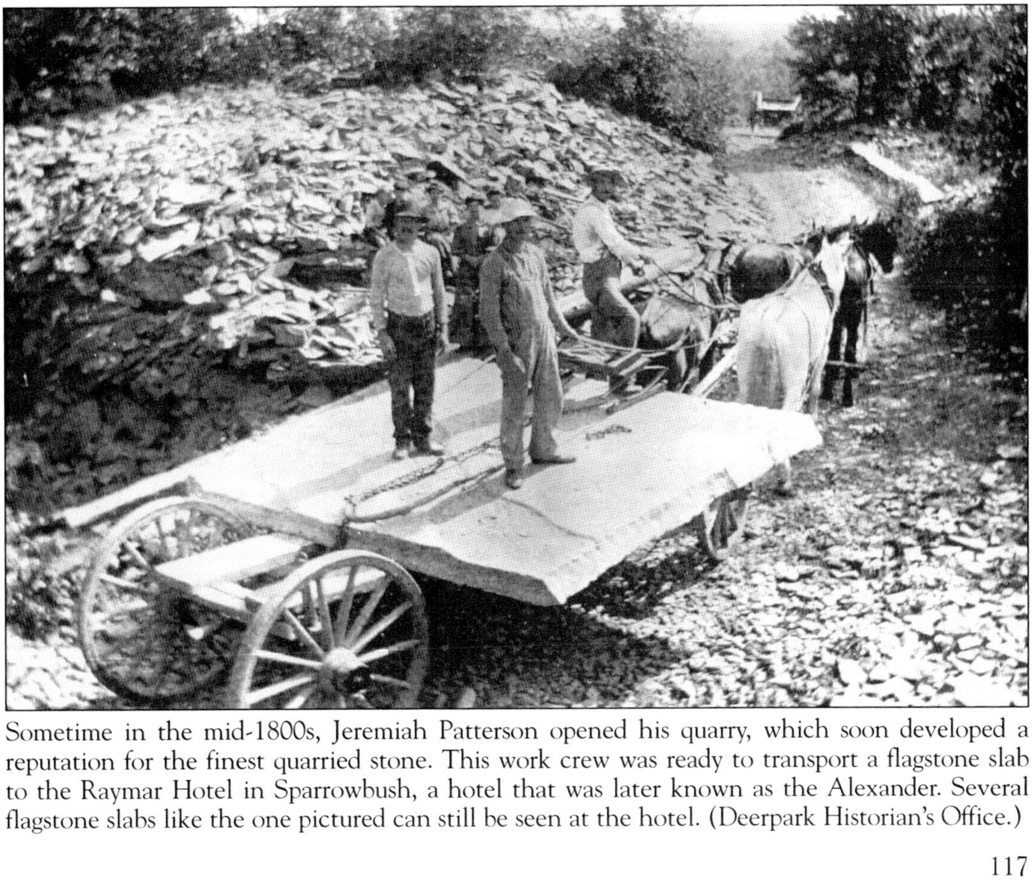

Sometime in the mid-1800s, Jeremiah Patterson opened his quarry, which soon developed a reputation for the finest quarried stone. This work crew was ready to transport a flagstone slab to the Raymar Hotel in Sparrowbush, a hotel that was later known as the Alexander. Several flagstone slabs like the one pictured can still be seen at the hotel. (Deerpark Historian's Office.)

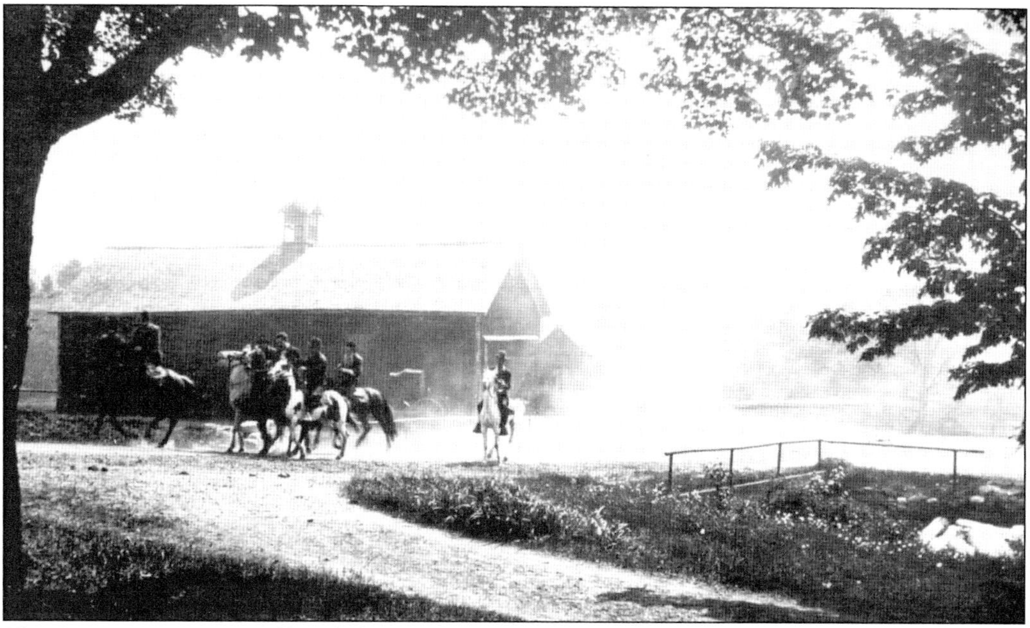

The Squaws Love was filmed by D.W. Griffith in Cuddebackville in 1911. It starred Mabel Normand, Kate Bruce, Dorothy West, and James Kirkwood. This barn is located off of the Guymard Turnpike. (Minisink Valley Historical Society.)

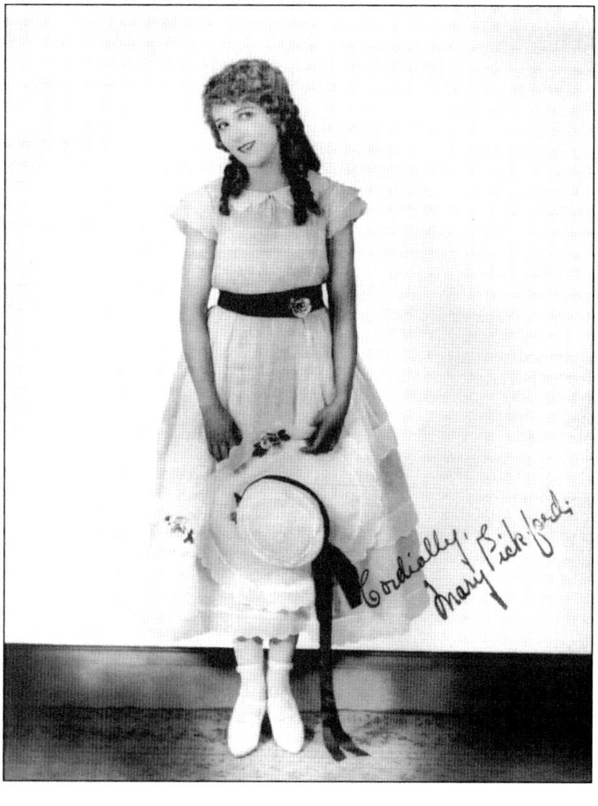

Mary Pickford, "America's Sweetheart," starred in silent films made in Cuddebackville between 1909 and 1911. (Neversink Valley Area Museum.)

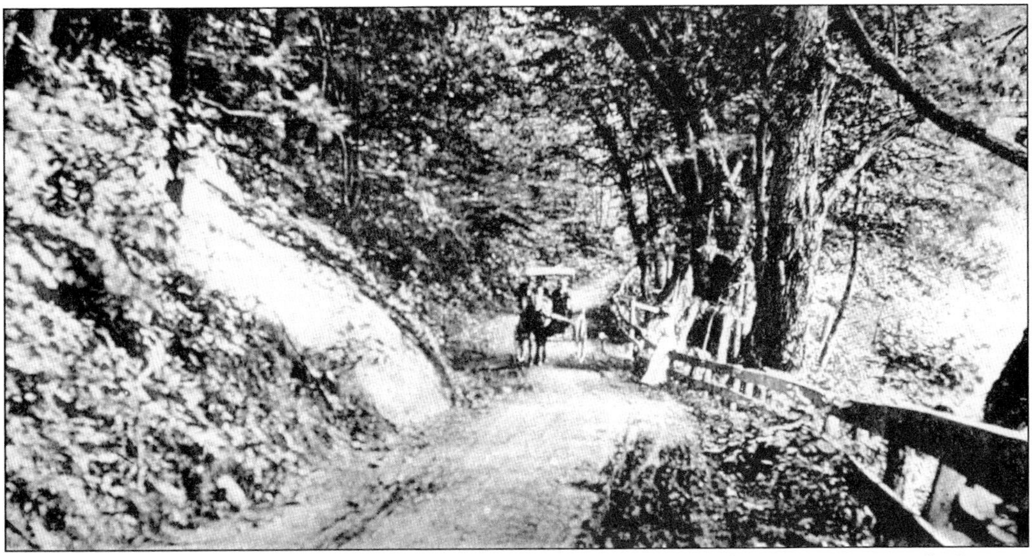

Neversink Drive was still a dirt road in 1905. Local lore has it that it was "a good place to spoon." This photograph was taken between today's Brown Swiss Farm and Indian Acres. (Author's collection.)

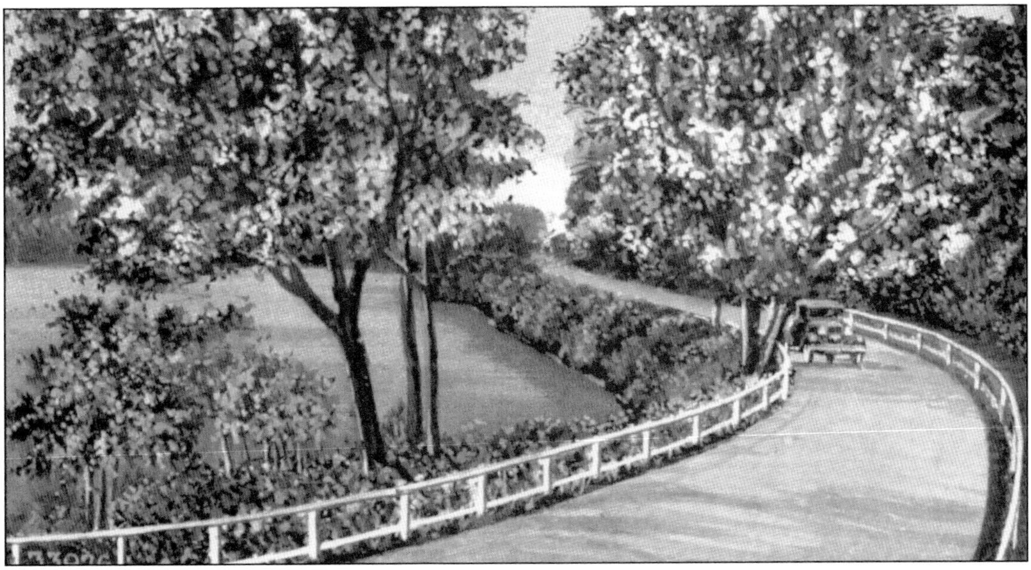

The Rio reservoir is the storage reservoir for the Orange and Rockland Utilities Power Plant. This road scene is probably near the beach. (Author's collection.)

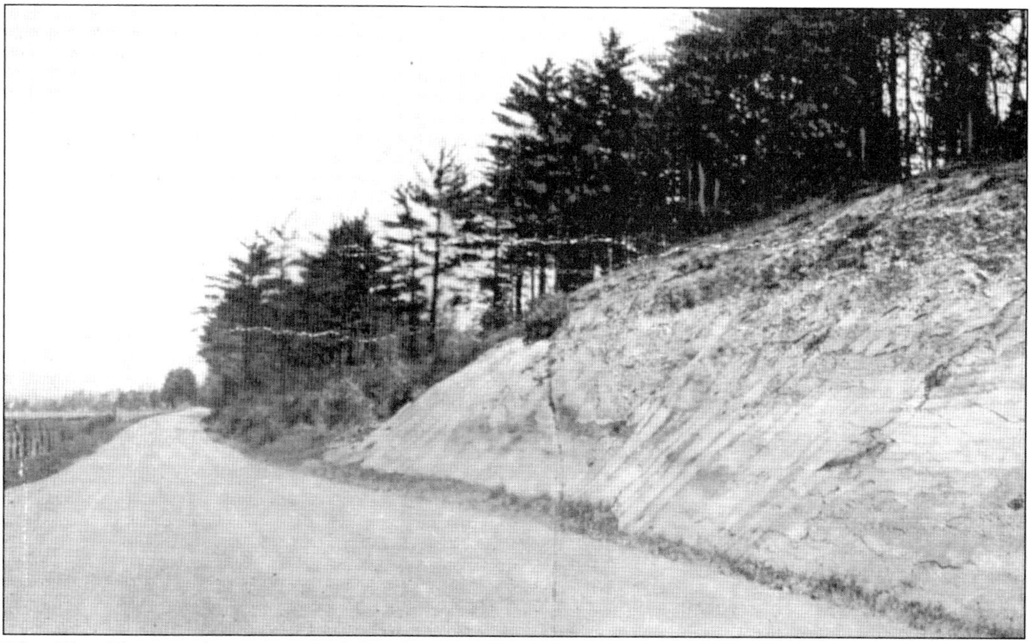

The Van Fleet rocks are named for the family that owned the land in this area. These rocks can be seen by people traveling south on Route 209 in Huguenot just before Orchard Lane. (Author's collection.)

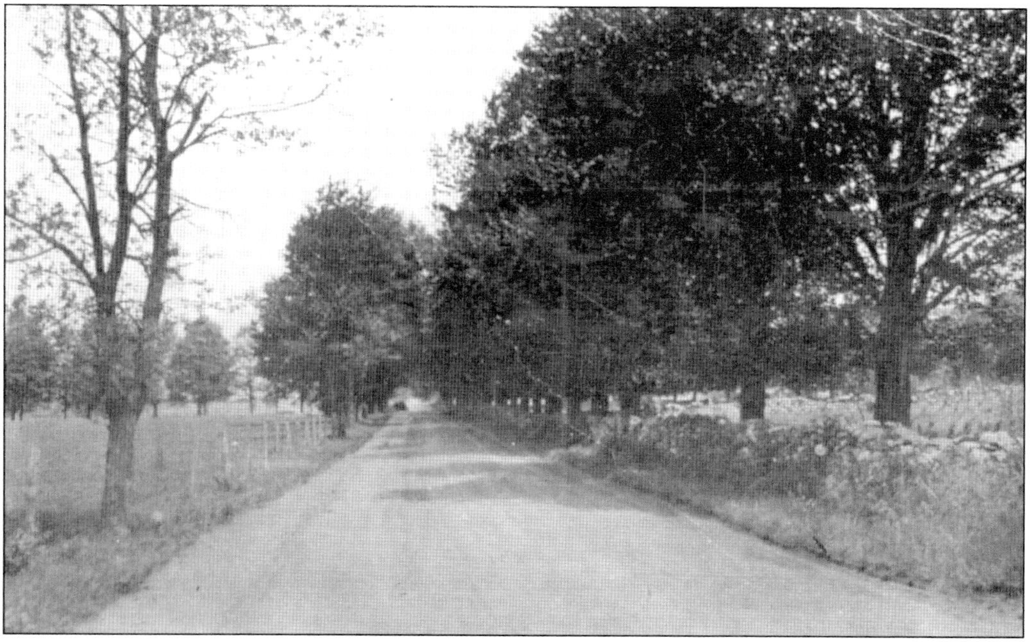

Pictured is an early view of farmland on the Huguenot Road (Route 209) before the road was paved and the land was developed. The photograph was taken between Tri-States Christian Camp (formerly Cejwin Camps) and Neversink Drive. (Author's collection.)

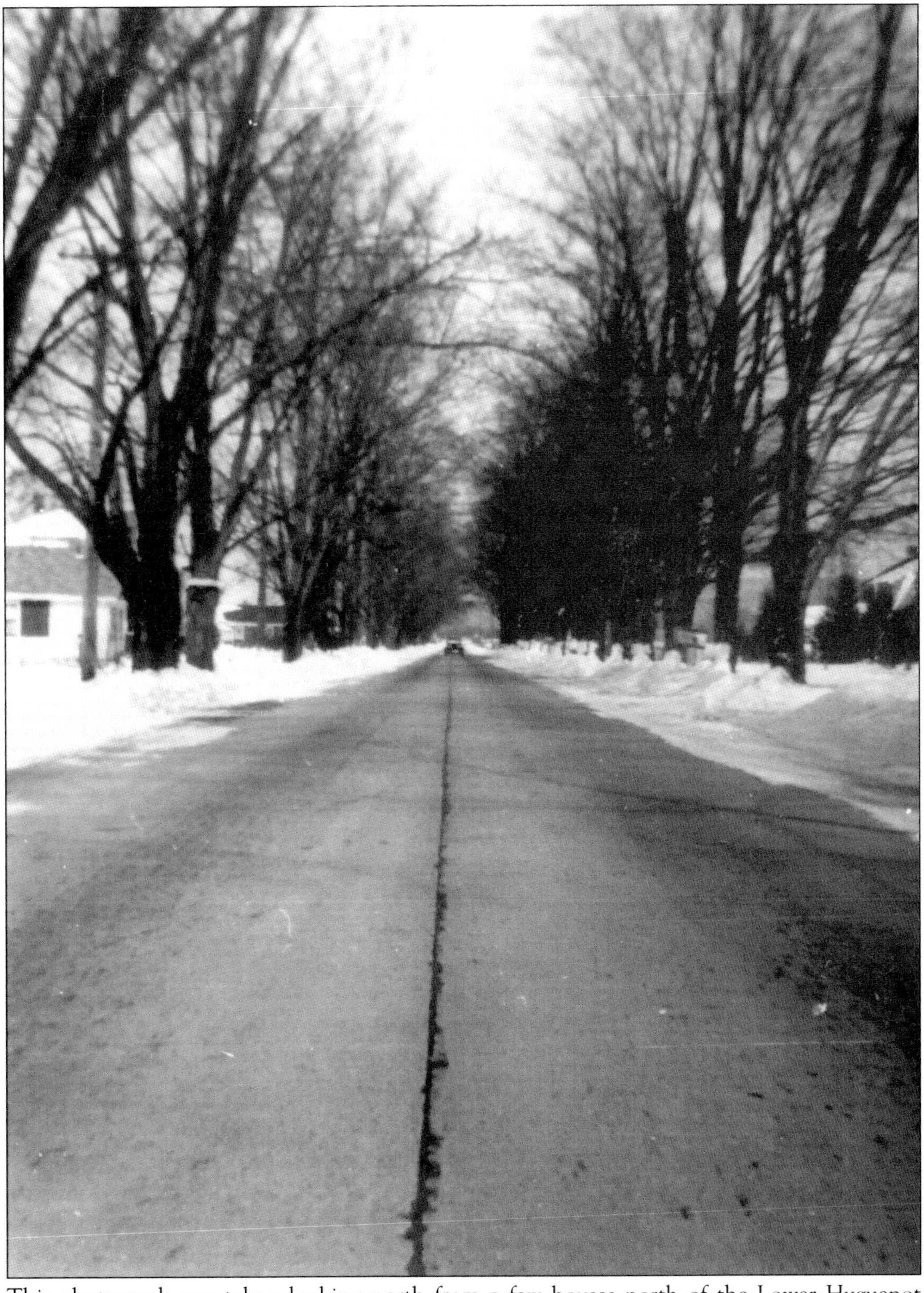

This photograph was taken looking north from a few houses north of the Lower Huguenot Schoolhouse (now Town Building No. 2) in February 1947. It shows a maple tree lined Route 209. The scene changed in the 1960s, when all of the trees were cut down to widen the road. (Diane Archer.)

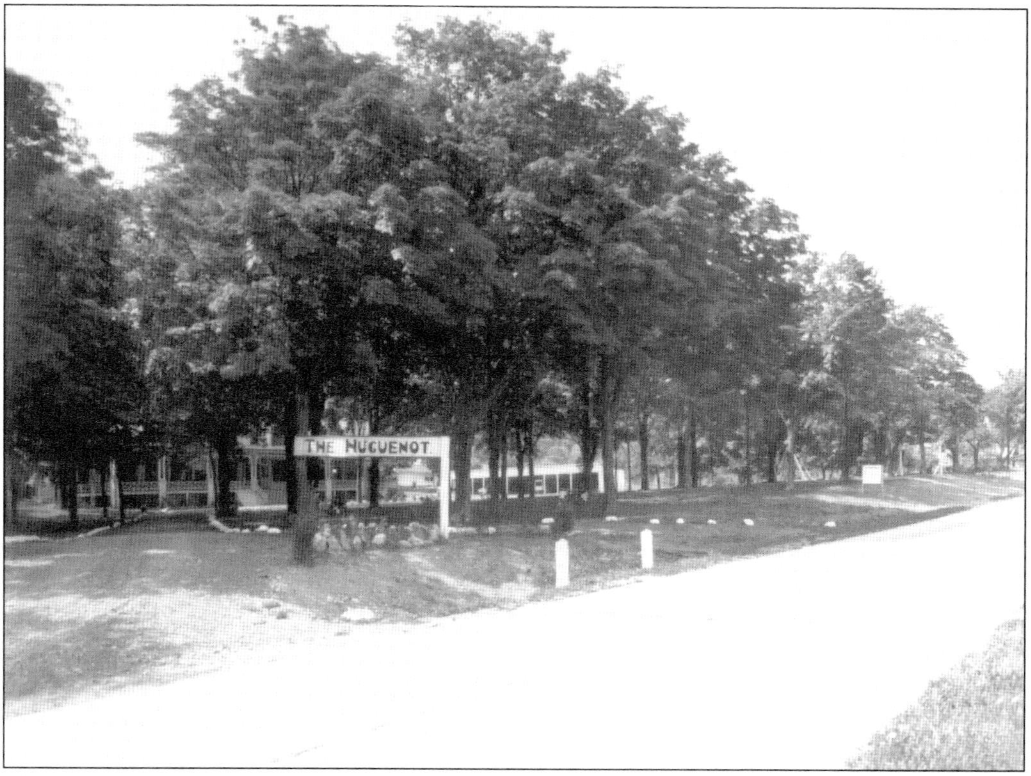

The Huguenot Road (Route 209) was known to be one of the finest roads in the country. This view was taken in front of the Hotel Huguenot, probably in the 1930s, not long after the roads were paved. (Deerpark Historian's Office.)

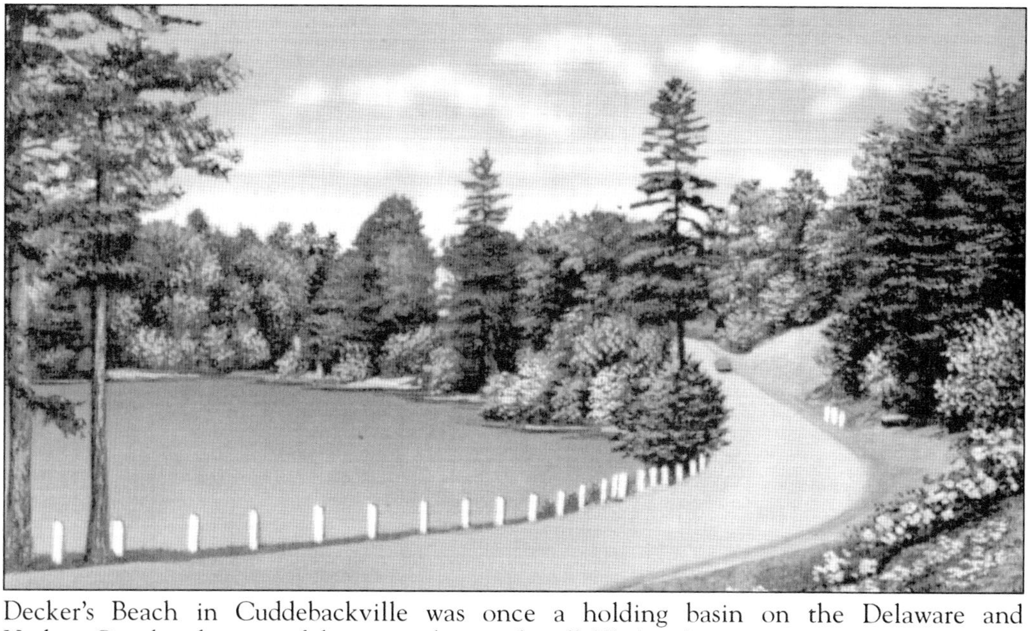

Decker's Beach in Cuddebackville was once a holding basin on the Delaware and Hudson Canal and is part of the one-mile stretch still filled with water, as it was in canal days. (Author's collection.)

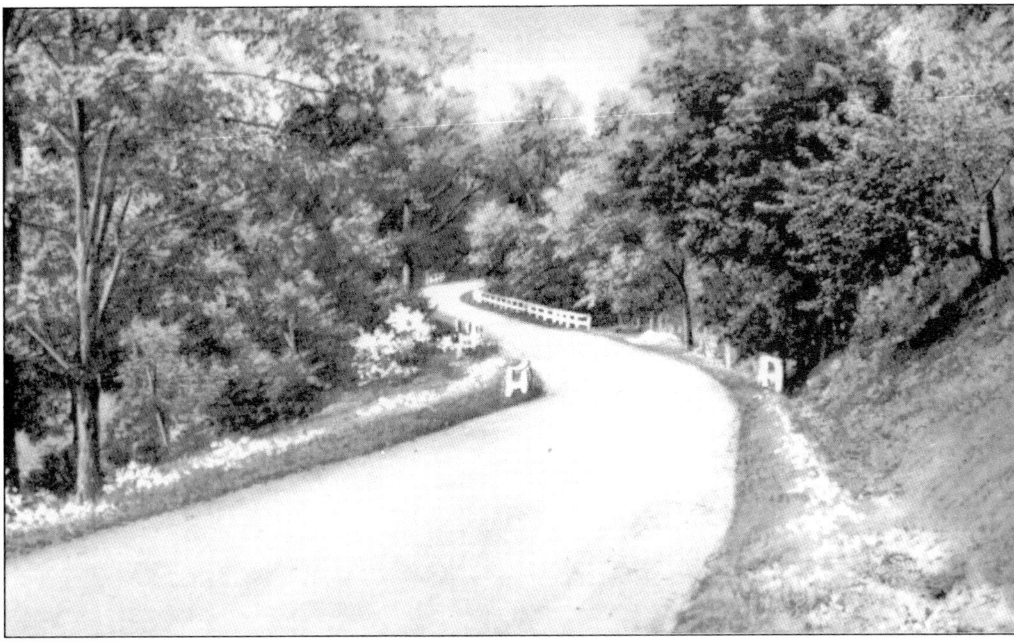

The Mount Hope and Lumberland Turnpike Road is Route 211 in Cuddebackville. On June 8, 1812, the New York State Legislature established the Mount Hope and Lumberland Turnpike Road Company, with an appropriation of $35,000. The road is between Wallkill and Narrowsburg on the Delaware River. The road was never completed to Narrowsburg and ended in Cuddebackville. (Author's collection.)

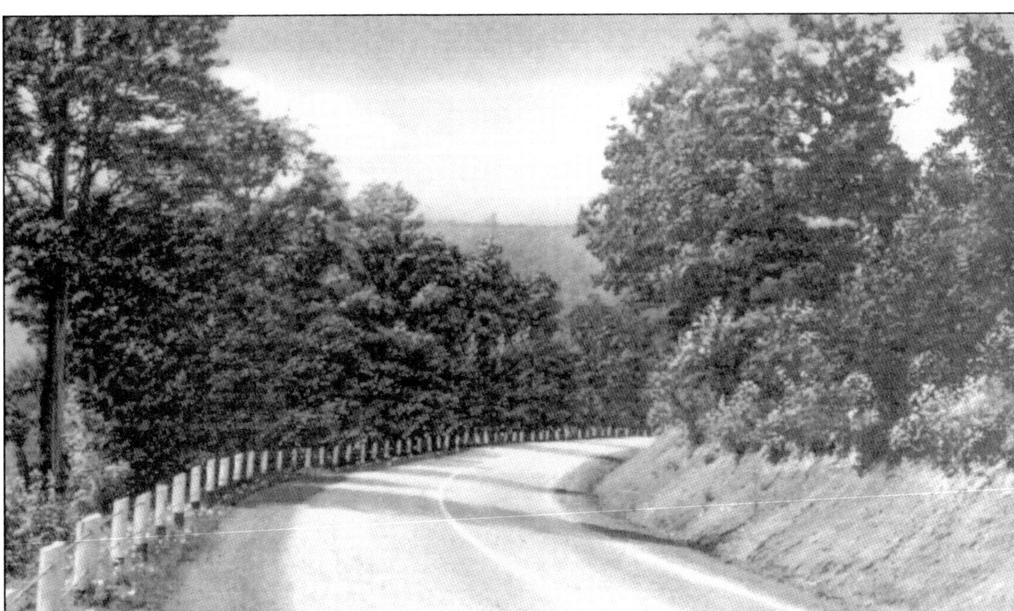

The picturesque country road in Cuddebackville depicted on this postcard is an artist's rendering of Prospect Hill Road. (Author's collection.)

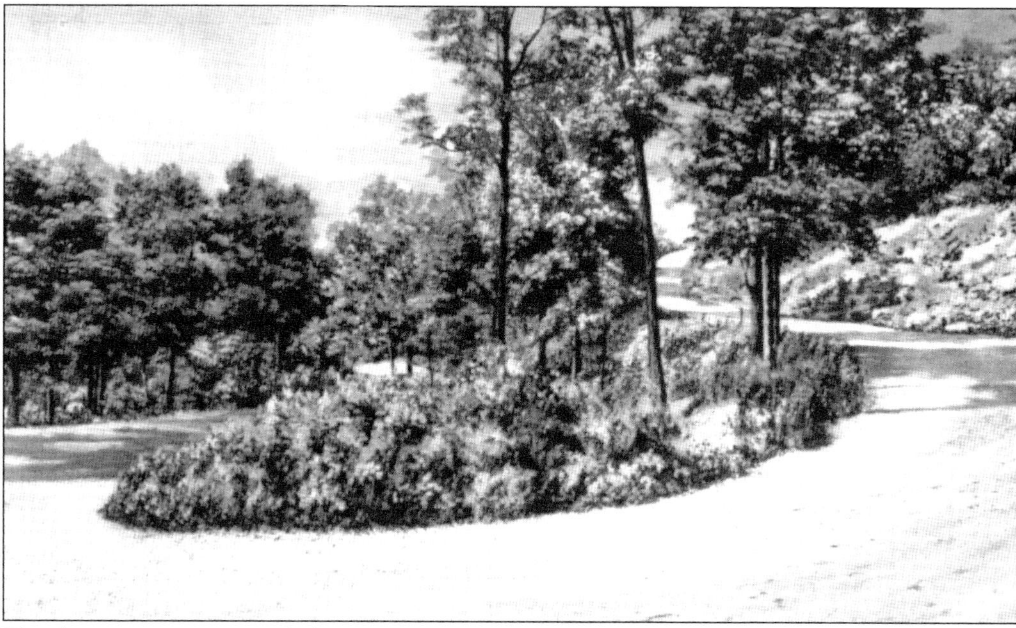

This hairpin curve is on Skyline Drive, the road to Point Peter. Picnicking up on Point Peter has been a family tradition dating back to the 1800s. (Author's collection.)

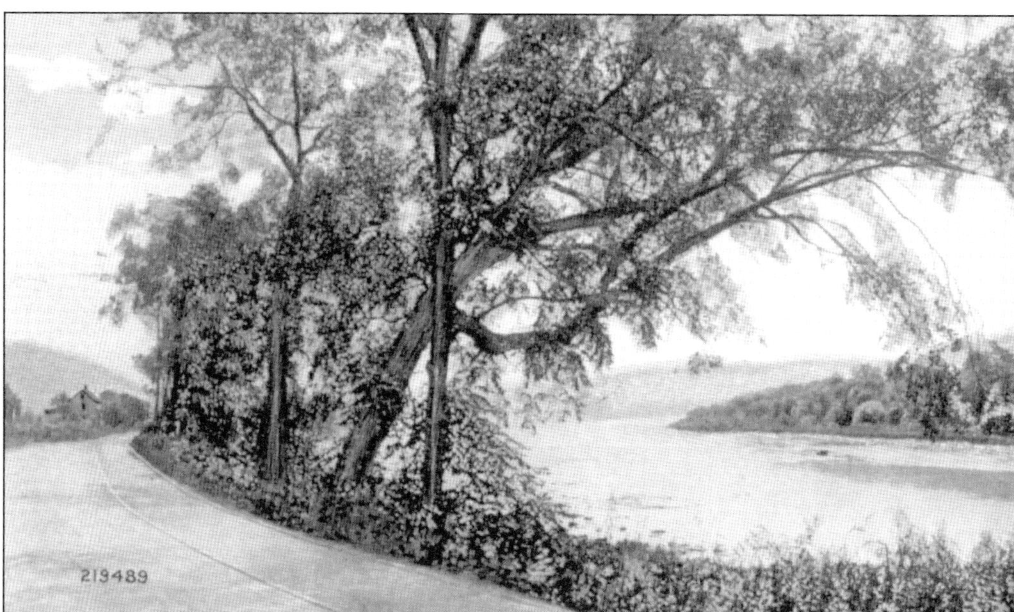

This postcard view shows trolley tracks along the banks of the Delaware River in Sparrowbush near the railroad bridge. A stagecoach line was started in the 1880s and discontinued by 1902, when the trolley tracks were laid. (Author's collection.)

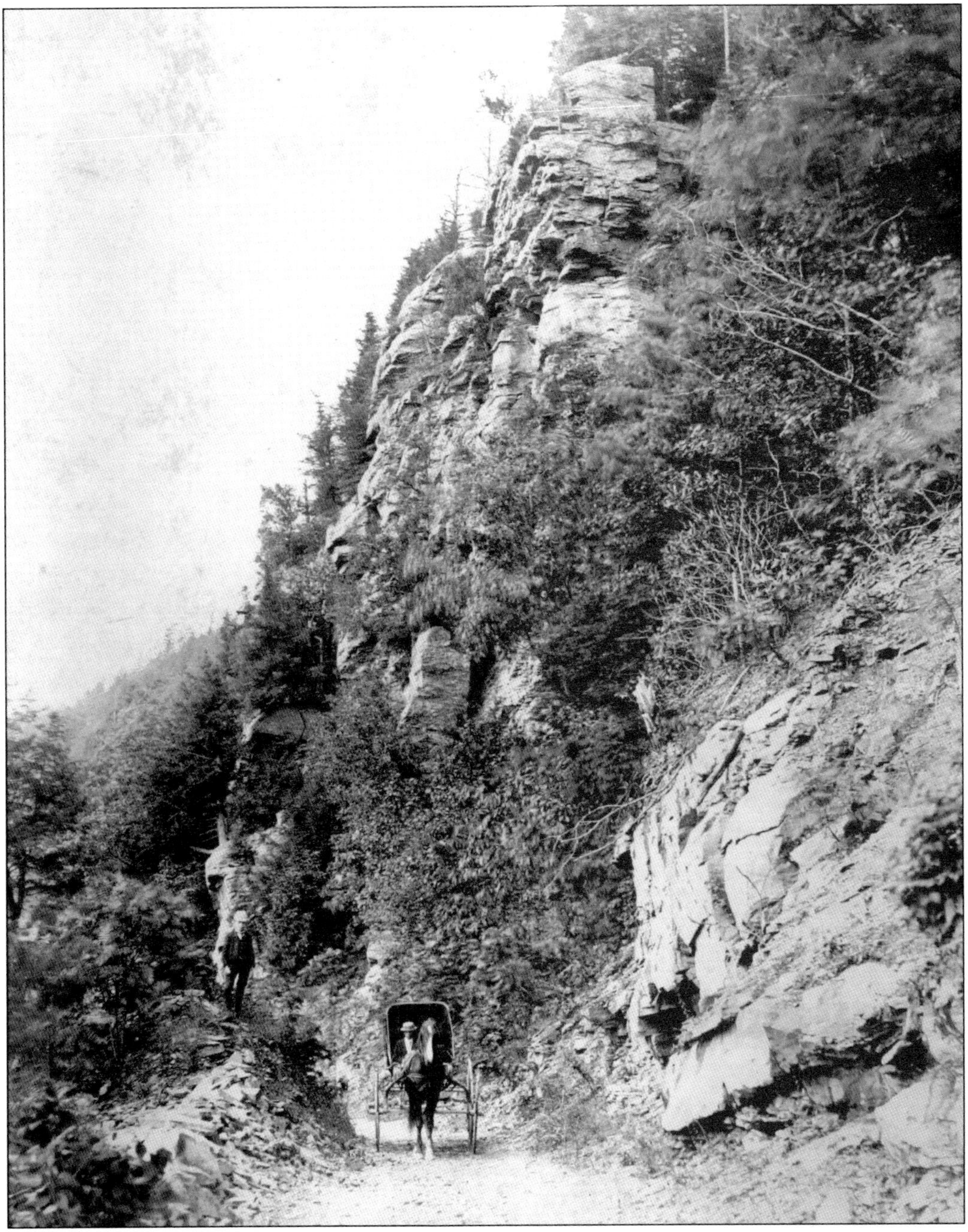

One of the most picturesque spots in the eastern United States, this incredible rock formation known as the Hawk's Nest in Sparrowbush has evolved from a foot trail in pioneer days to a modern roadway. The road was the passageway from Sparrowbush to Mongaup. This is one of the earliest photographs found, dated August 1889. The photograph was taken near the top of the S curves, and the road is only one wagon-width wide. (Matt and Carol Osterberg.)

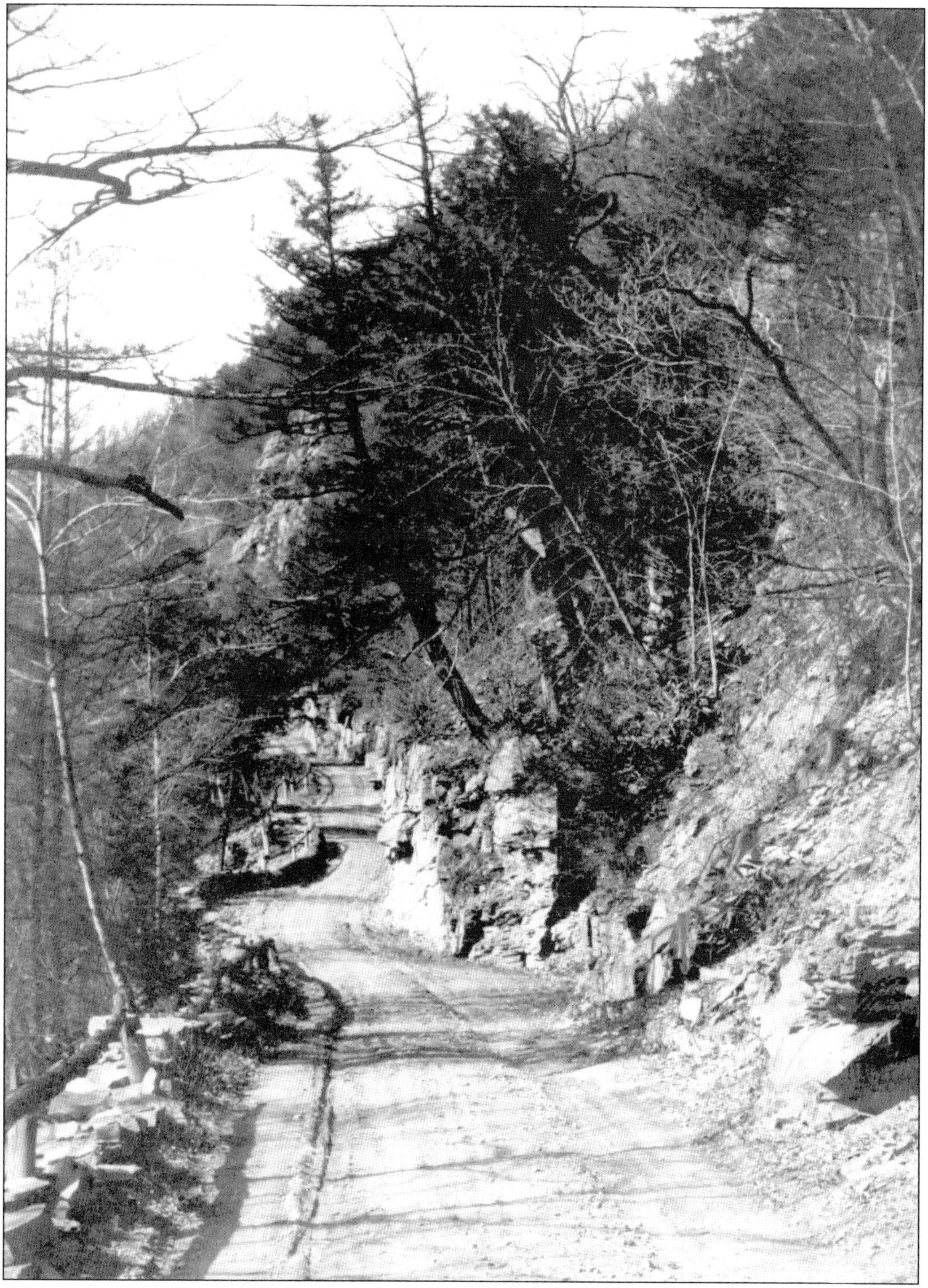

A few years later, in the 1890s, improvements in the Hawk's Nest Road (Route 97) in Sparrowbush are evident. Although the road is still unpaved, with deep wagon wheel ruts, we can see more cut stone walls, wooden side rails, and pull-offs. Because it was a one-lane road, pull-offs were very important. (Author's collection.)

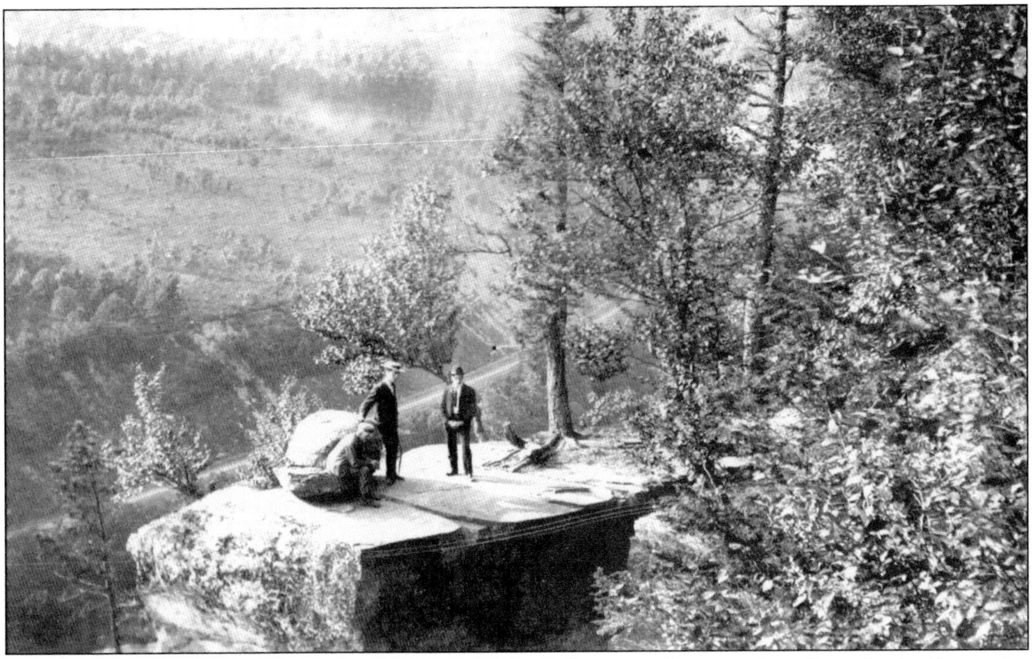

The Hawks Nest affords an incredible view. This photograph was taken from high above the roadway in the 1890s. Straight down is the Delaware River, the Delaware and Hudson Canal hugging its banks, and a fine view of Pennsylvania and the Erie Railroad tracks. (Minisink Valley Historical Society.)

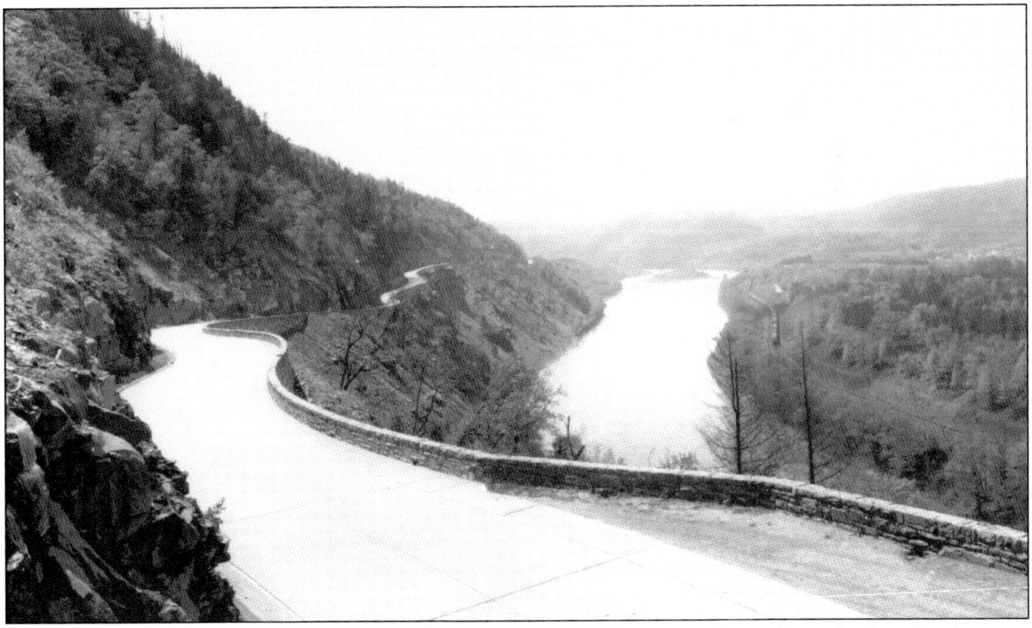

With increased automobile traffic, cars became more numerous. Something had to be done to improve the four-mile stretch of the Hawk's Nest hairpin curves. Construction began in 1932. Thousands of tons of crushed stone were used for building the roadway. On December 19, 1933, although not completely paved, the new Hawk's Nest was opened to traffic. This beautiful view was taken shortly after modernization. (Minisink Valley Historical Society.)

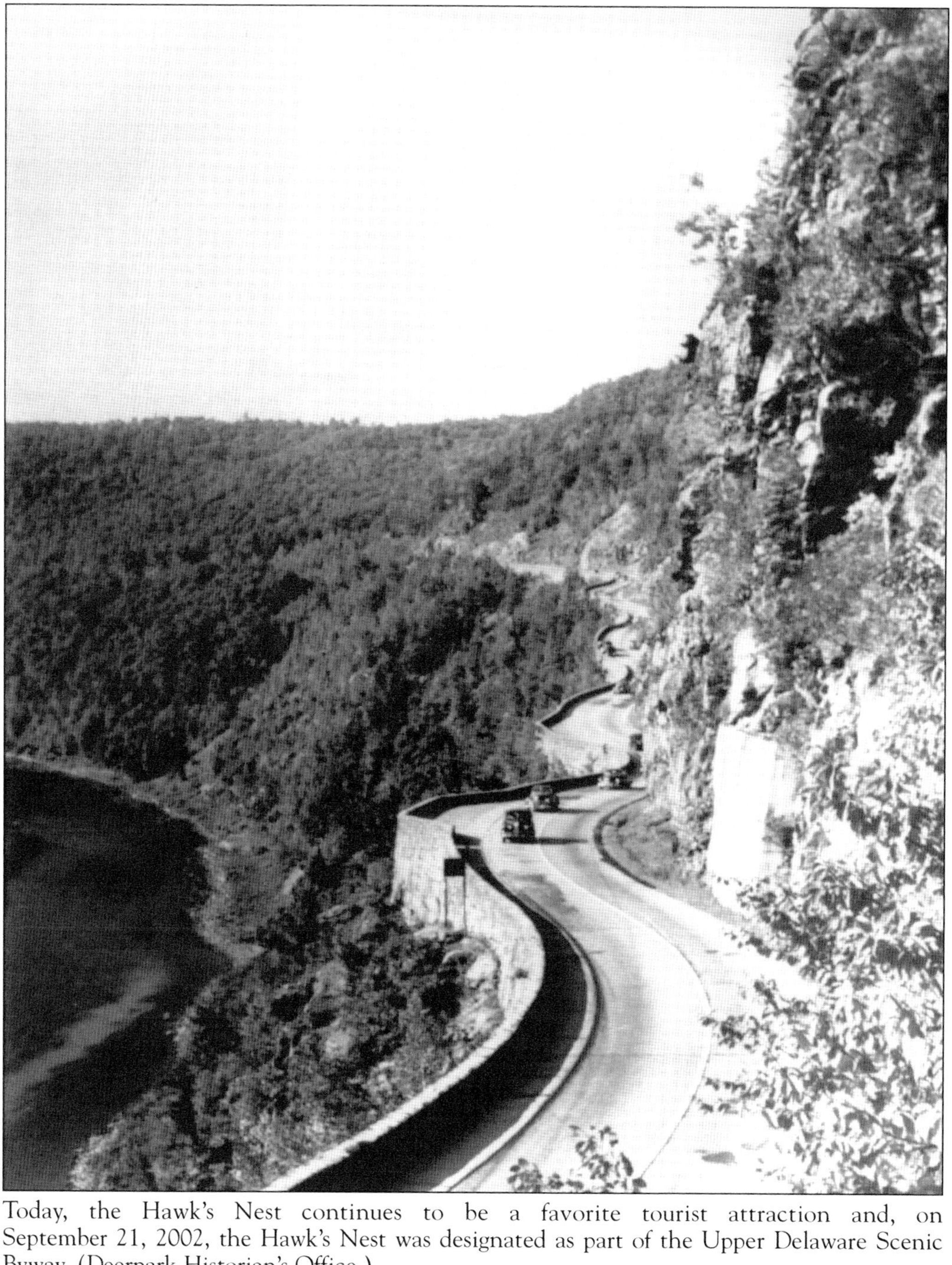

Today, the Hawk's Nest continues to be a favorite tourist attraction and, on September 21, 2002, the Hawk's Nest was designated as part of the Upper Delaware Scenic Byway. (Deerpark Historian's Office.)